George Q. Flynn

American Catholics & the Roosevelt Presidency

1932-1936

University of Kentucky Press
Lexington · 1968

Copyright © 1968 by the University of Kentucky Press, Lexington
Printed in the U.S.A.   Library of Congress Catalog Card No. 68-12968

for my wife

Contents

Introduction

In 1932 Franklin D. Roosevelt was elected president of the United States. Few Roman Catholics realized it at the time, but this event was to initiate a new era in their Church's place in American society. Disturbed and made insecure by the campaign of 1928,[1] the Roman Catholic Church, represented by the hierarchy and individual members, was to reach a degree of recognition and intimacy under Roosevelt that would have astounded their forefathers. This state of affairs was the result of two forces: the political acumen of Franklin Roosevelt and the largely fortuitous similarity between much of the New Deal's reform legislation and the social and economic teachings of the Church.

If, as one observer has remarked, "the Depression and Roosevelt years . . . were a providential opportunity for Catholics . . . to make their voices heard in changing the nation's social situation,"[2] it was no less a time when the president recognized the power and influence that could be exerted by American Catholics. Samuel Lubell has stated that it was Al Smith who in 1928 awakened the urban masses, largely Roman Catholic, to a political consciousness and a sympathy for the Democratic party. It should also be pointed out that subsequently it was FDR who maintained the allegiance of American Catholics toward the party by the recognition he extended them and the finesse with which he treated them.

It is also asserted that the New Deal provoked a true social consciousness among many Catholics. Lubell has stated: "The quickened pace of social change touched off by the depression and New Deal forced the Church leaders to become articulate on all sorts of questions which had lain dormant during the 1920's like the expanding role of the government, the sharpened class cleavage which the Roosevelt Revolution brought and the dramatic extension of trade unionism into the mass production industries where Catholic workers were so heavily concentrated."[3] But this opportunity to contribute to the economic dialogue was only one facet of the sense of belonging achieved by American Catholics under President Roosevelt. Unfortunately, the narrative of how Roosevelt exploited this drive to recognition has to be gained from indirect sources, since the president himself very seldom spoke from this point of view. Yet enough evidence exists to show that he was aware of American Catholics as a political force of no small consequence.

This book, however, attempts primarily to tell the story from the point of view of American Catholics and how they reacted to the New Deal in domestic and foreign affairs from 1932 to 1936.[4] Events of the 1930's in many cases evoked the same response from Catholics as they did from other American citizens. This study attempts to discuss Catholic reaction to the major events of the period and the reasons for their particular response.

[1]Among others, Richard Hofstadter, The Age of Reform (New York, 1955), 300, points out that Roman Catholics in the United States never really recovered from the 1928 "trauma" and that this had made impossible their "effort at assimilation" and attempts "at the achievement of full American identity." The election of a Roman Catholic president in 1960, however, seems to have completed the process of integration first started by Roosevelt. See Lawrence H. Fuchs, John F. Kennedy and American Catholicism (New York, 1967).

[2]Francis J. Lally, The Catholic Church in a Changing America (Boston, 1962), 48.

[3]Lubell, The Future of American Politics, 2d ed., rev. (New York, 1956), 236.

[4]The term "American Catholics" is used interchangeably with the term "the Catholic Church." Generally they imply the public opinions of the Church hierarchy, the Catholic press, prominent Catholic

While there may be certain disadvantages to such an internal approach, it should be clear that one must analyze the parts before understanding the whole.

My major thesis is that it was under Franklin Roosevelt and the New Deal that American Catholics were given recognition as a major force in society and were raised to "a new level of association . . . indicating a change in the 'official' American attitude toward the Church, and equally important, in the Church's disposition toward the government."[5] But this major thesis involves many subsidiary findings that will unfold with the story. For example, much New Deal reform legislation was accepted eagerly by American Catholics because it was presented to them by their leaders as an American version of the papal encyclicals. In this sense the New Deal liberalized American Catholics by showing them the relevance of their Church's teaching on social problems.

---

spokesmen, and various Church-affiliated groups such as the Knights of Columbus. The analysis is largely limited to these sources, since most Church archives for this period are still closed.

[5]This statement is made by Lally, The Catholic Church in a Changing America, 48, but he does little to support it with historical evidence. It is my hope that this present study will add the support of historical scholarship to what I consider a correct and penetrating observation. Other authors who have struck a similar theme include William V. Shannon, The American Irish (New York, 1964), 327, who speaks of new opportunity under Roosevelt, but who limits his analysis to American Irish. Allen Guttmann, The Wound in the Heart: America and the Spanish Civil War (New York, 1962), 45, says that members of the Catholic hierarchy had been trying to "accommodate themselves to American Society" for years, but only succeeded in the New Deal. At this time, the Church gained an importance it had "never enjoyed in any other administration." The appointments of James A. Farley and Joseph P. Kennedy, for example, made Catholics forget the bigotry of 1928. William E. Leuchtenburg, Franklin D. Roosevelt and the New Deal (New York, 1963), 332, recognizes that many new groups received recognition under FDR but, significantly, he says: "Equal representation for religious groups became so well accepted that, as one priest wryly complained, one never saw a picture of a priest in a newspaper unless he was flanked on either side by a minister and a rabbi." It might be added that for Catholics this equal time represented a gain in status.

One problem in a study of this kind is the use of group terms. It is important to note that when I speak of "the Catholic Church," I am referring to that institution on a purely secular level.[6] Some critics would deny any use of the term "American Catholic Church," because there is no one central controlling body in America and because each bishop is largely autonomous in his diocese. Furthermore, argue these critics, the bishoprics differ widely in problems, affluence, and ethnic makeup.[7] Yet it seems clear that there is enough centralization and community of attitude to permit the use of the term "American Catholic Church." This Catholic opinion can be garnered by studying the statements of the National Catholic Welfare Conference (NCWC)[8] which the bishops of the United States often use to publicize their collegiate attitude toward a problem, and by reading the Catholic press, which depends largely on the news service of the NCWC. Furthermore, the study of Will Herberg has clearly shown that there is a national element in the various American creeds. The Church may be universal, but it is also distinctly American.

My research for this study revealed a high degree of unanimity among the Catholic hierarchy, leading spokesmen of the Church, the Catholic press, and lay groups toward public questions such as American recognition of Russia and the effectiveness of New Deal legislation. Certainly I make no claim of unanimous opinion for American Catholics. There does seem to be, however, a great similarity in the opinions expressed by this "public mind" on key issues during the 1930's.

[6]See Will Herberg, *Protestant, Catholic, Jew: An Essay in American Religious Sociology* (New York, 1956), 15, for the same distinction.

[7]Thomas McAvoy, "The Catholic Church in the United States," in *The Catholic Church in World Affairs*, ed. Waldemar Gurian and M. A. Fitzsimmons (South Bend, Ind., 1954), 361.

[8]Recently reorganized and renamed the National Conference of Catholic Bishops.

There is also a problem in labeling individuals as spokesmen for one group when they may not be acting for that group at all.[9] Church membership is only one of many memberships claiming an individual's allegiance. The pluralism of American society makes difficult the delineation of one overriding motive for an individual action, and the much-maligned American "individualism" has permeated the Catholic's relationship with his Church and made blind obedience as outdated as the Inquisition.[10]

Such considerations have caused some students to reject entirely the concept of group allegiance when discussing the churches and politics. The term "Catholic vote" has proved very offensive to some and has been called "one of the greatest myths of American politics."[11] Undoubtedly this offense results from the implication that Catholics are a captive and precommitted segment of the public. Others say that the Church can no more influence its members to vote one way than can labor unions, and that much of the Church's political power is based on bluff.[12] Finally, historians have been accused of using in-

[9]R. M. Darrow, "Catholic Political Power: A Study of the Activities of the American Catholic Church on Behalf of Franco During the Spanish Civil War, 1936–1939" (unpublished Ph.D. dissertation, Columbia University, 1953), iii, admits the distinction of individual churchmen and the Church, but remarks: "This delicate problem of judgment hardly calls for refusing to recognize that the Church acts as an organized institution through denying its temporal existence."

[10]R. M. Darrow, "The Church and Techniques of Political Action," in Religion in American Life, ed. James W. Smith and A. L. Jamison (Princeton, 1961), II, 170-71.

[11]Thomas McAvoy as quoted in Peter H. Odegard, "Catholicism and Elections in the United States," in Religion and Politics, ed. Peter H. Odegard (New Brunswick, N.J., 1960), 125. See also Elmer Roper, "The Myth of the Catholic Vote," in Religion and Politics, 152; Rev. George B. Ford, Interview in Columbia University Oral History Project, 105, who says there is no Catholic vote because Catholics owe allegiance to the Church only in matters of faith and morals.

[12]Herbert C. Pell, Interview in Columbia University Oral History Project, 358, 360. Pell was New York Democratic state chairman during the 1920's.

sufficient data and weak conceptual tools in interpreting voting behavior.[13]

Yet the fact remains that practically all political analysts talk in terms of a "Catholic vote." It is also clear that Roosevelt was only one of many politicians who believed there was such a vote and acted accordingly.[14] Furthermore, there is no disputing the fact that many prominent Catholic figures and journals spoke in terms of influencing their coreligionists to vote a certain way. Most importantly, there is considerable evidence that the "Catholic Church's influence on the political attitudes of Catholics is pervasive and profound."[15] The attitudes of the churches form part of the climate of opinion in which politicians operate, and reactions are often on the basis of indirect pressure. Acceptance and advocacy of certain political attitudes by public representatives of the churches is "filtered through to their religious communities" in a wide variety of ways.[16] If a clergyman is ministering to a community that comprises the majority of a voting element in a city or district, he will automatically find that he shares political power with the politicians simply by virtue of his position as interpreter of the commonweal.

[13]Lee Benson, "Research Problems in American Political Historiography," in *Common Frontiers of the Social Sciences,* ed. Mirra Komarovsky (Glencoe, Ill., 1958), 114.

[14]James Farley and Thomas Corcoran are two others who accept the term. Farley, Interview with author, March 20, 1965, Washington, D.C.; Corcoran, Interview with author, July 15, 1965, Washington, D.C.

[15]John H. Fenton, *The Catholic Vote* (New Orleans, 1960), 56. Fenton, a political scientist, came to this conclusion after a statistical analysis of such issues as the birth control referendum in Massachusetts, approval of right-to-work laws in Ohio, and five different state elections in which a Catholic was running for high office. He concludes that Catholics are more susceptible to political influence because of their religion than are Protestants (see 82-83).

[16]Darrow, "The Church and Techniques of Political Action," 164, 165; Odegard, "Catholicism and Elections," 120, says, "It is not unlikely that some parishioners . . . simply follow the lead of their priest as an expression of group solidarity so frequently found among Catholics."

As Mahatma Gandhi is said to have remarked, "Those who say that religion has nothing to do with politics do not know what religion means." Neither do they know what politics means. Franklin Roosevelt was never guilty of such ignorance. He had great respect for the power of the American Catholic hierarchy, although perhaps a too simplified view of the Church's ability to shift votes.[17] The Catholic press, the hierarchy, prominent lay and clerical individuals, and various lay organizations did take stands on issues of national consequence during Roosevelt's presidency. To ignore the effect of such actions is to ignore a significant dimension of American politics and church history.[18]

[17]Farley points out that FDR clearly recognized the hierarchy's influence. Farley Interview.

[18]Darrow, "Catholic Political Power," 21, says the Catholic press in 1936 consisted of 134 newspapers, with a circulation of 2.3 million; 198 magazines, with a circulation of 4.6 million; and various other publications for a total circulation of 8.9 million. All these organs depended largely upon the NCWC news service for national coverage at this time according to Rev. George Higgins, NCWC, Interview with author, April 29, 1965, Washington, D.C. While most of the diocesan newspapers had rather limited circulation, they are valuable sources because they generally express the opinions of the local hierarchy.

Acknowledgments

Many debts have been incurred in the writing of this book. Professor Burl Noggle of the Department of History at Louisiana State University was a constant source of scholarly guidance. Acknowledgment must also be made for the assistance rendered by the librarians and archivists at the Franklin D. Roosevelt Library, Hyde Park, N.Y.; the Catholic University of America Library, Washington, D.C.; the David Walsh Collection at Holy Cross Library, Worcester, Mass.; the Manuscript Division of the New York Public Library; the Oral History Collection at Columbia University; the Seattle University Library; and the Manuscript Division of the Library of Congress. A special note of thanks is due the interlibrary loan staff at Louisiana State University whose full cooperation greatly facilitated my work. I am also indebted to my colleagues at Seattle University, Drs. Martin Larrey and Robert Saltvig, for reading the manuscript and making many helpful suggestions. The following individuals also assisted in sundry ways in the final product: Charles Crandell, Joseph C. Otto, Jr., Paul Reising, Jr., and Mrs. Helen Donoghue. Finally, the contributions of my wife, though often intangible, were indispensable. I, of course, am responsible for any errors or omissions contained within the following pages.

I

Toward the White House

FRANKLIN ROOSEVELT came to the presidency eminently suited to accept and appreciate the growing political maturity of American Catholics. His own religious convictions were amorphous enough to allow him a tolerance for doctrinal differences, yet formal enough to generate an appreciation for the hierarchical structure of the Catholic Church. Equally persuasive was his political experience with the Church in the state of New York as senator, as supporter of Al Smith in 1928, and as governor.

It is difficult enough to assess any man's personal religious convictions. When that man is as complex and enigmatic as Franklin Roosevelt, the task becomes especially foolhardy. We can easily set down the formal fact that Roosevelt was an Episcopalian, but what does this mean? He once admitted to Harold Ickes, his secretary of the interior, that this allegiance had developed primarily because his father had found it more convenient to attend an Episcopal church than a more remotely located Dutch Reformed church. He boasted of being Low Church and

of preferring a Baptist sermon to an Episcopalian one.[1]
Yet he was very proud of his own wardenship in the
Episcopal Church. Furthermore, he liked to draw attention to the fact that one of his relatives was a prince of
the Catholic Church. Archbishop James Roosevelt Bayley
of Baltimore was a cousin and known as "Rosey" Bayley
among the Roosevelts. FDR also boasted of his close personal relationship with James Cardinal Gibbons, another
member of the Catholic hierarchy.[2]

It is difficult to gauge Roosevelt's religious sincerity. He
was a man who could insist that his cabinet meet for
prayer before assuming public office, who could look
after the spiritual conversion of his own household staff,
and who could contribute financially to his own and
other churches in the Hyde Park area.[3] Yet he was also a
man who could joke about the relative political strength
of each religious group and how to balance them.[4]

The answer to this seemingly paradoxical attitude toward religion may be found in FDR's personal theology
and religious convictions. It seems clear that "in matters
of the soul Mr. Roosevelt was a conservative."[5] He accepted the basic tenets of Christianity with the certitude
of a fundamentalist. Frances Perkins, secretary of labor
during the New Deal, has written most perceptively on
this side of Roosevelt. She points out that the major problems of higher criticism of the Bible and "scientific dis-
coveries . . . bothered him not in the least."[6] It might be

[1]Harold Ickes, The Secret Diary of Harold Ickes (New York, 1954),
II, 290.

[2]Frank Freidel, "Roosevelt's Father," in The Franklin D. Roosevelt
Collector (Nov. 1952), V, 5.

[3]Grace Tully, F.D.R., My Boss (New York, 1949), 112, 354; Frances
Perkins, The Roosevelt I Knew (New York, 1946), 140.

[4]James A. Farley, Jim Farley's Story: The Roosevelt Years (New
York, 1948), 59.

[5]George N. Schuster, "Mr. Roosevelt," Commonweal, April 25,
1945, p. 38.

[6]Perkins, The Roosevelt I Knew, 140.

added that this lack of theological background may have permitted FDR the flexibility and receptiveness to all faiths, which made his presidency congenial to Catholics and others. Roosevelt himself gave some insight into his view on religion in a reply he made in March 1935 to a query regarding the religious affiliation of his ancestors. "In the dim distant past," he said, "they may have been Jews or Catholics or Protestants. What I am more interested in is whether they were good citizens and believers in God. I hope they were both."[7]

Franklin Roosevelt's political awareness of the Catholic Church started early in his career. When, as a member of the New York state senate in 1911, he attempted to lead a revolt against Tammany Hall control of the Democratic nomination to the United States Senate, he felt the barbs of the Catholic hierarchy. William F. Sheehan, the Tammany candidate, was an Irish Catholic. This, however, had little to do with Roosevelt's and the other insurgents' opposition to him. They simply felt that he was not the best man for the job. Yet Bishop Patrick A. Ludden of Syracuse, New York, condemned FDR and his friends as being motivated by "bigotry and the old spirit of Knownothingism."[8] Roosevelt quickly replied to this outburst, terming it "uncalled for, unnecessary and unfortunate." He denied that the controversy had any religious overtones and stated that the bishop did not know what he was talking about.[9]

[7]Samuel Rosenman, ed., The Public Papers and Addresses of Franklin D. Roosevelt (New York, 1938–1950), IV, 96. Roosevelt's views on religion seem to fit a pattern brilliantly outlined in Will Herberg, Protestant, Catholic, Jew: An Essay in American Religious Sociology (New York, 1956), 88, where the author observes that Americans have become dedicated not to one religion but to the idea that religion itself is good for society and that the most popular religion is the "American Way of Life."

[8]Vlastimil Kybal, "Senator Franklin D. Roosevelt, 1910–1913," in The Franklin D. Roosevelt Collector (Nov. 1951), IV, 13.

[9]Ibid., 14.

It was, of course, during the 1928 presidential campaign that Roosevelt became intimate with the problem of the Catholic Church's relationship to American public life. As an early and strenuous supporter of Alfred E. Smith, Roosevelt was squarely in the middle of the religious question. Before the campaign started, FDR did not think that Smith's Catholicism or his humble origins would prevent his election.[10] When the religious issue did crop up during the campaign, Roosevelt gave Smith political advice on how to answer some of the more sophisticated Protestant charges.[11] Roosevelt informally combated religious bigotry while vacationing at Warm Springs, Georgia, shortly before the election. Here he was astounded at the southern rural dweller's ignorance of Catholicism.[12] His private correspondence during this period (before 1928) was filled with letters answering charges that a Catholic should not be president of the United States.[13]

Roosevelt also took formal steps against the bigotry he saw developing in the campaign of 1928. Speaking at Binghamton, New York, on October 17, 1928, he made light of the issue by joking that some people were not opposed to Irish Catholics, only Roman Catholics.[14] Yet a few days later, on October 20, at Buffalo, New York, he spoke seriously on the question. Calling upon his experiences in Europe during World War I, he reminded his audience that no religious question was raised when American doughboys went to defend freedom, and those of all creeds died side by side. He hoped this great lesson

[10]Harold F. Gosnell, *Champion Campaigner: Franklin D. Roosevelt* (New York, 1952), 75.

[11]Edmund A. Moore, *A Catholic Runs for President: The Campaign of 1928* (New York, 1956), 72-73.

[12]Eleanor Roosevelt, *This I Remember* (New York, 1949), 40.

[13]Bernard Bellush, "Apprenticeship for the Presidency: Franklin D. Roosevelt as Governor of New York" (unpublished Ph.D. dissertation, Columbia University, 1950), II, 22.

[14]Rosenman, *Public Papers*, I, 20-21.

would not be forgotten. But if any man could remember the war experiences and still "cast his ballot in the interest of intolerance and of a violation of the spirit of the Constitution of the U.S.," then, concluded Roosevelt, "I say solemnly to that man or woman, 'May God have mercy on your miserable soul!' "[15]

With the thought of presenting an official complaint to a congressional committee at some time in the future, Louis Howe, FDR's personal secretary, systematically collected letters and documents that contained bigoted information against Smith, traced them to their source, and prepared a substantial file of evidence. Howe was assisted by Roosevelt's private secretary, Grace Tully—an Irish Catholic and former secretary to Patrick Cardinal Hayes of New York. This file was eventually forwarded to Washington, but no use was ever made of it.[16]

Ironically, it seems that while Smith's Catholicism hurt his chances for the presidency, FDR's defense of Smith and attacks on religious bigotry won for him the sympathy of many New York Catholics. While it is true that Louis Howe was worried because Roosevelt's defense of Smith and attacks on bigotry were being interpreted as attacks against Protestantism in general, it is also true that FDR received a plurality vote of 406,505 in New York City, which was only 32,000 less than the Smith vote. This support in New York City, combined with some upstate backing, was enough to elect Roosevelt as governor, succeeding Smith.[17]

Governor Roosevelt continued to receive the support of New York's Catholic element. One of the more outstand-

[15]*Ibid.*, 36-38.
[16]Grace Tully, *FDR*, 34; Eleanor Roosevelt, *This I Remember*, 40.
[17]Gosnell, *Champion Campaigner*, 90; Bellush, "Apprenticeship," III, 39. Needless to say, religion was not an issue in Roosevelt's campaign, but his defense of Smith certainly made him more attractive to New York Catholics.

ing instances where Catholics noted his favorable attitude was his signing of the Love-Hayes Bill in 1932. This bill made it unlawful to inquire into the religious beliefs of anyone seeking a teaching position in the public schools. The legislation had sprung from a charge by a Catholic woman of religious discrimination in hiring for public school teaching. All the Catholic newspapers in the state had supported the bill in their editorials and rejoiced at FDR's favorable action.[18]

In June 1929 Roosevelt spoke at Fordham University, a Jesuit institution in New York City, which was awarding him an honorary degree. In his address he praised those men and women who turned their backs on materialistic careers to devote their life to charity and the service of God. More important than FDR's theme, however, was the fact that when the Jesuit president of Fordham commented that Roosevelt was a man who might someday be president of the United States, the ten thousand in attendance cheered enthusiastically. It seemed that some American Catholics could look upon the presidential candidacy of Franklin Roosevelt with favor.[19] Yet before Roosevelt received the Democratic nomination, a number of factors entered the picture which helped to confuse and divide Catholic sentiment.

As the election year of 1932 dawned, it became clear that the Democrats had their best chance of winning the presidency since Woodrow Wilson's triumph in 1916. This fact was probably the main reason for Al Smith's decision to contest the nomination with Roosevelt. This put the Roosevelt forces in the embarrassing position of courting the support of those sections of the country that

[18]Brooklyn *Tablet,* March 26, 1932, p. 1.
[19]Frank B. Freidel, *Franklin D. Roosevelt* (Boston, 1952–1956), III, 72. Thomas Corcoran noted that it was impossible for Roosevelt not to be aware of the Church because of his political roots in New York. Interview with author, July 15, 1965, Washington, D.C.

had rejected Smith in 1928. The ensuing fight for the nomination produced a bitter reaction among many eastern Catholics, and after the convention Roosevelt devoted a major effort to woo them back into the Democratic fold.

Catholic reaction to the news that Smith had decided to seek the nomination in 1932 was ambiguous. Some Catholic political analysts felt that his entrance on the scene would stop the "Roosevelt Express" and that Smith had a good chance to win both the nomination and the election.[20] Furthermore, James Farley had found spotty support for Smith in his tour of the country. Smith's strong showing in the Massachusetts and Pennsylvania primaries indicated that to many Easterners he was still a hero. But Farley noted that the Smith sentiment "comes mostly from ardent Catholic admirers and in some instances from strong wet advocates."[21]

Not all Catholics were in favor of Smith's running again in 1932. The Reverend John A. Ryan, author, scholar, teacher, and leading Catholic social thinker throughout the 1930's, remembered the vicious bigotry of 1928 and was reluctant to do anything to revive this spirit.[22] The editor of the *Catholic World,* the Reverend James Gillis, was worried about the constitutional crisis that might result from another Smith campaign. After all, if Smith should be rejected again on the basis of his religion, Gillis felt the constitutional clause that no religious test be required for office would prove meaningless. This editor seriously questioned whether the nation could

---

[20]C. W. Thompson, "Today and Next November," *Commonweal,* June 1, 1932, p. 119; *Extension,* XXVII (June 1932), 24-25.

[21]James A. Farley, *Behind the Ballots* (New York, 1938), 84; William E. Leuchtenburg, *Franklin D. Roosevelt and the New Deal* (New York, 1963), 7; J. Joseph Huthmacher, *Massachusetts People and Politics, 1919–1933* (Cambridge, 1959), 237.

[22]Ryan to Thomas R. Lynch, Feb. 5, 1930, John A. Ryan Papers, Catholic University of America, Washington, D.C. The Ryan Papers are arranged chronologically by date of correspondence.

stand another display like that of 1928. Yet on second thought he felt it might be better to clarify the issue once and for all.[23] This crisis in confidence of the constitution was shared by other Catholics.

Another indication of the division of Catholic sentiment toward the Democratic nomination was the number of prominent Catholic laymen who worked actively for Roosevelt. Frank P. Walsh, a well-known New York attorney and Catholic layman, supported FDR before and at the convention. Senator Thomas J. Walsh of Montana, later selected to be Roosevelt's attorney general, also worked to secure the nomination for FDR at Chicago.[24] Irish Catholic politicians, such as Farley, Edward J. Flynn of the Bronx, and James M. Curley of Boston, were essential cogs in the Roosevelt machine. Colonel P. H. Callahan, a Kentucky businessman and influential Catholic layman, had urged Roosevelt long before 1932 to make the race. Callahan was of the opinion that Smith had received a pro-Catholic vote in 1928 and should give someone else a chance in 1932.[25] *Commonweal,* a national Catholic magazine edited by laymen, pledged neutrality in the race for the Democratic nomination, but it could not refrain from speaking of Roosevelt as a man whose "strength may be said to lie in a happy blend of skill and knowledge." The editor also played up the governor's great familiarity with the problems of agriculture and taxation.[26]

Yet it was also clear that Roosevelt was taking a calculated risk by basing his nomination on the support of the

[23]*Catholic World,* CXXXIV (March 1932), 734.

[24]Walsh to Ewing Y. Mitchell, Jan. 19, 1932, Box 134, Frank P. Walsh Papers, New York Public Library; Clipping of "National FDR League for President," Box 405, Thomas J. Walsh Papers, Division of Manuscripts, Library of Congress.

[25]FDR to Callahan, Dec. 5, 1929, in *F.D.R.: His Personal Letters,* ed. Elliott Roosevelt (New York, 1947–1950), III, 93.

[26]May 4, 1932, p. 3.

southern wing of the party. Of course, Smith's popularity in the East made such strategy logical. But when Roosevelt's antiprohibition speech of 1932 was accepted without a protest in the South, the New York *Times,* a "Smith paper" in 1928, could editorialize that this proved the South's defection from the Democratic column four years previous had been for religious reasons. "The same people who rejected a 'wet' Smith have now accepted a 'wet' Roosevelt, because the latter is not a Catholic."[27]

Roosevelt was soon labeled the candidate of the southern bigots by certain Catholic sources, who pointed out that the antieastern wing of the party was behind him.[28] One of Smith's more reckless supporters even tried to document this accusation by forwarding to the delegates at Chicago copies of letters purporting to show that the Ku Klux Klan was supporting FDR in the South. F. B. Summers and C. W. Jones were named as two Klansmen who had solicited other Klansmen to support FDR in Georgia. Both Roosevelt and Farley dismissed these charges as ridiculous.[29]

These scattered attacks seemed to have little effect on the governor's drive for the nomination. It was true that FDR was counting on the support of those elements in the Democratic party which had rejected Smith at the polls in 1928. But this support did not require extensive proselytizing by FDR. Many southern delegates were antagonized by Smith's and by National Chairman John J. Raskob's attempts to precommit the party to an antiprohibition stand before the convention met. Raskob's antiprohibition and high-tariff philosophy pushed many southern conservatives into the Roosevelt camp.[30] It was also true that

---

[27]June 21, 1932, p. 8.
[28]C. W. Thompson, "The New Portent at Chicago," *Commonweal,* July 13, 1932, p. 282.
[29]New York *Times,* June 21, 1932, p. 8.
[30]Frank Freidel, *F.D.R. and the South* (Baton Rouge, 1964), 30.

FDR was known as a friend of Catholics in New York, had defended Catholicism in 1928, and had considerable support from Irish Catholics in the East.[31] The Roosevelt forces could assume that the attitude of the *Catholic World* did not represent that of American Catholics: "The Democratic party should show its hand. . . . If the democratic delegates reject Smith without giving some bona fide reason for his 'unavailability,' all the world will know that they have rejected him because of his religion. In that case the party writes itself down a coward and an enemy to religious liberty and it deserves all the beatings it has ever had or will ever get."[32]

During the convention, some of Roosevelt's advisers realized that something must be done to overcome the bitterness aroused among many eastern Catholics by the rejection of Smith. Furthermore, Roosevelt himself realized that although the South and West might give him the nomination, the big electoral votes of the East would be needed to win the presidency. Edward Flynn, one of Roosevelt's closest friends, suggested that the vice-presidential nomination go to someone who would appease the northeastern Catholics. This proposal was rejected, and John Nance Garner, who was described by the *Catholic Mirror* as a "representative of perhaps bigotry's banner state," was picked because Roosevelt needed the Texas delegation for the nomination.[33]

Evidence of Catholic bitterness over the convention results mounted as the delegates left Chicago to return home. Members of the Massachusetts delegation were heard to mutter they would not vote for the "Klan candidate."[34] The Catholic press also gave indications of dis-

[31]Huthmacher, *Massachusetts*, 230-39.
[32]*Catholic World*, CXXXIV (March 1932), 737.
[33]Oscar Handlin, *Al Smith and His America* (Boston, 1958), 166. See *Michigan Catholic*, July 14, 1932, p. 4, for the suggestion that Senator Walsh of Montana be chosen as vice-presidential nominee.
[34]Huthmacher, *Massachusetts*, 239.

pleasure with the Roosevelt nomination. The *Ave Maria,*
published at Notre Dame, said that William G. McAdoo
deserved the boos he received from the Chicago galleries
when he helped Roosevelt at the convention.[35] The
Chicago diocesan paper, *New World,* wondered why the
Democrats made "a concerted effort to shut out of the
convention even mention of a Catholic candidate." But
why bother, mused the editor, when they already had the
Catholic vote "in their pocket"?[36] The *Catholic Mirror* of
Springfield, Massachusetts, announced that bigotry was
"a steamroller in 1932" and that the Democrats had less
excuse for it than the Republicans. The party had denied
Smith the nomination simply because of his religion and
had compounded its offense by choosing as vice-presidential nominee a man from one of the most bigoted states in
the union.[37] The *Italian News* commented that the Democratic party of Al Smith had nothing in common with the
forces that nominated Franklin Roosevelt in Chicago.[38]

The spirit of resentment building up in segments of the
Catholic population was apparent to neutral observers.
The New York *Times* editorialized on the bitterness and
spirit of rebellion that was evident among Catholic voters
of Connecticut and Massachusetts. Arthur Krock, noted
political analyst for the paper, expected FDR to lose Massachusetts in November.[39]

One of the most surprising manifestations of this Catholic bitterness was the development of a movement to
vote for Norman Thomas, the Socialist candidate, as a
protest. Hoover, as the beneficiary of the bigotry of 1928,
had little public support. The Thomas movement first
came to public attention when C. W. Thompson wrote an

[35]Cited approvingly by the *Michigan Catholic,* July 28, 1932, p. 4.
[36]July 22, 1932, p. 4.
[37]*New York Times,* Oct. 25, 1932, p. 10; Huthmacher, *Massachusetts,*
242.
[38]Huthmacher, *Massachusetts,* 239.
[39]Sept. 5, 1932, p. 10; Oct. 25, 1932, p. 10.

article for *Commonweal,* in which he debated the propri-
ety of a Catholic's voting for a Socialist. He concluded
that since the Democrats were ruled by southern bigots,
Catholics might well vote for Thomas "with a clear conscience." Thompson portrayed Thomas as a defender of
religious liberty and no tool of Russia.[40] Anthony J. Beck,
editor of the *Michigan Catholic,* wrote from Detroit that
there was strong sentiment in that section of the country
for Thomas from both laymen and clergy.[41] Father John
Ryan, when asked for advice, was reluctant to deny a
Catholic's right to vote for Thomas or even to doubt the
wisdom of doing so.[42]

An indication of the proportions of the Catholic movement for Thomas is the storm of opposition it called
forth. Ryan's reluctance was not shared by other Catholic
sources, who were quick to condemn what they saw as a
dangerous movement. The editors of *Commonweal* could
not even agree with the position taken by their contributor, C. W. Thompson. They pointed out that the Socialist
offered "an all embracing philosophy which was entirely
naturalistic." A vote for Thomas might not mean acceptance of socialism but it was a dangerous flirtation.[43] Another national Catholic magazine, *America,* published by
the Jesuits, was even more vigorous in its opposition. The
socialist view of the world was, it declared, totally alien
to the Catholic view. Furthermore, Thomas was in favor
of recognizing the Soviet Union, a move that should be
strenuously opposed. In the opinion of the editor of
America, Catholics were forbidden to vote for Thomas
"even in the phantom form of a 'protest vote.' "[44]

---

[40]Thompson, "Will Catholics Vote for Thomas?" *Commonweal,*
Aug. 31, 1932, pp. 422-24.
[41]Beck to Ryan, Sept. 25, 1932, Ryan Papers.
[42]Ryan to Rev. Francis J. Martin, Feb. 1933, Ryan Papers.
[43]Sept. 7, 1932, pp. 437-38.
[44]Gerard B. Donnelly, S.J., "Can Catholics Vote Socialist?" *America,* Oct. 15, 1932, p. 32; *America,* Sept. 10, 1932, p. 536.

On a more local level, several diocesan papers came out against what they considered growing sympathy for Norman Thomas in their midst. The geographic locations of these papers give some indication of the widespread nature of this movement. The Boston *Pilot* said that the great interest in Thomas exhibited by Catholics could only be an indication of a lack of enthusiasm for either Roosevelt or Hoover. Yet the editor felt that a Socialist vote would be dangerous and unwise. The mail received by the Denver *Catholic Register* indicated a growing preference for Thomas among its readers; the editor, however, felt that it would be best for his readers to vote for one of the major candidates. A vote for Thomas would be a wasted one. The *Michigan Catholic,* published in Detroit, admitted that a number of intelligent Catholics had expressed a desire to vote for Thomas, but the editor cautioned them against such a move. The Socialists had a cosmology, he explained, which would replace religion, and it would be dangerous to support them at the polls. The *Catholic Messenger* of Davenport, Iowa, was even more blunt about the matter: Socialists were anti-Christian, and a "vote for the Socialist ticket is a vote for the recognition and approval of the actions of the Russian Soviet."[45]

If the protest vote for Thomas was not enough to worry Democratic leaders, they also had to contend with Republican attempts to exploit the dissatisfaction of Catholic voters over the rejection of Smith. Paul Y. Anderson, writing in the *Nation,* August 3, 1932, suggested that eastern Republicans were busy telling Smith supporters in New York, New Jersey, and Massachusetts that FDR workers had used anti-Catholic propaganda in the South and West to gain the nomination over Smith. One

[45]Boston *Pilot*, Nov. 5, 1932, p. 4; Denver *Catholic Register*, Nov. 6, 1932, p. 1; *Michigan Catholic*, Sept. 29, 1932, p. 4; *Catholic Messenger*, Aug. 18, 1932, p. 2.

Catholic editor observed that this campaign was not limited to the East and that it was proving surprisingly effective among Catholics.[46] Apparently the campaign was serious enough to cause Farley to speak out against it before the State Democratic Convention of Rhode Island on October 7, 1932. He accused Republicans of reviving the religious issue with a new angle and pleaded with Catholics not to let Republicans put them in the same position as the bigots of 1928.[47]

It appears, however, that very few Catholics put stock in this attempt to label Roosevelt as anti-Catholic. Some called the evidence supporting the claim so meager that only an idiot would fall for it. Others resented the fact that the party which benefited most from bigotry four years ago would attempt to do so again, only in reverse. The attempt to use vice-presidential nominee Garner as a scapegoat for southern bigotry of 1928 was described as "detestable business." Finally, this campaign's assumption that Catholics voted for religious reasons was especially irksome to some Catholics.[48]

The actions of Al Smith were also important in cutting the ground out from under the attempts to deprive Roosevelt of Catholic support in 1932. Roosevelt realized that he would need the big electoral support of the East. And it was in the East that Smith had his most loyal supporters.[49] After the Chicago convention, Smith had mumbled something about being a party man but had done nothing publicly to support the ticket. Roosevelt's advisers,

[46]*Extension*, XXVII (Oct. 1932), 23.
[47]New York *Times*, Oct. 8, 1932, p. 2.
[48]Cleveland *Universe Bulletin*, Sept. 1, 1932; *Extension*, XXVII (Oct. 1932), 23; *Catholic Transcript*, Aug. 18, 1932, p. 4; *America*, Aug. 13, 1932, p. 439.
[49]See Bellush, "Apprenticeship," II, 24, where it is noted that in 1928 FDR had confided to a friend that failure to nominate Smith would cause great defections in the East from the Democratic party because of the "blind, hero-worshiping following" he had.

among them Felix Frankfurter, tried to promote a reconciliation between the two New Yorkers.[50] In August, vice-
presidential candidate Garner visited Smith in New York.
Their conversation was private, but in a statement immediately following the meeting Garner, "with tears in
his eyes," took an apologetic attitude about the defection
of Texas in 1928 and condemned religious bigotry in general. In the meantime, Senator David I. Walsh of Massachusetts, a close friend of Smith, was trying to persuade
the ex-governor to support FDR for the sake of the party.
Whatever the consequences of these actions, Roosevelt
and Smith did join forces to support the nomination of
Herbert Lehman for governor of New York. The newspapers carried pictures of them shaking hands. Such cama-
raderie was a source of elation to Farley and Howe. They
felt it would eliminate the possibility of any Irish Catholic defection from the ticket in November.[51]

Smith campaigned for Roosevelt in the East. After the
ex-governor's first speech in Newark, New Jersey, some
newspapermen complained because he injected the religious issue of the 1928 campaign into the 1932 campaign.
But there was no question that the crowds still appreciated him. Although slow in warming up, Smith eventually
came around to full support for FDR.[52] The apogee of his
efforts for the party was reached in Boston on October
27. There, speaking to fifteen thousand people, he closed
his address with a remark interpreted as a rebuttal to the
anti-Catholic rumors being used against Roosevelt.

[50]FDR to Frankfurter, Sept. 14, 1932, in *F.D.R.: His Personal Letters*,
ed. Elliott Roosevelt, III, 301.
  [51]Rexford G. Tugwell, *The Democratic Roosevelt* (New York, 1957),
245; Huthmacher, *Massachusetts*, 241-42; Clipping of Boston *Advertiser*, July 2, 1932, in Scrapbook No. 48, David I. Walsh Manuscripts,
Holy Cross College, Worcester, Mass.; *Catholic Transcript*, Nov. 10,
1932, p. 4, in which the editor insists that it was Garner who won
Smith over to campaign for FDR.
  [52]New York *Times*, Oct. 28, 1932, p. 1.

"There can be," Smith said, "no bigotry and there can be no resentment in the Catholic heart. It cannot be there."[53] The New York *Times* called Smith's tour of Massachusetts a triumph and pointed out that "priests were in the forefront of every crowd eager to clasp his hand and state their approval of his speech."[54]

It is difficult to assess the effect of Smith's efforts on Catholic voters. It seems clear that after Maine went Democratic in its mid-September election, most political professionals in the East saw a walkaway for Roosevelt in November, with or without Smith's help. In Massachusetts, after some initial hesitation, Senator David Walsh came out strongly for the ticket, and he seems to have played an important role in swinging the Bay State into the Democratic column.[55]

Yet it is also clear that Smith's support of Roosevelt was looked upon by some Catholic sources as a final benediction to the candidate. *Commonweal* remarked in September that "the show is in jeopardy until Al Smith makes up his mind to join." The *Michigan Catholic* and the *Catholic Herald* felt that reconciliation of Smith and Roosevelt would deal a deathblow to the whispering campaign which was attempting to exploit religious feeling.[56] Father John Ryan had been approached early in the campaign about endorsing Roosevelt and thereby undercutting the anti-Catholic campaign being waged in the East. Ryan was now told by these same Catholic sources that the issue was no longer in doubt because of the

[53]Quoted by Huthmacher, *Massachusetts*, 248.

[54]Oct. 29, 1932, p. 1.

[55]Huthmacher, *Massachusetts*, 245; Clipping of Boston *Advertiser*, July 2, 1932, Scrapbook No. 48, David Walsh Papers; Farley, in retrospect, says Smith did help in the East but that the Roosevelt camp was not overly concerned with the possibility of Irish Catholics defecting. Interview with author, March 20, 1965.

[56]*Michigan Catholic*, Oct. 13, 1932, p. 4; *Catholic Herald* (Milwaukee), Oct. 13, 1932, p. 4.

splendid reaction to Smith's New England campaign. John McHugh Stuart, a Democrat and journalist for the New York *Herald and Sun,* wrote, "Smith's endeavor makes doubly sure that we will have in the White House . . . a knowledgeful friend and intelligent champion of the social and economic doctrines recommended to us by Authority and experience."[57]

In spite of these indications, it appears certain that Roosevelt would have received considerable Catholic support regardless of the actions of Smith. The economic crisis was only one of a number of things working in his favor. First, there was a natural tendency to view Hoover as the man who had profited by the anti-Catholicism of 1928. Roosevelt, on the other hand, had defended Smith and presented a posture of tolerance in 1928. Furthermore, Roosevelt was intimate with many prominent Catholics, and two of his chief advisers, Farley and Flynn, were Catholics.[58]

Perhaps the most attractive thing Roosevelt did during the 1932 campaign—from the Church's point of view—was to quote from the papal encyclical *Quadragesimo Anno* of Pius XI in a speech at Detroit, October 2, 1932. Roosevelt called the encyclical "just as radical as I am," and "one of the greatest documents of modern times." FDR quoted the pope as follows: "It is patent in our days that not alone is wealth accumulated, but immense power and despotic economic domination are concentrated in the hands of a few, and that those few are frequently not the owners but only the trustees and directors of invested funds which they administer at their good pleasure. . . .

[57]Stuart to Ryan, Oct. 29, 1932, Ryan Papers.
[58]Harold F. Gosnell, *Champion Campaigner,* 131; *New World,* July 15, 1932, p. 1, reminded its public that Roosevelt was a distant relative of Mother Elizabeth Ann Seaton, foundress of the Sisters of Charity and a "distinguished figure in Catholic Church history in this country."

This accumulation of power, the characteristic note of the modern economic order, is a natural result of limitless free competition, which permits the survival of those only who are the strongest, which often means those who fight most relentlessly, who pay least heed to the dictates of conscience."[59]

The fact that a presidential candidate had quoted approvingly from a papal encyclical had an immediate effect on American Catholics. To one editor, this demonstrated that at last Catholic social teaching was having an effect in the country.[60] Another felt that Roosevelt could not be accused of radicalism by his opponents, since he was no more radical than the pope.[61] To some, his actions, implying "endorsement of some fundamental principles of Christian social reform," required great courage. This public service would, suggested one editor, go down as the most important remark of the entire campaign. Roosevelt's condemnation of laissez faire capitalism gave hope that perhaps he was a man really concerned with social justice.[62]

The obvious significance of FDR's Detroit remarks for American Catholics was seen by John M. Stuart, a politically active New Yorker and friend of Father John Ryan. Stuart wrote Ryan asking the priest to comment on the Detroit speech and promising to publicize his remarks in New England, "where I fear there is likely to be a recognizable defection of our people through tribal pride."[63] Ryan had received a similar query from the Reverend Bryan J. McEntegart of Omaha. Furthermore, Roosevelt

[59]Rosenman, *Public Papers*, I, 778.
[60]*Catholic Herald*, Dec. 15, 1932, p. 4.
[61]*America*, Oct. 15, 1932, p. 31.
[62]*Michigan Catholic*, Oct. 6, 1932, p. 4; *Commonweal*, Oct. 12, 1932, p. 545; Denver *Catholic Register*, Nov. 20, 1932, p. 1.
[63]Stuart to Ryan, Oct. 3, 1932; Ryan to Stuart, Oct. 5, 1932, Ryan Papers.

himself had written Ryan asking that the priest give some professional advice to Raymond Moley to be used in the campaign. Despite this contact, Ryan had not at first viewed Roosevelt's candidacy with exuberance. The priest had preferred Newton Baker for the Democratic nomination. But by September he was writing the Honorable W. F. Connolly of Detroit, who had published an article on why Catholics should support Roosevelt, on how much he admired the latter's views. Ryan suggested they be given wide publicity by the Democratic National Committee.[64] Yet Ryan refused to help the Democratic cause directly by writing on the similarity between Roosevelt's views and the papal encyclicals. Privately he admitted that FDR was obviously familiar with the Catholic documents and had accepted "important parts of its [Quadragesimo Anno] philosophy." He also felt that Roosevelt's Commonwealth Club address in San Francisco was in harmony with Catholic teaching, but he did not wish to contribute an article on these conclusions. He felt his position as a member of the National Catholic Welfare Conference prohibited any direct political action. Instead, Stuart was sent copies of old articles by Ryan in which Hoover's policies were criticized.[65]

Ryan was not the only prominent Catholic who considered Roosevelt the best choice in 1932. Frank Murphy, mayor of Detroit and later attorney general, supported FDR long before the Chicago convention and worked actively for his nomination.[66] Frank P. Walsh of New York had been appointed by Governor Roosevelt to the New

[64]Francis L. Broderick, The Right Reverend New Dealer: John A. Ryan (New York, 1963), 208; Ryan to Connolly, Sept. 17, 1932, Ryan Papers.

[65]Ryan to Stuart, Oct. 13, 1932, and Oct. 18, 1932, Ryan Papers.

[66]Richard D. Lunt, "The High Ministry of Government: The Political Career of Frank Murphy" (unpublished M.A. thesis, University of New Mexico, 1962), 63.

York Power Authority and had supported the governor for the presidential nomination in 1932.[67] The already famous radio priest of Detroit, the Reverend Charles E. Coughlin, came out early in support of Roosevelt. On a visit to New York City with Frank Murphy in the spring of 1932, the priest offered his services to support FDR's theory of government.[68]

When the votes were finally counted in November, the fears of the Roosevelt camp seemed largely exaggerated. Franklin Roosevelt was the overwhelming victor. He received 27,821,857 votes to 15,761,841 for Hoover and carried forty-two states with 472 electoral votes. Of the seventy-seven northern counties with large Catholic populations, which Smith swung out of the Republican camp in 1928, the vast majority supported Roosevelt in 1932.[69] In Boston, Roosevelt did better among Irish and Italian voters than had Smith.[70] The new president showed impressive strength in the twelve largest urban areas in the United States, areas with big Catholic populations. Among others, he carried Boston, Massachusetts; Cook County (Chicago), Illinois; Orleans Parish (New Orleans), Louisiana; Wayne County (Detroit), Michigan; St. Louis, Missouri; Milwaukee, Wisconsin; and New York City by impressive majorities.[71]

It seems clear that the vast majority of American Catholics supported FDR at the polls in 1932. The reason for

[67]Walsh to Lewis Howe, Dec. 9, 1931, Box 134, F. P. Walsh Papers. Archbishop Glennon of St. Louis had remarked that Walsh presented an impressive speech for FDR. William P. Harvey to Walsh, Aug. 1932, Box 134, F. P. Walsh Papers.

[68]Freidel, Franklin D. Roosevelt, III, 285.

[69]Samuel Lubell, The Future of American Politics, 2d ed., rev. (New York, 1956), 37. Lubell also points out that fifty-seven of these counties remained Democratic in every presidential election from 1928 to 1948.

[70]Huthmacher, Massachusetts, 250-51.

[71]Edgar E. Robinson, They Voted for Roosevelt (Stanford, 1947), 20, 82, 103, 110, 120, 130, 149, 180.

this support is more elusive. One author attributes it to no more than "a reasonable expectation of future favors."[72] This interpretation seems inadequate. Clearly the crisis of the depression and the desire for change affected Catholics as it did most other Americans. Although much in Roosevelt's program appealed to Catholics, it seems impossible to isolate a "Catholic vote" in the Democratic mandate.

[72]Daniel F. Cleary, "Catholics and Politics," in *Catholicism in America: A Series of Articles from the Commonweal,* ed. J. O'Gara (New York, 1954), 98.

2

Catholic Social Thought in 1932

WHEN Franklin Roosevelt entered office in 1932, American Catholics had a social philosophy with which to interpret the measures of the New Deal. The state and content of this social thought was the cumulative result of three elements forged in the preceding fifteen years: the "Bishops' Program for Social Reconstruction" of 1919, the papal encyclical *Quadragesimo Anno* of 1931, and the work of Church liberals such as John A. Ryan and Dorothy Day. It was these elements that Catholics drew upon when they faced the depression of the 1930's. This is not to say that Catholic priests and laymen had not been concerned with social problems before 1929. Rather, the depression acted as a catalyst to their views and they became bolder in espousing them.[1]

In 1919 the bishops of the United States published a document that spelled out a program of "social reconstruction." The program was so radical that one prominent businessman felt that socialism had found a home in the Catholic Church.[2] Specifically, the bishops called for minimum-wage laws and governmental intervention in the economy to crush monopolies. For labor they advocated unemployment insurance, health insurance, old-age insurance, and government recognition of labor's right to organize. Other measures that they sponsored included public housing developments, legal safeguards relating to women's work and child labor, and a share by labor in management and ownership.[3]

The impact of this document can be seen in retrospect. By 1945 John T. McNicholas, archbishop of Cincinnati, was eulogizing Archbishop Schrembs, late bishop of Cleveland, by stressing that the latter had signed the bishops' program of 1919. Of the twelve major proposals offered in 1919, all but one had become federal law.[4] A member of the Roosevelt administration, Solicitor General Robert H. Jackson, remarked in 1939 that "liberal political thinking in America has been profoundly influenced by the 'Bishops' Program of Social Reconstruction.' . . . What suffering might have been spared to men had the voice of the Bishops been heeded by those who came to power in 1920 instead of having to wait for the disaster-born administration of 1933."[5]

Another document to which Catholics had reference during the depression and the New Deal was the papal encyclical *Quadragesimo Anno* by Pope Pius XI, written in 1931.[6] This document played a pivotal role in Catholic

[1]Aaron Abell, "The Catholic Church and the American Social Question," in *The Catholic Church in World Affairs*, ed. Waldemar Gurian and M. A. Fitzsimmons (South Bend, Ind., 1954), 396.

[2]John Tracy Ellis, *American Catholicism* (Chicago, 1956), 142-43.

[3]Francis L. Broderick, *The Right Reverend New Dealer: John A. Ryan* (New York, 1963), 104-106; Ellis, *American Catholicism,* 142.

[4]Ellis, *American Catholicism,* 143.

[5]Quoted in William V. Shannon, *The American Irish* (New York, 1964), 326.

[6]The document's actual title was "On Reconstructing the Social Order," and was a supplement to the famous encyclical *Rerum Novarum* of Leo XIII (1891).

interpretation of the New Deal. The general theme of the encyclical was a condemnation of laissez faire capitalism. Pius XI reiterated certain thoughts of an earlier document by Leo XIII. Leo had rejected the old watchdog concept of the state and had called on government to "put forth every effort so that through the entire scheme of laws and institutions . . . both public and individual well-being may develop spontaneously out of the very structure and administration of the State."[7] He had also encouraged the organization of unions to protect the rights of the laborer. Pius reaffirmed these ideas, but he also developed new principles of his own. He began by distinguishing the "twofold character of ownership of goods." The right of private ownership he defended, but he distinguished this from the use of ownership, declaring that the latter should be manifested with due regard for the common good as defined by the state.[8] While denying the claims of both Manchesterist and Socialist, the pope did agree that "the riches that economic-social developments constantly increase ought to be so distributed among individual persons and classes that the common advantage of all . . . will be safeguarded."[9] He called for a living wage for labor sufficient to support both the worker and his family. "Opportunity to work [should] be provided to those who are able and willing to work."[10]

The pope rejected capitalism as the answer to man's ills. He denied the value of unlimited and free economic competition because, in truth, a dictatorship had grown out of this system. "It is obvious that not only is wealth concentrated in our times, but an immense power and despotic economic dictatorship is consolidated in the

[7]Quoted in *Quadragesimo Anno* (National Catholic Welfare Conference edition, 1942), 12.
[8]*Ibid.*, 19-20.
[9]*Ibid.*, 23.
[10]*Ibid.*, 28.

hands of a few." Furthermore, these few did not really own the property but were only the "managing directors," who nevertheless were all but unlimited in their disposition of this power. "Free competition has destroyed itself; economic dictatorship has supplanted the free market; unbridled ambition for power has likewise succeeded greed for gain; all economic life has become tragically hard, inexorable, and cruel."[11] As a substitute for this competitive system, the pope called for industrial partnership: the cooperation of both labor and capital in the formation of vocational guilds. Although broad in concept, this goal of vocational groupings was to be the criterion by which many Catholics estimated the worth of the New Deal.[12]

Since the turn of the century, the Reverend John A. Ryan had been teaching and writing about the Church's concern for social justice. In 1906 he published one of his many books on the rights of labor. This one called attention to the papal insistence that the worker be paid a living wage. As a faculty member at the Catholic University of America, and later as director of the Social Action Department of the National Catholic Welfare Conference, Ryan was consistently pressing for a more vigorous Catholic social movement. He played a large role in drafting the bishops' statement of 1919. Dorothy Day was the moving force behind the Catholic Worker organization. A former Communist, Miss Day preached a primitive form of Christian activism expressed by voluntary poverty and acts of charity.[13]

[11]*Ibid.*, 37-38.

[12]Aaron I. Abell, *American Catholicism and Social Action: A Search for Social Justice, 1865–1950* (New York, 1960), 263.

[13]Edward Marciniak, "Catholics and Social Reform," in *Catholicism in America: A Series of Articles from the Commonweal*, ed. J. O'Gara (New York, 1954), 123-24. For an excellent discussion of Catholic social thought and the men who formulated it, see David J. O'Brien, "American Catholic Social Thought in the 1930's" (unpub-

Whatever the source of their information, one thing is clear: By 1932 many American Catholics, both lay and clergy, were generally appalled at the economic situation that existed and were calling vigorously for radical reform of the economic and social structure of the country. This concern was reflected in a joint statement by the American hierarchy, published on November 12, 1931, under the auspices of the National Catholic Welfare Conference. The bishops expressed sympathy for those suffering from the depression, blamed unrestricted individualism for the economic dislocation, and offered detailed cures for the situation. For one thing, they called for the study and application of *Quadragesimo Anno* by all elements of society. For another, they insisted that "the wealthy are obligated in conscience to contribute for the relief of those who suffer and the more so because the system under which they suffer has yielded wealth to others." Specifically taking a cue from Ryan, this meant a living wage for labor and a more equal sharing of profits. The bishops also expressed their conviction that "federal and state appropriations for relief in some form will become necessary." They proposed a joint conference of labor, business, and the government to deal with the depression.[14]

The National Catholic Welfare Conference (NCWC), which had sponsored the bishops' remarks, was a ten-year-old organization that had sprung from the National Catholic War Council. This latter group had been formed

---

lished Ph.D. dissertation, University of Rochester, 1965). He points out that, despite the work of men like Ryan, Catholic social thought was still an insignificant movement before the depression. Furthermore, although the economic crisis did make Catholics receptive to papal teaching on social justice, there was never any agreement on the particular implementation of the encyclical's rather general statements. See O'Brien, v, 83, 387.

[14]Raphael M. Huber, ed., *Our Bishops Speak: National Pastorals and Annual Statements of the Hierarchy of the United States, 1919–1951* (Milwaukee, 1952), 194-96.

during World War I to enable the Catholic hierarchy to support more effectively the United States involvement in the European conflict after 1917. In essence the group was a national conference for Catholic affairs. It was directed by the bishops of the United States through a council which met frequently each year. Between meetings, the work of the NCWC was carried on by a permanent staff of priests and laymen. Located in Washington, D.C., and influenced by such Catholic liberals as the Reverend John A. Ryan and the Reverend John J. Burke, the NCWC played a large role in the discussion of public affairs.[15]

One month after the bishops issued their statement, other evidence appeared of growing Catholic dissatisfaction with Hoover's method for solving the depression. Father Ryan of Catholic University and the Social Action Department of NCWC made an appearance before a senate committee. As a first step in combating the depression, Ryan called for five billion dollars in federal public works to provide relief from unemployment.[16] In the meantime, his assistant in NCWC, the Reverend Raymond A. McGowan, issued a joint statement with the Reverend James Myers of the Federal Council of Churches of Christ in America, and Rabbi Edward L. Israel of the Central Conference of American Rabbis. Echoing the bishops' statement, these men called for a more equal distribution of wealth and income. They deplored the practice of some businesses to cut wages during the economic crisis. "It is now time," read their statement, "that the engineering principle of planning . . . should be extended to the control of entire industries and of industry in general."[17]

[15]Daniel Callahan, *The Mind of the Catholic Layman* (New York, 1963), 86-87; Broderick, *Right Reverend*, 235-36. NCWC continues to be active today as the National Conference of Catholic Bishops.
[16]*Catholic World*, CXXXIV (Dec. 1931), 366.
[17]Quoted in *ibid.*, 623.

Over and over, prominent Catholics were heard demanding more positive action by the federal government in combating the depression. Father Charles Coughlin of Detroit called for a rejection of the idea that the state should interfere with its citizens as little as possible.[18] The Reverend Francis J. Haas, director of the National Catholic Conference of Social Work, addressing his students on July 1, 1932, in Philadelphia, called for an end to clichés such as "balanced budget" and "no dole." He suggested instead an emergency program of massive federal spending and a high surtax on large incomes and inheritances.[19] In an Independence Day address to the American Legion of Washington, D.C., the Reverend Edmund A. Walsh, vice president of Georgetown University, called for a new concept of capital. He pointed out that the best way of preventing the advance of communism in this country is to give the laborer a wage above his immediate worth to provide insurance against unemployment and old age. "The few people who control all the money in the country," said Walsh, "have a choice of giving up some of it or having the government conscript it, or [seeing] a mob rob them."[20] The Reverend Joseph A. Cashen of Duluth, Minnesota, speaking on the radio under the sponsorship of the Federated Trades Assembly, March 4, 1932, called for "active, adequate, and effective intervention by the United States Government" to end unemployment and decentralize the wealth of the nation.[21]

The eighteenth annual convention of the National Conference of Catholic Charities (NCCC), held September 25-

---

[18]Shannon, *American Irish*, 296, calls Coughlin "a path breaker and propagandist for the radicalism of the subsequent New Deal" and says the priest prepared Irish Catholics for an intellectual acceptance of the New Deal as being in the tradition of the Church.

[19]Brooklyn *Tablet*, July 9, 1932, p. 1.

[20]*Ibid.*, July 16, 1932, p. 2.

[21]*Ibid.*, March 12, 1932, p. 1.

28, 1932, at Omaha, Nebraska, provided an opportunity for Catholics to speak out on the emergency facing the country. The Very Reverend A. J. Muench at St. Francis, Wisconsin, rejected the rugged individualism concept of business and the laissez faire philosophy of government. He called for a redistribution of wealth on a broader base. Furthermore, the Sherman Act needed revision, for "only on the basis of cooperation can rational planning of production and distribution be made a reality." Muench was quick to make clear that the planning he called for should come not from the state, but from the "industrial and trade units themselves."[22]

Catholic laymen at the conference also spoke out on the situation. Frank P. Walsh, chairman of the New York State Power Commission, said that the efforts of credit extension and public works being pursued by President Hoover were wholly inadequate to meet the demands of relief. Wartime measures were called for, insisted Walsh. He also urged a rejection of the theories of the English classical economists with their iron laws and suggested a return to the guild system of the Middle Ages as a way out of the depression.[23]

James Fitzgerald, another layman at the conference and an official of the St. Vincent de Paul Society in Detroit, took this occasion to castigate Hoover's relief policies as inadequate. Fitzgerald felt that Hoover's assumption that local initiative should be the major source of relief was erroneous. The Reconstruction Finance Corporation was supposed to provide funds in an emergency. In fact, Fitzgerald commented, few funds were being distributed. He felt the administration should realize that federal relief

[22]National Conference of Catholic Charities, *Proceedings, 1932–1941* (Omaha, Nebr., 1932–1941), 18th annual convention, 1932, p. 204, hereafter cited as *NCCC Proceedings.*
[23]*Ibid.,* 11.

funds were needed immediately and that "necessity knows no law."[24]

James F. Murphy of Detroit, president of the NCCC Omaha conference, rejected the idea that "blind economic forces" were the cause of the depression. On the one hand he condemned the "ruthless free competition which ends inevitably in economic dictatorship," and the procrastination of the government in "mobilizing the resources of the nation for relief." Yet Murphy insisted that he was also against excessive centralization and bureaucracy of government.[25]

Indeed, many Catholic spokesmen took a rather radical reading of the depression and of the action needed to combat it. In their interpretation they were influenced by the belief that the ideas expressed in the encyclical of Pius XI held the answer to the American dilemma. For example, the National Catholic Alumni Federation undertook the sponsorship of regional meetings to promote social justice. In New York City on November 20, 1932, a call went out for a crusade based on the encyclicals of Leo XIII and Pius XI. The goals of these meetings were twofold: to educate American industrialists to the fact that modern capitalism had failed, and to promote the acceptance of papal principles by the entire nation. The three main speakers at the New York meeting were the Reverend James M. Gillis, editor of the *Catholic World,* Wilfrid Parsons, S.J., editor of *America,* and the Reverend John A. Ryan. Father Gillis predicted a vast social upheaval in America if capitalism did not reform. Father Parsons condemned laissez faire economics, and Father Ryan said American capitalism was committing suicide by stressing production over consumption.[26]

[24]*Ibid,* 28-33.
[25]*Ibid.,* 4-6.
[26]New York *Times,* Nov 21, 1932, p. 19.

Father Ryan had been an early exponent of the idea that the papal encyclicals could help solve the economic crisis. He pointed out that public authorities were obliged to take positive steps for the general welfare and that the state should care for the poor and provide relief.[27] He stressed the fact that national planning was advocated by Pope Pius XI and that individualism was "a blind alley."[28]

Father Parsons was another propagator of the encyclicals. He lamented how few American Catholics realized that the pope had condemned concentration of wealth and rugged individualism—phrases that Parsons associated with the Hoover regime. The priest felt that the pope's call for an abolition of antitrust laws and the rejection of the free competition philosophy behind such laws was especially timely for American consideration.[29] Parsons' magazine, *America,* called the Democratic platform of 1932 "a hodge-podge of economic theory," and boasted that only Pius XI was bold enough to go to the root of the depression—laissez faire economics. The editor proudly remarked that "Pius XI remains the most radical in social economics among all the public men of our age."[30]

Other voices joined the chorus stressing the relevance of the pope's encyclical to the depression. Mayor Frank Murphy of Detroit spoke before the International Federation of Catholic Alumni at a meeting in New York City in November 1932. The mayor chose the papal encyclicals as his topic and emphasized their applicability to the current economic crisis.[31] The Catholic Central Verein of America,

[27]Ryan, "National Responsibility in the Present Crisis," *Catholic World,* CXXXVI (Nov. 1932), 169.
[28]Ryan, "After the Depression," *Catholic Action,* Jan. 1932, p. 5; also *NCCC Proceedings,* 1932, p. 20.
[29]Parsons, "The Pope and the Depression," *Catholic Mind,* XXX (June 22, 1932), 244.
[30]July 9, 1932, pp. 320-21.
[31]Brooklyn *Tablet,* Nov. 26, 1932, p. 1.

at its seventy-seventh general convention in St. Louis, August 19-24, 1932, passed a resolution calling for the reconstruction of society along the lines of vocational groups as laid down by *Quadragesimo Anno*.[32]

Another theme in the growing Catholic demand for economic reform was a bitter criticism of American capitalism. Already some of this had been made evident in the remarks of Ryan and Parsons. Catholic editors soon joined in this criticism. One editor said that if the depression proved anything, it proved "that the enormously wealthy men of the world are not its wise men."[33] Father Gillis used the editorial pages of the *Catholic World* to disassociate publicly the Catholic Church from capitalism, although he admitted the right of private property. He felt that the depression should certainly make clear to all that "injustices" and "mad incongruities" were "inherent in the capitalistic system." To dismiss all attempts at reform as "communistic" was folly and revealed an inordinate fear complex.[34]

The speakers at the Catholic Alumni Federation meeting of 1932 took the occasion to attack American capitalism. Father Gillis continued his criticism and accepted the fact that a social revolution, altering the old class structures, was beginning in the United States. His only question was how much violence would accompany the revolution. According to Gillis, capitalists had treated labor worse than an animal. Father Parsons pointed out that the existing economic structure "actually had produced nothing but unlimited competition and unlimited opportunity for avarice and greed." Father Ryan remarked that capitalism had committed suicide by its nar-

[32]*Central-Blatt and Social Justice* (official journal of the Catholic Central Verein), Sept. 1932, pp. 173-75.
[33]Denver *Catholic Register,* Aug. 14, 1932, p. 1.
[34]*Catholic World,* CXXXIII (May 1931), 231-32; (July 1931), 487-88.

row policies. He branded as a delusion the attempt to blame the depression on the normal cycles of business. Joseph A. Porcelli of Fordham University took the opportunity to call for laws to force industrialists to practice social justice.[35]

During the early 1930's Catholics were offered more than one forum for expressing their social views. In Detroit, Father Coughlin was developing the base for his Union of Social Justice with an emphasis on federal control of finance. For those who found his program either too vague or hysterical, there was the Catholic League for Social Justice. This group was the outcome of a meeting early in 1932 of Catholic teachers, industrialists, and economists, held under the auspices of the National Catholic Convert's League, to study the depression. It was announced at the meeting that the Calvert Associates, publishers of *Commonweal*, were forming a League of Social Justice to promote the "study and application of the teachings of Pius XI." The leading spirit in this movement was Michael O'Shaughnessy, an oil executive and journalist. In October 1932 the league received the endorsement of Cardinal Hayes of New York.[36]

O'Shaughnessy set the tone and goals of the new organization soon after he began publication of the *Social Justice Bulletin*, the league's official monthly organ. He outlined a plan to bring the United States out of the depression. He envisioned the formation of trade associations of all industrial units, which would provide health and accident insurance for members. These associations would also work for stabilization of production and prices. All trade associations would be under a directorate composed of management, labor, and the consumer. A

[35]"A Warning to Capitalists," 1932 clipping in Ryan Papers; *Catholic World*, CXXXVI (Dec. 1932), 367.
[36]Abell, *American Catholicism*, 242.

government tribunal would be set up to decide labor-management disputes and would have veto power over the directorate.[37]

It is impossible to estimate the influence of O'Shaughnessy and his group. They were small in number and had little publicity. It is known that his plan was circulated among the members of Roosevelt's new cabinet. Furthermore, the National Catholic Alumni Federation adopted some of O'Shaughnessy's ideas and during the 1930's called for trade association as a means of promoting economic stability.[38]

After Roosevelt's victory in November 1932, individual Catholics offered a variety of suggestions for action by the new administration. John Ryan wrote Raymond Moley that things were looking up because Hoover was getting out. He expressed hope that Roosevelt would be what he appeared—a man who knew the importance of restoring the purchasing power of the people and who would concentrate on redistribution rather than expansion of production.[39] Meanwhile, Richard Dana Skinner, associate editor of *Commonweal*, addressed the Knights of Columbus in New York and said that antitrust laws must be repealed because they promoted ruthless competition, a prime cause of the depression.[40] Frederick Siedenburg, S.J., dean of Detroit University, gave a presidential address before the Illinois Conference of Social Work in which he called for an "economy of abundance" to replace the "economy of scarcity" under which the United States was then operating. The common good must replace the selfishness of the capitalist. Socialization of production and distribution should come about by

[37]*Ibid.*, 245-46.
[38]*Ibid.*, 245; Brooklyn *Tablet*, Feb. 20, 1932, p. 1.
[39]Ryan to Moley, Nov. 29, 1932, Ryan Papers.
[40]Brooklyn *Tablet*, Dec. 10, 1932, p. 3.

evolution rather than revolution. Old-age insurance, minimum wage laws, and workmen's compensation were only a few things needed. Siedenburg, in a tone that was shared by many American Catholics, concluded, "If need be, the Government must pour out its billions for relief and for Government work."[41]

By early 1933 it appeared that a large segment of American Catholics were favorably disposed toward the vigorous type of leadership Roosevelt would soon offer them.

[41]Quoted in the National Catholic Welfare Conference *News Service,* Urbana, Ill., Dec. 5, 1932, hereafter cited as *NCWC News Service;* Brooklyn *Tablet,* Dec. 10, 1932, p. 1.

3

Support for Roosevelt's Program

As the character of the new president and his program unfolded during 1933, both president and program met enthusiastic response from many American Catholics. Undoubtedly much of this can be explained in terms of simple economic needs and the desire to support anything that promised a relief to the current distress. Yet more than this was involved in Catholic support for Roosevelt and the New Deal. Bishops, priests, and laymen evaluated the president and his program in adulatory terms. Some of their enthusiasm was unquestionably heightened because Catholic spokesmen and the Catholic press presented the reform legislation of the New Deal as being based on, and embodying, Catholic social teaching; in particular, the ideas of the papal encyclicals. On his part, Roosevelt demonstrated an acute awareness of his Catholic backers and managed to solidify this support through his cordial relationship with the American hierarchy, his availability to the Church, and his patronage policies.

One of the most surprising aspects of the Church's support for the president was the wide spectrum of opinion which it represented. The American Catholic hierarchy became Roosevelt boosters even before his program was under way. William Cardinal O'Connell of Boston, dean of the hierarchy, praised the president in a speech in April 1933 and called him a godsent man who was willing to sacrifice all for the good of the country. By November 1933 the cardinal was writing of the "wonderful degree of success" Roosevelt had achieved in restoring confidence to the American people.[1] Patrick Cardinal Hayes of New York, an old acquaintance of the new president, dined with him before the inaugural as a guest of James Farley, and spoke reassuringly of Catholic support for the president's program. After the inaugural Hayes spoke glowingly of FDR as "crystallizing the sentiments of the country in meeting the grave problems [of the depression]."[2] The following year Hayes, speaking at the Manhattan College commencement in James Farley's honor, praised the president for his spirit and vision. The cardinal concluded, "We ought to rejoice that everything he [Roosevelt] tries to do . . . will come to a happy success."[3]

George Cardinal Mundelein of Chicago was an early and enthusiastic supporter of Roosevelt. The president made contact with Mundelein in characteristic fashion. Senator David I. Walsh of Massachusetts had remarked to Roosevelt that Mundelein was an avid autograph hunter

[1]O'Connell, *Recollections of Seventy Years* (Boston, 1934), 370; Boston *Pilot*, May 6, 1933, p. 1; Brooklyn *Tablet*, April 8, 1933, p. 2.

[2]James A. Farley, *Jim Farley's Story: The Roosevelt Years* (New York, 1948), 34; New York *Times*, March 22, 1933, p. 19; Farley says that Hayes probably wanted to reassure the president on the Church's cooperation, even though Smith had lost the nomination. Interview with author, March 20, 1965, Washington, D.C.

[3]New York *Times*, June 13, 1934, p. 19.

and would greatly prize adding the president's to his collection. Roosevelt took the occasion of the cardinal's an-
niversary in the priesthood to send him a short note of
congratulations. Mundelein was truly touched by this bit
of thoughtfulness by the "busiest man in the land" and
called the note "the finest gift I could possibly receive."
He requested a private visit with the president to pay his
respects for the fine achievements already made during
FDR's first month in office.[4] The Catholic press duly reported the fact that the cardinal visited the White House
in May.[5]

Cardinal Mundelein's role as an apologist for the New
Deal was to expand throughout the 1930's, and he came
to play an important role in soliciting support for the
international diplomacy of Roosevelt before World War
II. In 1933, however, the cardinal concentrated upon urging cooperation with the president's domestic program. In
an address delivered before the Chicago Council of Catholic Women on October 12, 1933, the cardinal praised
FDR for showing "more friendly sympathy to the Church
and its institutions than any occupant of the White House
in half a century."[6] This type of sentiment seemed to be
shared by the Vatican. Bishop Gannon of Erie, Pennsylvania, reported that in a private conversation the pope
had expressed to him high praise for President Roosevelt
and his deeds.[7] Meanwhile, in the United States the cho-

[4]FDR to Mundelein, April 22, 1933, and Mundelein to FDR, April
26, 1933, *Selected Materials from the Papers of Franklin D. Roosevelt
Concerning Roman Catholic Church Matters,* microfilmed at the
Franklin D. Roosevelt Library at Hyde Park, N.Y., June 1955, 3 reels,
Louisiana State University; hereafter cited as *Sel. Mat.*

[5]Brooklyn *Tablet,* May 20, 1933, p. 2.

[6]Quoted in *NCWC News Service,* Oct. 13, 1933; see also Brooklyn
Tablet, Oct. 21, 1933, p. 4; Samuel Rosenman, ed., *The Public Papers
and Addresses of Franklin D. Roosevelt* (New York, 1938–1950), II,
22-23. Thomas Corcoran admitted being a courier from FDR to
Mundelein in the period preceding World War II. Interview with
author, July 15, 1965, Washington, D.C.

[7]New York *Times,* Aug. 12, 1933, p. 12.

rus of episcopal praise continued unabated. Archbishop Edward J. Hanna of San Francisco, chairman of the Bishops' Administrative Committee of the NCWC, spoke for the entire hierarchy of the United States when he proclaimed Catholic support for the president's recovery efforts.[8] Roosevelt thanked the bishop for his expressions of support, which had been forwarded to the White House through the Reverend Michael J. Ready of NCWC.[9] According to Bishop Karl J. Alter, of Toledo, Ohio, Roosevelt's inaugural address breathed "the spirit of Our Holy Father's recent encyclical 'Quadragesimo Anno.'" This, said the bishop, augured the acceptance by America of Catholic social teaching.[10]

In September 1933, over the national facilities of the Columbia Broadcasting System, American Catholics heard Bishop Bernard J. Mahoney of Sioux Falls, South Dakota, praise the New Deal. The bishop, pointing to Roosevelt's preinaugural visit to church with his cabinet, concluded that "Christ will not fail one who made such a conspicuous profession of faith."[11] At the same time, William A. Hickey, bishop of Providence, Rhode Island, called upon the Catholics of his diocese to support the New Deal. He added: "I have been profoundly impressed with the evidence of God's hand in the unfolding and execution of our President's economic program." The bishop gladly offered whatever influence he had to solicit support for the administration because its policies were "absolutely in harmony with the best economic and religious and patriotic principles."[12]

At the same time William Cardinal Dougherty of Phila-

[8]Clipping of the *Echo* (Buffalo, N.Y., [n.d.]), in Reel 3, *Sel. Mat.;* Col. P. H. Callahan to Louis Howe, March 20, 1933, Reel 2, *Sel. Mat.*
[9]*Catholic Action,* April 1933, p. 17.
[10]Printed statement of Bishop Alter, March 7, 1933, Toledo, Ohio, in Reel 3, *Sel. Mat.*
[11]Quoted in *NCWC News Service,* Chicago, Sept. 11, 1933.
[12]Quoted in *NCWC News Service,* Providence, R.I., Sept. 8, 1933.

delphia expressed his regard for President Roosevelt. Dougherty's sentiments, however, grew more out of concrete political matters than from general principles. He was concerned over what he considered a discriminatory clause in the administration's new revenue act. The bill would, according to the cardinal, single out certain religious congregations for taxation. He wrote Roosevelt of his displeasure and warned that Catholics would resent such a clause. FDR replied by suggesting that Dougherty forward his objections to the chairman of the Ways and Means Committee of the House. The objectionable clause was eventually eliminated and the cardinal attributed this to FDR's intervention.[13]

Other members of the hierarchy who commented favorably on the new president included Archbishop Mc-Nicholas of Cincinnati, Archbishop Michael J. Curley of Baltimore, and Bishop Henry P. Robiman of Davenport, Iowa.[14]

Various influential elements of the Catholic population reiterated the hierarchy's support for President Roosevelt. The Reverend John A. Ryan remarked that the actions of FDR were epochal,[15] and the Reverend Wilfrid Parsons, editor of *America*, wrote that President Roosevelt was pursuing a noble goal in trying to convince business to organize for the common good.[16] The Reverend Jones I. Corrigan, speaking on the Boston radio network, said that God was obviously answering FDR's prayer because na-

[13]Dougherty to FDR, telegram, Dec. 23, 1933; FDR to Dougherty, Jan. 11, 1934; Dougherty to FDR, March 2, 1934, OF 137-A Income Taxes, Box 19, The Franklin D. Roosevelt Papers, Hyde Park, N.Y.

[14]Brooklyn *Tablet,* March 11, 1933, p. 1; March 16, 1933, p. 8; *Catholic Herald,* April 3, 1934, p. 1.

[15]John A. Ryan, *Social Doctrine in Action: A Personal History* (New York, 1941), 247; Francis L. Broderick, *The Right Reverend New Dealer: John A. Ryan* (New York, 1963), 213.

[16]Wilfrid Parsons, "The Church and the Modern World," *Catholic Mind,* XXXI (June 8, 1933), 206.

tional recovery was taking place.[17] William C. Murphy, writing in *Commonweal*, pictured Roosevelt as a conservative politician. Rather than being the image-breaker pictured by his enemies, the president was fighting to prove the ability of democracy to face any emergency.[18] Perhaps the highest individual tribute to President Roosevelt was rendered by the Most Reverend W. D. O'Brien, who pointed out that the United States always received God's help in time of crisis. Thus, in 1933, "Almighty God raised up FDR—the Apostle of the New Deal."[19]

Major Catholic organizations were also enthusiastic in their support of the new president. The president of the International Catholic Truth Society, the Reverend Edward L. Curran, wrote to Roosevelt praising his leadership and high moral determination.[20] When the National Catholic Alumni Federation, representing fifty Catholic colleges and universities in the United States, held its national convention in New York City, June 20-24, Edward Dare, a high-ranking member, transmitted to President Roosevelt copies of a resolution that praised and endorsed the New Deal.[21] The Catholic Daughters of America, through their supreme regent, Mary C. Duffy, sent copies of their resolutions pledging assistance to the president and expressing their confidence in him. These resolutions were passed at the national convention in Colorado Springs, July 7, 1933, by a group that claimed a membership of 200,000.[22] The *Social Justice Bulletin*, organ of the Catholic League for Social Justice, spoke of the obvious influence of Pius XI on the president, and the

[17]Boston *Pilot*, Oct. 21, 1933, p. 1.
[18]William C. Murphy, "The New Deal in Action," *Commonweal*, May 5, 1933, pp. 11-13.
[19]W. D. O'Brien, "The New Deal in Religion," *Extension*, May 1934, p. 7.
[20]Curran to FDR, April 19, 1933, Reel 1, *Sel. Mat.*
[21]Dare to FDR, July 21, 1933, Reel 3, *Sel. Mat.*
[22]Duffy to FDR, telegram, July 7, 1933, Reel 3, *Sel. Mat.*

Polish Roman Catholic Union expressed similar sentiments at the Union's triennial convention held in Springfield, Massachusetts.[23] Various Knights of Columbus
groups praised the president's determination and decisive
action.[24]

The Catholic press was almost unanimous in its approval of Roosevelt's first hundred days in office. *Commonweal* expressed the predominant feeling when it said:
"All Catholics who desire to give practical effect to the
principles of social justice laid down by Pope Pius XI will
see that . . . Roosevelt's opportunity to lead . . . is likewise the Catholic opportunity to make the teachings of
Christ apply to the benefit of all." The Denver *Catholic
Register* had much the same to say for the New Deal. The
New Deal should be supported because it had sprung
from Catholic sources. "The *Register* and other powerful
mouthpieces of the Catholic Church in this country,"
commented this editor, "have made the NCWC social action program so insistent that the government is now going to try it out, as the only real cure." The Brooklyn
Tablet called FDR's every action "motivated by a Christian philosophy which moves forward in the right direction." *Extension* magazine said that the new president
had done more in his brief tenure than had most of his
predecessors during their entire time in office.[25]

Yet in the praise lavished upon President Roosevelt by
the Catholic press, certain comments indicate that some

[23]*Social Justice Bulletin*, no. 8, Aug. 16, 1933, in Reel 1, *Sel. Mat.*;
New York *Times*, Sept. 15, 1934, p. 18.
[24]Knights of Columbus Council to FDR, telegram, March 8, 1933,
OF, Box 1, Roosevelt Papers.
[25]*Commonweal*, Nov. 16, 1932, p. 58; Denver *Catholic Register*,
June 29, 1933, p. 4; March 9, 1933, p. 4; Brooklyn *Tablet*, May 13,
1933, p. 9; *Extension*, XXVII (May 1933), 13-14. These same optimistic notes were also struck by the following Catholic newspapers:
Catholic Herald, March 23, 1933, p. 4; Boston *Pilot*, June 24, 1933,
p. 4; *Catholic Transcript* (Hartford, Conn.), May 25, 1933, p. 4.

had only a superficial awareness of the principles of the New Deal. The editor of *America* praised FDR's inaugural address but at the same time called for frugality in government, something Roosevelt had mentioned in the campaign. The editor of the Davenport *Catholic Messenger*, who supported the New Deal, was most attracted by the president's plan to balance the budget. The *News Service* of the NCWC sent out cryptic stories indicating that the Democratic program, giving great power to the president, was "foreshadowing the curtailment of a number of Federal activities which have shown an unprecedented growth in the past two decades." The *News Service* pointed to FDR's governorship of New York as an indication that he was a strong believer in "the protection of States' rights against Federal encroachment." The Denver *Catholic Register* had perhaps the most farfetched interpretation of events. Its editor said that if the country was saved from economic disaster it would be because the Catholic Church had succeeded in "putting over her economic program." The Church had her best chance in history under Roosevelt. Furthermore, there was now "a real chance" for a large federal spending program for relief because "Al Smith is the power behind the throne and Al has the Catholic slant."[26]

Clearly, most Catholic spokesmen were generous in their praise of the New Deal and of President Roosevelt. The reasons for this generosity are not readily apparent. The spokesmen themselves often pointed to contradictory tendencies in the New Deal when finding things to praise. Compare, for instance, the position of Father John Ryan, who anticipated federal direction of the economy, with the remarks of certain editors who expected frugality and

[26]*America*, March 18, 1933, p. 565; *Catholic Messenger*, March 30, 1933, p. 2; NCWC *News Service*, Feb. 13, 1933; *Catholic Herald*, March 16, 1933, p. 4; Denver *Catholic Register*, March 2, 1933, p. 4.

limited governmental intervention. Yet one consistent theme, which was superficial enough to gain widespread backing, was the idea that Roosevelt was enacting the social encyclicals of the popes.

During 1933 the Catholic press constantly presented the New Deal as an American version of the papal encyclicals. This campaign began with an interpretation of Roosevelt's inaugural address. As one editor remarked, the great similarity of FDR's speech to *Quadragesimo Anno* made it clear that "the new President has really grasped the spirit of that document." His program "is merely a practical application of the Papal principles for social reconstruction."[27] Both the pope and the president assigned blame for the present crisis to the same cause— the unscrupulous practices of business.[28] The *Catholic Times* of London, quoted widely in the United States, even went so far as to arrange the remarks of President Roosevelt and Pope Pius XI in parallel columns, to demonstrate that both men condemned capitalism. The similarities, felt the author, showed that FDR had not merely quoted the papal encyclical in the campaign as would a shallow politician, but had done so as a sincere student of its principles. He concluded: "The Roosevelt plan of social reconstruction is the Catholic plan."[29]

After Roosevelt had been in office for one month, a few Catholic editors felt that their first impressions of the president had been confirmed. The goals of Leo XIII and Pius XI were being sought by business, labor, and the government. The similarity of Roosevelt's ideas to those of Popes Leo XIII and Pius XI was, wrote a Cincinnati newspaper, especially apparent in the call for the aboli-

[27]Denver *Catholic Register*, March 12, 1933, p. 1.

[28]*Catholic World*, CXXXVII (April 1933), 107.

[29]Quoted by the *Catholic Herald*, March 30, 1933, p. 4; Denver *Catholic Register*, March 23, 1933, p. 4.

tion of child labor and for the establishment of minimum hours and wages for labor.[30] This similarity justified enthusiastic support of the president's program by American Catholics. In Milwaukee the New Deal was seen as the fulfillment of years of Catholic teaching, as expressed by the popes.[31] Indeed, the Christian social justice which seemed to be behind the New Deal could be traced only to the encyclicals of the popes. The recognition by FDR that labor deserved more consideration in our society was rooted in papal thinking.[32]

Some prominent Catholic sources, strangely ignoring the contributions of the Protestant social gospel movement, even insisted that without the groundwork laid by the Catholic Church, the New Deal would not have been received so well by the people. Commenting on a speech by Secretary of Interior Harold Ickes, in which he rejected rugged individualism, one editor remarked that "the seed sown by Leo XIII is beginning to grow into a mighty tree."[33] A. J. Hogan, S.J., president of Fordham University, felt that Catholic social thinking had helped people accept the New Deal. He thought it obvious that the administration was familiar with the papal plan. Such men as John Ryan, Michael O'Shaughnessy, and Charles Coughlin, said Hogan, had "prepared the way for acceptance of the New Deal by Catholics" by familiarizing them with the papal encyclicals.[34] The Reverend John F. O'Hara, vice president of Notre Dame University, echoed the sentiments expressed by Father Hogan, that FDR was expounding the social teachings of the Church. Speaking to the Knights of

[30]*Catholic Herald*, April 20, 1933, p. 4; Brooklyn *Tablet*, April 22, 1933, p. 3; *Catholic Telegraph* (Cincinnati), July 27, 1933, p. 4.
[31]*Catholic Herald*, July 27, 1933, p. 4.
[32]Brooklyn *Tablet*, July 29, 1933, p. 1; *America*, Aug. 5, 1933, p. 411; *Michigan Catholic*, Aug. 3, 1933, p. 4.
[33]*America*, Nov. 18, 1933, pp. 146–47. A hyperbolic tone was frequently present in Catholic evaluations.
[34]*NCCC Proceedings*, Oct. 1–4, 1933, pp. 50–52.

Columbus in Waterbury, Connecticut, Father O'Hara remarked that President Roosevelt "discovered Catholic economics for us," and that he used the encyclicals constantly. The priest speculated that perhaps some rich Catholics would now finally learn from the president of the United States the Church's teaching on wealth.[35]

Leaders of Catholic lay organizations contributed their support to the thesis that the New Deal was based on Catholic teaching. Edmond B. Butler, president of the National Catholic Alumni Federation, wrote a letter to the heads of alumni groups of Catholic colleges in the United States, urging them to support the New Deal. The reason why they should support the program was obvious. "The principles for which we have argued," wrote Butler, "and which were laid down for us in the encyclicals, *Rerum Novarum* and *Quadragesimo Anno,* seem for the first time in the history of our country, to be guiding the National Administration during this formative period." Catholics must ensure the success of this experiment. Indeed, "it is the duty of every educated Catholic . . . to take an active part," argued Butler.[36] He was supported in this line of reasoning by William J. McGinley, supreme secretary of the Knights of Columbus, who in October 1933 was received by Pope Pius XI in Rome. As McGinley was leaving the papal apartments, he expressed the thesis that President Roosevelt was being inspired in his deeds by Christian teaching, foremost of which was the encyclical of the reigning pontiff.[37]

The American hierarchy exhibited the same exaggerated notion of the influence of Catholic social teaching.

[35]*NCWC News Service,* Jan. 22, 1934; Ryan to Father George M. Sanvage, Jan. 29, 1934, Ryan Papers.

[36]*NCWC News Service,* July 17, 1933; New York *Times,* July 14, 1933, p. 8.

[37]*NCWC News Service,* Oct. 6, 1933; the editorials of the NCWC, carried over its *News Service,* also reiterated this theme, see April 17, 1933.

John Mark Gannon, bishop of Erie, Pennsylvania, urged the Catholic Daughters of America, at their convention in Colorado Springs, to help President Roosevelt put through his program. The bishop felt that the president was "thoroughly acquainted with the principles laid down by our Holy Father in his many encyclicals." Furthermore, he was trying to implement these principles in the New Deal. In fact, the New Deal was the papal program in practice.[38] Edmond Heelan, bishop of Sioux City, Iowa, wrote the priests of his diocese that they should find a certain satisfaction in the fact that President Roosevelt was using the papal teachings as the basis of his program of recovery. Bishops John A. Duffy of Syracuse, New York, and Michael J. Gallagher of Detroit, Michigan, were two more members of the hierarchy who praised Roosevelt's program and felt that it was based on the encyclicals. Gallagher even went so far as to say that Catholics had a solemn obligation to support the New Deal.[39]

The question naturally arises as to how much of this comment was simply wishful thinking on the part of American Catholics. Were they simply projecting their desires or was there solid evidence to support their belief that the New Deal came from Catholic sources? Before making a judgment on this, it might be well to discover whether or not the administration was really familiar with the papal encyclicals.

Evidence does exist which demonstrates that Roosevelt did have some knowledge of the Church's social program. During the campaign of 1932, he had quoted from *Quadragesimo Anno*. Furthermore, he had received a letter from Richard Dana Skinner of New York, with whom he appears to have been on a first-name basis, in which Skinner commented on the wisdom of quoting from the

[38]"News Letter," *NCWC News Service,* July 10, 1933.
[39]*Ibid.,* Feb. 19, 1934; Brooklyn *Tablet,* Aug. 19, 1933, p. 2.

papal document. Skinner sent FDR an article on *Quad-ragesimo Anno* by the Reverend Wilfrid Parsons and sug-gested that a study of it be made as a basis for social action against the depression. Roosevelt replied by refer-ring Skinner to brain truster Raymond Moley, but ad-mitted that he was interested in the ideas projected by the encyclical.[40] After the election, Skinner wrote to the president-elect again on the subject of the encyclicals. This time he spoke of winning Catholics' support to the "industries control idea" by convincing them that FDR's program was identical with the plan of Pope Pius XI. This was a tempting suggestion, but there is no evidence that Roosevelt personally pursued such a policy.[41]

There are other signs that Roosevelt was at least cogni-zant of the message of the encyclicals. The Reverend Charles Coughlin, undoubtedly exaggerating, boasted in the pages of the *Catholic Universe Bulletin* of Cleveland that he had "sat down with Mr. Roosevelt and read the encyclical over to him page by page."[42] Michael O'Shaughnessy, founder of the Catholic League for Social Justice, received a letter from Henry Wallace, secretary of agriculture, in which the latter spoke of having read *Quadragesimo Anno* and of being very impressed with it. Wallace said that he had discussed the encyclical with others in the administration.[43] The editor of *America,* Father Parsons, wrote of also having discussed *Quad-ragesimo Anno* with President Roosevelt. At the time, ac-cording to Parsons, Roosevelt had said that the encyclical

[40]Skinner to FDR, Aug. 3, 1932, and FDR to Skinner, Dec. 27, 1932, PPF, Box 229, Roosevelt Papers.

[41]Skinner to Louis Howe, June 13, 1933, OF 76-B, Box 4, Roosevelt Papers. Thomas Corcoran says that members of the administration were all aware of the encyclical. Interview with author, July 15, 1965.

[42]Quoted in *NCWC News Service,* Aug. 14, 1933.

[43]*America,* July 1, 1933, p. 292. Wallace admitted a familiarity with the encyclical in a letter to the author, Jan. 23, 1964.

was "too radical for him."[44] Donald Richberg, legal counsel of the National Reconstruction Administration in 1932, had also made a study of the program outlined by Pius XI.[45]

On a number of occasions, members of the president's official family publicly associated the New Deal with the papal encyclicals. Henry Wallace was the most prominent and persistent exponent of the idea that Roosevelt was only putting into practice the age-old social ideas of the Church.[46] In a 1934 speech before the World Alliance for International Friendship in New York City, Wallace made a point of the identity between the New Deal's attempt to balance agricultural and industrial prices and the ideas expressed by Pius XI.[47] The secretary reiterated this theme in a speech to the National Conference of Catholic Charities in Cincinnati, October 1934. He remarked that the New Dealers "are traversing ground in detail which has been described in more general terms in certain of the Papal encyclicals."[48]

Perhaps the most judicious conclusion that can be drawn from all this evidence is that while FDR and his advisers knew of the papal program, their knowledge was in the context of general American reform ideas. Some of these ideas were restatements of old Progressive movement principles. It seems clear that the New Deal would have developed even if the popes had not spoken. Of course, this observation does not minimize the importance of the support that Catholics gave Roosevelt in the 1930's in terms of papal encyclicals. In addition, however,

[44]*America*, June 2, 1934, pp. 174-76.
[45]Leo J. Hassenauer to John A. Ryan, April 11, 1934, Ryan Papers. Hassenauer was a business associate of Richberg's.
[46]Brooklyn *Tablet*, June 2, 1934, p. 10.
[47]*Ibid.*, Dec. 15, 1934, p. 3; *Monitor* (San Francisco), Dec. 22, 1934, p. 1.
[48]*NCCC Proceedings*, Oct. 7–10, 1934, p. 66.

there were other reasons for Catholics to welcome FDR and his program.

For one thing there was the appointment policy adopted by the new administration. Many American Catholics were hungry for recognition by appointment to a high post in the federal government. One month before Roosevelt was elected, Catholics attending St. Patrick's Cathedral in New York City heard the Reverend Henry F. Hammer complain that there was a conspiracy afoot to "keep Catholic men and women out of high national office." Father Hammer complained bitterly that a man could not "be a good Catholic and be a bad citizen." In December 1932 one Catholic author lamented the fact that there had been so few Catholics in past presidential cabinets. But he was optimistic for the future because he felt that the bitter experience of 1928 should have purged everyone of bigotry.[49]

There was some justice in this charge of discrimination. To most Catholics, it seemed impossible that only four of their coreligionists had been qualified to serve in all presidential cabinets from 1789 to 1932. Furthermore, only six Catholics had ever served on the Supreme Court. During the Republican rule of the 1920's, only one lower judicial appointment out of every twenty-five had gone to a Catholic.[50] While it may appear absurd to apportion federal appointments on the basis of percentage strength in a political party, such demands had previously been made by others. The statistics were real and were grist for the Catholic mill.

Under Franklin Roosevelt these trends were to be reversed sharply. Two Catholics, James A. Farley and

[49]Hammer is quoted in the New York *Times*, Oct. 17, 1932, p. 13; Richard J. Purcell, "Catholics in the President's Cabinet," *America*, Dec. 17, 1932, pp. 252-53.

[50]John Tracy Ellis, *American Catholicism* (Chicago, 1956), 149; Peter H. Odegard, "Catholicism and Elections in the United States," in *Religion and Politics*, ed. Peter H. Odegard (New Brunswick, N.J.,

Thomas J. Walsh, were appointed to the cabinet. Catholics were given an average of one out of every four judicial appointments during FDR's entire term in office. As one historian has stated, under Roosevelt the Irish Catholic was given a chance to ascend from his vulgar role as local party boss to more glamorous positions with the federal government.[51]

The appointments of Farley as postmaster general and Walsh as attorney general were a source of pride to many Catholics. Of course, many expected Farley to receive an appointment because of his fine work during the nomination race and presidential campaign.[52] Others speculated that there might be even more Catholics appointed to the cabinet. When Roosevelt named Walsh as attorney general, it was noted that although he was a Catholic, there was good reason for the appointment because of his progressive record as a senator and because of his prosecutor's role in the Teapot Dome Scandal.[53]

The announcement of the Farley and Walsh appointments provoked a favorable response from the Catholic press. The NCWC wire service sent out a story by Thomas E. Kissling, in which he pointed out that, for the first time in the history of the United States, two Catholics would serve simultaneously in a presidential

---

1960), 121; Samuel Lubell, The Future of American Politics, 2d ed., rev. (New York, 1956), 83.

[51]William V. Shannon, The American Irish (New York, 1964), 331. Shannon points to such men as Thomas G. Corcoran, John McCormick, Joseph E. Casey, James A. Farley, Edward J. Flynn, Joseph P. Kennedy, and Frank Murphy as representing a young generation of Irishmen who were brought to national prominence by Roosevelt. James Farley admitted a certain satisfaction in being the first Catholic in a presidential cabinet in the twentieth century. Interview with author, March 20, 1965.

[52]Shannon, American Irish, 372, reminds us that Roosevelt started the tradition of giving the post of national chairman of the Democratic party to an Irish Catholic.

[53]Rexford G. Tugwell, The Democratic Roosevelt (New York, 1957), 267.

cabinet.[54] Pictures of the two men were splashed all over the diocesan press. Colonel P. H. Callahan of Louisville, Kentucky, a prominent Catholic layman with a sharp political sense, made a survey of Catholic press reaction to the story. He forwarded to Louis Howe, presidential secretary, the news that most Catholic papers in the United States gave very favorable notice to the appointments.[55]

The cabinet appointments were only one sign of increased Catholic recognition from Roosevelt. Equally satisfying to American Catholics were the diplomatic positions handed out. Two appointments were particularly important: that of Frank Murphy, mayor of Detroit, as governor-general of the Philippines, and that of Robert H. Gore as governor of Puerto Rico. The Murphy appointment was a combination of diplomatic need and political reward. The Philippines were largely Catholic in population, which made the appointment of Murphy especially suitable. Furthermore, Murphy had worked long and hard for Roosevelt during the campaign. Roosevelt's brother-in-law G. Hall Roosevelt wrote to the president about Murphy's loyalty, pointing out that apart from the mayor's many qualifications, he also had "tremendous Catholic influence." Murphy's personal desire for the Philippine position was also a factor in his selection.[56]

The reaction of the Catholic press to the appointment was characteristic. Murphy's picture was printed on many front pages, and it was noted that he was the first Catho-

[54]*NCWC News Service,* March 4, 1932. This unique event failed to materialize when Walsh died unexpectedly before taking office.

[55]Callahan to Howe, March 10, 1933, Reel 2, *Sel. Mat.;* the Brooklyn *Tablet,* March 4, 1933, and the Boston *Pilot,* March 11, 1933, both carried front-page stories. After Walsh's death, the Boston *Pilot* gave major emphasis to the significance of a Catholic funeral being held in the state chambers with prominent churchmen and the president being present. March 11, 1933, p. 1.

[56]Richard D. Lunt, "The High Ministry of Government: The Political Career of Frank Murphy" (unpublished M.A. thesis, University of New Mexico, 1962), 66.

lic to hold the position. With the Murphy appointment, wrote one editor, "President Roosevelt has added another Catholic to the list of those already occupying conspicuous places in his administrative family."[57] The appointment of Robert Hayes Gore as governor of Puerto Rico met a similar response. Gore had nine children, a fact that was a source of ironic amusement to some Catholics, for the previous Puerto Rican governor had been sympathetic to the planned parenthood group on the island.[58] The editor of the Brooklyn *Tablet* felt that the Murphy and Gore appointments indicated that "days of fairness, as well as intelligence, are being inaugurated at Washington."[59]

Besides these appointments of prominent lay Catholics to public office, a number of priests had been enlisted in support of New Deal projects. Most prominent of these were John A. Ryan and Francis J. Haas. Ryan was on the Advisory Council of the United States Employment Service and the Advisory Committee of the Subsistence Homestead Division in the National Reconstruction Administration.[60] Roosevelt appointed Haas a member of the National Labor Board on October 7, 1933. The priest had previously been a member of the Labor Advisory Committee under the National Industrial Relations Act. Later, Haas would serve as labor representative on the General Code Authority, as a member of the National Committee on Business and Labor Standards, and as one of the three members of the Labor Policies Board of the Works Progress Administration.[61]

[57]Quoted in *NCWC News Service*, April 10, 1933; Brooklyn *Tablet*, April 15, 1933, p. 1.

[58]*America*, May 20, 1933, p. 146; Boston *Pilot*, May 20, 1933, p. 11.

[59]May 13, 1933, p. 9.

[60]Broderick, *Right Reverend*, 213; Hon. Frances Perkins to Ryan, Aug. 5, 1933, Ryan Papers.

[61]Roosevelt to Haas, telegram, Oct. 7, 1933, and Roosevelt to Haas, Dec. 18, 1935, Correspondence-personal, 1932, and Miscellaneous, Haas Papers at Catholic University, Washington, D.C.; Rev. Michael J. Ready to Stephen Early, Dec. 17, 1935, Reel 2, *Sel. Mat.*

Across the country, in the summer of 1933, the Catholic clergy swung their support behind the NRA. A number of priests served as members of regional boards of the NRA. Archbishop Edward J. Hanna of San Francisco was chairman of a presidential committee to deal with longshoremen's strikes. This role of the clergy in the early days of the New Deal justified Father Ryan's statement in late 1934 that "there are more Catholics in public positions, high and low, in the Federal Government today than ever before in the history of the country."[62]

Did Roosevelt make these appointments with an eye on the Catholic vote? There is little explicit evidence of this but certainly his actions were interpreted in a way that was politically profitable. Roosevelt began a trend toward using Catholics at high levels of government and this trend was recognized by prominent Catholic spokesmen. It is not insignificant that Colonel P. H. Callahan could send to Louis Howe numerous clippings of diocesan papers praising Catholic appointments, and that the Knights of Columbus of New York City and of New Hampshire should send congratulatory telegrams on the cabinet appointments of Farley and Walsh.[63] The *News Service* of the NCWC denied that there was any substantial basis for the assumption that religion played a part in FDR's appointments, but it also pointed out that "President Roosevelt has gone further than most, if not all, his predecessors in nominating Catholics for important posts."[64] The Brooklyn *Tablet* expressed pride that it had predicted that Roosevelt would show more "regard" for Catholics and that the old policy of nonrecognition would be discarded.[65] A more hardheaded line was taken by the

---

[62]Ryan to James Moran, Sept. 28, 1934, Ryan Papers.

[63]William Flynn to Roosevelt, March 17, 1933, and Charles Doherty to Roosevelt, telegram [n.d.], OF, Box 28, Roosevelt Papers; Callahan to Howe, March 10, 1933, OF 76-B, Box 4, Roosevelt Papers.

[64]April 10, 1933; April 17, 1933.

[65]Dec. 30, 1933, p. 7.

Michigan Catholic, whose editor felt that Catholics should not act like children because they had gained recognition in the presidential cabinet appointments. The new recognition was no more than just for a group representing one-sixth of the country's population. Yet this editor could not deny that FDR deserved much credit for changing the former policy of exclusion.[66]

If President Roosevelt's appointment policy helped his image among American Catholics in 1933, of added significance were the direct contacts he sought with the Church during his first year in office. His two most notable public contacts were his acceptance of an honorary degree from Catholic University of America in June and his speech at the annual meeting of the National Conference of Catholic Charities in October.

Roosevelt received his honorary degree on June 14 in Washington, D.C.[67] The major speech of the occasion was made by Patrick Cardinal Hayes, archbishop of New York. The cardinal prefaced his remarks with congratulations to a president who was "moving forward with courage and intelligence" to combat the crisis of the depression. "Your actions," the cardinal continued, "spring from but one motive, namely, the advancement of the Common Good." The remainder of the speech was an elaboration on this theme of the "Common Good." He pointed out that while private associations might do much to curtail unfair competition and ruthless business practices, this was not enough. Something was needed which would represent the interest of all the people; this was where the federal government entered the picture. The govern-

[66]March 2, 1933, p. 4.

[67]This honor had been arranged by Rev. Maurice Sheehy and James Farley. Sheehy had approached Farley with the idea and the latter had urged FDR to accept the honor. Farley, Interview with author, March 20, 1965. Later Sheehy and Archbishop James H. Ryan called on FDR to extend a formal invitation. Sheehy, Letter to author, Nov. 16, 1963.

ment should protect individual rights and promote human welfare, for these were "activities which cannot adequately be carried on by private efforts." The extension of the government into many areas of society should be viewed as a good trend, just as laissez faire was a bad trend. Certain individual rights might be curtailed by this action, but such restrictions could be justified on the basis of the common good. Furthermore, in time of crisis, citizens should not expect the government to be bound by precedents but should expect bold strokes of experimentation. Centralization of power may be necessary, and "one clear, confident voice can save hundreds from panic."[68]

President Roosevelt, who had not planned to speak, was moved by the auspicious occasion to offer a few impromptu remarks. He referred to the cardinal as an old friend and neighbor, and commented that his own presence among the "great dignitaries of the Church" plus the fact that it was Flag Day made a "happy combination."[69]

What appears as a rather dull academic gathering was, instead, for the Catholics who viewed the event, a moment of pride. FDR had been impressed with Cardinal Hayes's address and requested a copy. The cardinal obliged two days later and, in an accompanying letter, thanked the president for "the wonderful tribute you paid to the Catholic people of America by your distinguished presence and kindly words."[70] The Catholic press was quick to echo these sentiments. Even the banal remarks made by the president were recorded with scriptural care. One editor remarked that Cardinal Hayes's endorsement of the New Deal was seconded by all American Cath-

[68]Address on "The Common Good," by Patrick Cardinal Hayes at Washington, June 14, 1933, copy in Reel 3, *Sel. Mat.*
[69]*Catholic World,* CXXXVII (July 1933), 493.
[70]Hayes to Roosevelt, June 16, 1933, Reel 3, *Sel. Mat.*

olics.[71] To some, FDR's appearance indicated "a change for the better in the public mind toward the Church." The president himself manifested "a splendid feeling of good will" toward the Church, in contrast to the neglect suffered by the Church from the last four presidents.[72] One Catholic priest in Detroit felt that giving Roosevelt an honorary degree was inadequate. The Reverend Charles E. Coughlin wrote the president that "a thousand such honors could never manifest the gratitude which the American people owe you for what you have already accomplished."[73]

The second public manifestation of Roosevelt's rapport with the Church was in connection with the annual meeting of the National Conference of Catholic Charities, held in New York City during October 1933. At the opening session of the meeting, Harry Hopkins addressed the gathering on "National Trends in Relief." More important, however, was the appearance of President Roosevelt to give the main address at the final dinner of the convention. Patrick Cardinal Hayes was the first speaker of the evening and again he praised Roosevelt's leadership. Hayes called for a new social order of justice with a wider distribution of ownership, higher wages, and fewer hours. The cardinal declared the formation of trade associations to be a major step forward and commented that if these groups were just in their actions, the federal government would not have to oversee them. But in any case, such justice must prevail. The cardinal concluded his remarks with a strong statement on the responsibility of the government for the public welfare: "In fact, the claims of the common welfare on ownership are so strong that the

[71]*Pax,* official organ of Benedictine Missionary Fathers, July 1933, pp. 126-27; *Commonweal,* June 30, 1933, p. 227.

[72]Brooklyn *Tablet,* June 24, 1933, p. 9.

[73]Quoted in Peter Morris, "Father Coughlin and the New Deal" (unpublished M.A. thesis, Columbia University, 1958), 24.

State, though it enjoys no right to abolish the private
ownership of property, is justified, with due regard to the
natural and divine law, in adjusting this ownership and
controlling its use so as to bring it into harmony with the
interests of the public good."[74]

After this speech, which seemed to endorse much of
Roosevelt's efforts, Monsignor Robert F. Keegan, secretary to Cardinal Hayes and a leader in the NCCC, introduced the president. Keegan spoke of FDR's "clear
vision" and "accurate appreciation" of the evils of laissez
faire capitalism. He ended his introduction by declaring,
"We love him [Roosevelt] for the man and friend he is."[75]

Roosevelt thus began his address with assurance of support from the NCCC. His speech stressed the need for
continued relief work by private agencies; the federal
government could not carry the load alone. Furthermore,
the success of relief work depended to a large degree on
personal contacts that were better achieved by small private associations. Private church relief was also important because, said the president, the people believe
"spiritual values count in the long run more than material
values." Pursuing another theme, the president remarked
that all attempts by governments to interfere with the
right of religious worship had failed and would continue
to fail because such interference contradicted a basic human need. In conclusion, FDR expressed optimism about
the ability of the United States to overcome its current
difficulties. In terms undoubtedly selected for his Catholic
audience, Roosevelt remarked: "With every passing year I
become more confident that humanity is moving forward
to the practical application of the teachings of Christianity as they affect the individual lives of men and
women everywhere."[76]

[74]Address of Patrick Cardinal Hayes, Oct. 4, 1933, Reel 3, *Sel. Mat.*
[75]*Ibid.*
[76]Rosenman, *Public Papers*, II, 379-81.

The president's speech was received enthusiastically by many Catholics. Monsignor Keegan later wrote to FDR thanking him for the inspiration and encouragement he had given the NCCC.[77] Aloysius J. Hogan, S.J., president of Fordham University, felt that there was growing evidence that "Catholics had given a soul to the New Deal."[78] One editor considered FDR's mere presence at the NCCC meeting "a stirring tribute to the Church's efforts to help our fellowmen."[79] Before a Council of Catholic Women meeting in Chicago, Cardinal Mundelein referred to Roosevelt's appearance at the NCCC in glowing terms. The cardinal called the president a physician who had prevented an uprising in the United States and who would cure the nation's ills. Even *Osservatore Romano*, the Vatican newspaper, and an especially authoritative source for the American Catholic press, praised Roosevelt's remarks on the necessity of religion in all social works.[80]

As Roosevelt spoke in New York City, other members of the administration were also addressing Catholic groups on the New Deal. Brooks Hays, Stanley Reed, and Arthur J. Altmeyer of the Social Security Board addressed a gathering of Catholics in Peoria, Illinois, and asked for support of the New Deal.[81] Church leaders gave Roosevelt enthusiastic backing on the basis of his personal attitudes and actions and because of certain general

[77]Keegan to Roosevelt, Oct. 9, 1933, PPF 628, Roosevelt Papers.
[78]Quoted in *Columbia*, Nov. 1933, p. 7.
[79]Brooklyn *Tablet*, Oct. 7, 1933, p. 9.
[80]Cited by *Catholic Herald*, Oct. 25, 1933, p. 1. The *New World* of Chicago was even more enthusiastic. In an editorial entitled "Coming into Our Own," the paper stressed the fact that FDR's appearance at the NCCC meeting was one more bit of evidence that Roman Catholics were no longer considered outsiders. The old idea of the Catholic Church as the prime defender of the status quo was being rejected. Roosevelt's appearance had indicated that "Catholic social teaching is making headway far beyond what is commonly thought." *New World*, Oct. 13, 1933, p. 4.
[81]Brooklyn *Tablet*, Oct. 12, 1933, p. 9.

principles of his program. Lacking a highly unified and explicit social program of their own, however, it was questionable whether such unanimous support would be expressed for the actual implementation of the legislative details of the New Deal.

4

Finance and Agriculture

IN their reaction to Roosevelt's handling of fiscal and agricultural problems, American Catholics exhibited at once a sense of radicalism and of nostalgia. Most Catholics welcomed the attempts by the administration to curtail the power of Wall Street and to regulate the currency. They also supported agricultural reforms, but here there was less desire for rigid federal regulation.

American Catholics shared the relief experienced by their fellow citizens when Franklin Roosevelt began his term of office by closing the banks of the nation to prevent their internal collapse. They hoped that Roosevelt would have the courage to withstand the assault that they felt would soon be launched upon his policies by the "money powers."[1] While the bank holiday and subsequent Reform Act were viewed by some Catholics as authoritarian in tone, others praised the measures as steps necessary to curb the greed of wealth. This was, wrote the *Catholic Herald,* a "New Deal in which the cards are not stacked by greed and power against the people and their government."[2]

When FDR attempted to relieve the depression by manipulating the amount of gold content in the dollar, Catholics shared the confusion of most citizens. Some of them, however, felt that Roosevelt's measures of calling in gold and restricting the importing of it were mere commonsense.[3] Al Smith condemned the currency manipulation as producing "baloney dollars," but Smith, for several reasons, failed to swing Catholic opinion against FDR's dollar policy. To begin with, Smith's defection on this issue was more than compensated for by the support the president received from Father Coughlin, the radio priest of Detroit. Coughlin wrote to FDR in October, approving the stabilization of gold at $31.75 an ounce and the dollar at 65 cents.[4] He fully supported FDR's attempts at manipulation. This support led Coughlin to attack the ideas of Smith. The priest chose a November 27 rally in New York City to defend the president's policy against the Smith charges. While expressing regret at having to correct such a gentleman as Smith, Coughlin felt that it was "Roosevelt or ruin." In his public address, Coughlin implied that Smith was attacking Roosevelt's monetary policies because the ex-governor wanted a loan from J. P. Morgan for the Empire State Building.[5]

While many Catholics shared Coughlin's doubts about the validity of Smith's criticism, few liked the priest's personal attack on the 1928 standard bearer. As one student of the period has noted, "A situation which dis-

[1]Denver *Catholic Register,* March 9, 1933, p. 1.
[2]*Catholic Herald,* March 23, 1933, p. 4; *Commonweal,* March 22, 1933, p. 563; *Catholic World,* CXXXVIII (Dec. 1933), 257-59.
[3]*Extension,* XXVIII (July 1933), 21.
[4]Coughlin to Roosevelt, telegram, Oct. 4, 1933, OF 229, Box 3, Roosevelt Papers.
[5]Lowell Dyson, "The Quest for Power: Father Coughlin and the Election of 1936" (unpublished M.A. thesis, Columbia University, 1937), 20; Peter Morris, "Father Coughlin and the New Deal" (unpublished M.A. thesis, Columbia University, 1938), 42; *Commonweal,* Dec. 8, 1933, p. 144.

closed the nation's leading Catholic layman and its most widely known clergyman calling each other names was discomforting to many Catholics."[6] Yet it was evident that Roosevelt's measures had support from others besides Coughlin. Some Catholics admitted that FDR's formula for recovery might be ineffective but they quickly pointed out that "his objective is ethically sound, and sound in common sense."[7] Father John Ryan thought the fears by some individuals of excessive inflation were exaggerated. Although he did not mention Smith by name, Ryan announced that he was opposed to direct inflation but that he saw little in Roosevelt's program to indicate that this policy had any backing in the administration.[8] This fear of inflation was shared by the Reverend John Burke, secretary of the NCWC, who praised Roosevelt's decision to veto the Patman Veteran's Bonus Bill because it was inflationary.[9]

One popular reaction to Roosevelt's fiscal policy was expressed by *Commonweal* magazine. After praising FDR's decision not to abide by the findings of the London Economic Conference, the editors announced that the central thesis of the New Deal's monetary policy was "public control, through the government, of money and credit, rather than the system of banker's control." This particular policy, the editors continued, was "in line with the assumptions of Pope Pius XI, expressed in *Quadragesimo Anno.*"[10]

Interesting for the light it throws on Catholic thought are the comments provoked by the United States Senate investigation of Wall Street pursuant to passage of legis-

[6]Dyson, "The Quest for Power," 20. See also Denver *Catholic Register,* Nov. 30, 1933, p. 1; Brooklyn *Tablet,* Dec. 9, 1933, p. 11.

[7]*Commonweal,* Dec. 15, 1935, p. 170.

[8]Ryan to Ray E. Jones, Feb. 17, 1933, Box 3; Ryan to G. P. McEntee, Dec. 13, 1933, Box 4, Ryan Papers.

[9]Burke to Roosevelt, May 27, 1935, Reel 2, *Sel. Mat.*

[10]July 21, 1933, p. 297.

lation to regulate the stock market. The Securities Act, passed in May 1933, gave the Federal Trade Commission more control over the issuing of new securities, required more information on the solvency of new stock, and made liability for misrepresentation more specific. The passage of this law was made easy by the public support engendered as a result of a Senate investigation of Wall Street which had been started by Hoover, and which was carried on with great zeal in 1933 by its chief counsel, Ferdinand Pecora of New York.

The Administrative Committee of the NCWC, representing the views of the American hierarchy, supported the Pecora investigations and FDR's policy of policing Wall Street.[11] The official organ of the Knights of Columbus also came out in support of the investigation and of Roosevelt's stand. The magazine *Columbia* felt that the American press was trying to whitewash Wall Street. The editor expressed a note of class feeling when he pointed out that J. P. Morgan got a better press because of his wealth.[12]

Elements of the Catholic press joined the call for a correction of the evils revealed by the Pecora investigation. A cure was needed. Whether this cure took the form of inflation, rejection of the gold standard, or a dose of "baloney dollars" was considered beside the point.[13] When Congress finally passed the Federal Securities Act to control some of the problems, one editor thought it would stand for some time because it was based on sound morality. By this he meant that the law put both the buyer and seller of securities on common ground.[14]

Finance, however, was only one of the major problems facing the New Dealers in 1933. Equally significant were

[11]*Catholic World,* CXXXVIII (Dec. 1933), 3.
[12]April 1933, pp. 11, 13.
[13]*Catholic Herald,* Dec. 7, 1933, p. 4.
[14]*Catholic Messenger,* Feb. 3, 1934, p. 2.

the difficulties of the American farmer. Although most of the Catholic population in the United States resided in urban areas, the Church had early addressed itself to the plight of the farmer who was suffering from the depression. The main source of Catholic thought on agriculture was the Rural Life Bureau of the NCWC, led by the Reverend Edgar Schmiedeler. Schmiedeler, together with other Catholic priests and bishops, was to formulate the Church's attitude toward the farm problem. While not an elaborate or detailed plan, the philosophy behind Catholic thinking on agriculture was sufficiently unique to permit its isolation as a type of Catholic agrarianism.

As early as July 1932, Schmiedeler had stated the aims of the Rural Life Bureau as being "the preservation and enrichment of the farm home."[15] It was a recurring theme for many Catholic thinkers that farming afforded a better opportunity to lead a truly Christian life. This romanticizing of the farmer could be traced back at least to the time of Thomas Jefferson.[16] For these Catholics the chief benefit of rural living was the social stability it promoted. Equally for them, life in the city was conducive both to unstable personal relations and to atheism. An urbanite was more susceptible to atheism because of his "contact with brick and mortar, with concrete and steel—the things of man—[rather] than with nature, and nature's beauties—the things of God." Thus spoke Schmiedeler to a group of Catholic teachers in Kansas in 1936.[17] Another popular theme in Catholic discussions of rural life was the tendency to attribute the rise in birth control to the crowded living conditions in the city. Farm families, in contrast, were generally large. Using these ideas, some Catholics began to urge a back-to-the-land movement in the 1930's.

[15]Quoted in the Boston *Pilot,* July 30, 1932, p. 5.
[16]Paul R. Conkin, *Tomorrow a New World* (Ithaca, N.Y., 1959), 12.
[17]Quoted in *Catholic Action,* Aug. 1936, p. 5.

Such a movement was endorsed by the Administrative Committee of the NCWC in a statement on April 25, 1933, and by the Catholic Rural Life Conference in October 1933.[18] The bishops on the Administrative Committee pointed out that the depression was partly the result of the industrial revolution, which had pushed people off the farm into crowded cities inadequate to support them. As a remedy, the bishops called for a return to the independent life of the farm.[19] Other Catholics expressed the fear that the depression would force more farmers into the city and thereby turn them into "aimless, drifting, proletariat."[20] Some criticized the ruthless capitalism and laissez faire attitude of the government as having contributed to the depression. But they also tended to categorize the "fostering of the drift of population from the country-sides to the slums of great cities" and the "denial to the farmer of a just and stable price for his products," as other evils of the existing economic system.[21]

During the 1932 presidential campaign, Catholics showed a distinct interest in the farm problem. F. P. Kenkel, director of the Catholic Central Verein of St.

[18]*NCWC News Service*, Oct. 19, 1933; Conkin, *Tomorrow*, 28, says "never before in the history of the United States had back-to-the-land been so popular" as in 1932. The CRLC was started in 1923 and advocated "property as a right and a responsibility, denounced farm tenancy, advocated subsistence farming, and . . . attempted to guide the back-to-the-land movement." See *ibid.*, 25; see also Raymond P. Witte, *Twenty-five Years of Crusading* (Des Moines, 1948).

[19]Raphael M. Huber, ed., *Our Bishops Speak: National Pastorals and Annual Statements of the Hierarchy of the United States, 1919–1951* (Milwaukee, 1952), 296-97. This statement of the Administrative Committee was signed by the archbishop of San Francisco, Edward J. Hanna; archbishop of Cincinnati, John T. McNicholas; archbishop of St. Paul, Minn., John G. Murray; bishop of Cleveland, Joseph Schrembs; bishop of Pittsburgh, Hugh C. Boyle; bishop of Fort Wayne, Ind., John F. Noll; bishop of Kansas City, Mo., Thomas F. Lillis.

[20]*Catholic Herald*, Sept. 8, 1932, p. 4.

[21]James F. Murphy, Presidential Address at 18th Session of NCCC, *Proceedings*, Omaha, Nebr., Sept. 25–28, 1932, p. 6.

Louis, Missouri, wrote that the American farmer should be acutely aware of the effect on him of the future economic planning that was being discussed in the campaign.[22] Father John Ryan was impressed with the ideas set forth by Roosevelt in his speech at Topeka, Kansas, during the campaign. Here Roosevelt had promised to reorganize the Department of Agriculture, to lower taxes for farmers, and to pass laws for federal financing of farm mortgages and for a voluntary domestic allotment plan to relieve surpluses.[23] To Father Ryan the domestic allotment plan looked like the best way to help the farmers by obtaining better prices for staple agricultural products. He hoped that Roosevelt would support the idea if elected and only regretted that the candidate had not been more clear in his advocacy of the plan.[24]

Ryan had good reason to be disturbed by FDR's vagueness on the question. When the Reverend W. Howard Bishop, president of the Catholic Rural Life Conference, wrote to the Democratic candidate, he enclosed a resolution of his organization which endorsed the domestic allotment plan as the best way to give needed relief to the farmers. Father Bishop asked Roosevelt what his plans were in this matter. Roosevelt replied through his secretary that he was not as yet completely committed to a definite plan for agriculture, but he referred Father Bishop to the campaign speech at Topeka.[25] After the 1932 election, Catholic agricultural thought still centered on the domestic allotment plan. Some accepted it because they thought it would create the least disturbance in the

[22]F. P. Kenkel, "The Farmer and Economic Planning," *NCCC Proceedings*, 1932, p. 200.

[23]James M. Burns, *Roosevelt: The Lion and the Fox* (New York, 1956), 142.

[24]Ryan to Prof. W. L. Wilson, Sept. 17, 1932, Ryan Papers.

[25]Frank O'Hara, "The Voluntary Domestic Allotment Plan," *Catholic World*, CXXXVI (March 1933), 641-48; *Catholic Messenger*, Dec. 1, 1932, p. 1.

world's prices. It was better than surplus dumping, which might produce retaliatory trade measures by foreign nations.[26] By January 1933 Father Ryan was supporting the idea of parity payments as being the best method of raising agricultural prices.[27] Others felt that no adequate adjustment of agricultural prices could be hoped for without a simultaneous plan to provide work and better wages for the city labor expected to consume the farm products.[28] It was also recognized, however, that the debt-ridden condition of the farmer had to be changed before any scheme to raise prices could be effective. Further, wrote one Catholic editor, "since Society and the State both sinned by permitting land to be treated as mere chattel, they should now provide for the reduction of farm mortgages."[29]

The Catholic hierarchy also made it clear that it supported immediate aid to the farmer. In June 1933 a group of bishops meeting in Cincinnati advocated local and regional cooperation by farmers to offset the flux in world prices. They pointed out that a healthy rural economy was the foundation for any national recovery. In a statement of first principles, the bishops remarked: "The first duty of the farmer is not to produce, but to live, and to live in a manner befitting his worth as a man and his dignity as a child of God."[30]

In order to live, however, the bishops realized that the farmer would need higher prices for his produce. A reform of the United States economic system was required to produce this rise. The farmer must be protected against the instability of the open market. Going this far, how-

---

[26]*Central-Blatt and Social Justice,* Jan. 1933, p. 303.
[27]Ryan to D. P. Hughes, Jan. 10, 1933, Ryan Papers.
[28]*Catholic Herald,* Feb. 9, 1933, p. 4.
[29]*Central-Blatt and Social Justice,* April 1933, p. 11.
[30]Bishops of the Cincinnati Province, "Agriculture and Catholic Principles," *Catholic Mind,* XXXI (July 8, 1933), 252-60.

ever, the bishops clearly pointed out that they were not calling for the industrialization or collectivization of American agriculture. Realizing that cooperation and government assistance would be necessary to relieve the farmer, the bishops were nevertheless vague on specific remedies. Actually their position presented them with a dilemma. On the one hand, they wanted to preserve at all cost the individualism and independence of the farmer. Yet they also saw the need for cooperation and state assistance if the independent farmer was to survive.[31]

This was the state of Catholic agrarian thought when the Congress approved the agricultural policies of the New Deal. The major agricultural measure was the Agricultural Adjustment Act, passed on May 12, 1933, which curtailed production and established parity prices. Farmers were granted payments for voluntary reduction of crops. A tax on processors of farm products was the source of relief money. Farm mortgages could be refinanced through Federal Land Banks at lower interest rates. The entire law was to be carried out by an Agricultural Adjustment Administration under the secretary of agriculture, Henry Wallace.[32]

Henry Wallace had strong support among important elements of the Catholic Church. Foremost among his backers was the Reverend Maurice S. Sheehy, a faculty member at Catholic University and a close friend of Father John Ryan. Sheehy had remarked that "few per-

[31]*Ibid., passim;* see also *Catholic Action,* July 1933, p. 4. The bishops who signed this statement included Archbishop John T. McNicholas of Cincinnati; Bishop James J. Hartley of Columbus, Ohio; Bishop Joseph Chartrand of Indianapolis; Bishop Joseph Schrembs of Cleveland; Bishop Michael J. Gallager of Detroit; Bishop Francis W. Howard of Covington, Ky.; Bishop Alphonse J. Smith of Nashville; Bishop John F. Noll of Fort Wayne, Ind.; Bishop Karl J. Alter of Toledo, Ohio.

[32]William E. Leuchtenburg, *Franklin D. Roosevelt and the New Deal* (New York, 1963), 48, 51, 52.

sons in American public life know better and agree more
completely with the Catholic conception of social justice
than Mr. Wallace."[33] The secretary of agriculture, said
Sheehy, had quoted the papal encyclicals of Pius XI and
Leo XIII on numerous occasions. Sheehy felt certain that
Wallace was using the papal teachings in his approach to
the farm problem.[34]

Other Catholics watched the debate on the farm bill
with mixed emotions. *Commonweal*, quite frankly confused as to the theory behind the Agricultural Adjustment
Act, called it "a very good substitute for a jig-saw puz-
zle." While deploring the paternalism it seemed to establish in agriculture, the editor accepted it as an experiment
and admitted that something drastic had to be done in
this area.[35] Father Ryan felt the bill might help the
farmer. When the processing tax feature of the act was
attacked as being unconstitutional by Professor Edwin W.
Kemmerer of Princeton, Ryan defended the administration's position. The priest had certain doubts about AAA
but felt that Roosevelt's spirit of experimentation was to
be applauded. William F. Montavon, director of the Legal
Action Department of the NCWC, called the AAA a good
plan but was afraid it imposed too heavy an administrative burden on President Roosevelt and Secretary Wallace.[36]

A few Catholics took a more positive stand in support of
the bill. Listeners of the weekly Boston radio program "The
Catholic Truth Hour" heard Jones I. Corrigan, S.J., an-

[33]M. S. Sheehy, "Henry A. Wallace and the Papal Encyclicals,"
clipping from *Daily Tribune* (Dubuque, Iowa [n.d.]), in Reel 3, *Sel.
Mat.*

[34]*Ibid.;* Sheehy was to support Wallace's bid for the vice-presi-
dency in 1940, Sheehy, Letter to author, Nov. 16, 1963.

[35]April 5, 1933, pp. 620-21.

[36]William F. Montavon, "Constructive Work of the 73rd Congress,"
Catholic Action, Aug. 1933, pp. 7-10; Francis L. Broderick, *The Right
Reverend New Dealer: John A. Ryan* (New York, 1963), 212-13.

nounce that the AAA had "saved agriculture by substituting planned control for anarchy."[37] The annual convention of the Catholic Rural Life Conference (CRLC), held in Milwaukee on October 19, 1933, adopted resolutions endorsing the AAA and subsistence farming. The CRLC also called for speed in implementing farm relief.[38] The Reverend Edgar Schmiedeler, director of the NCWC Rural Life Bureau, went on the radio in November 1933 to praise the agricultural program of the New Deal. He called the AAA "a charter of economic equality with the city" for the farmer. He admitted that much was yet to be done, but he praised the results thus far accomplished by Roosevelt as "a foundation whereon to build a rural life worthy of America."[39]

Naturally there were elements in the Catholic population that disagreed with Father Schmiedeler's praise of the AAA. Father Coughlin wrote to FDR in August 1933 that the proposals of the AAA were "foolish" and embodied "puerile policy" and an "asinine philosophy."[40] In California, the San Francisco *Monitor* applauded the New Deal's attempt to relieve farm mortgages but felt the idea of paying rent for unused land was absurd. The editor was convinced that AAA would mean the end of the American farmer. The rural population would be forced into the city to be exploited by industry as cheap labor.[41]

As the control policies of the Agricultural Adjustment Administration unfolded, there arose considerable opposition among certain segments of the population. Father Coughlin and others looked with disfavor upon the destruction of crops and pigs. Father Ryan, however, was more generous in his observations. To a friend's query

[37]Quoted in the Boston *Pilot,* Oct. 21, 1933, p. 1.
[38]*NCWC News Service,* Oct. 26, 1933.
[39]Quoted in *Catholic Action,* Nov. 1933, p. 5.
[40]Morris, "Father Coughlin," 29.
[41]Sept. 16, 1933, p. 10, and Aug. 16, 1933, p. 1.

about the moral obligation to use excess food to feed poor foreign nations, Ryan replied that for such a noble deed to have any effect it would have to be continued over a long period. He thought "it would be very difficult to prove the existence of such a moral obligation." Ryan did not think that American farmers were obliged to feed foreigners from their surplus.[42] The *Catholic Farmer* of Wisconsin also came to the defense of Wallace and the AAA. The editor defended both the secretary and the president against charges of excess waste in solving the farm problem, but he did fear that the "radical farm bloc" in Congress might force the administration into a more totalitarian approach to the rural depression. It would not do, he felt, to have the government telling the farmer what, and how much, to plant.[43]

By the end of 1934, most American Catholics could echo the sentiments expressed in November by the CRLC at their annual meeting in St. Paul. The conference adopted a resolution that commended the efforts of the New Deal "to bring debt relief to the American farmer." But the CRLC also realized that other areas of the farm problem were still unresolved.[44]

At the annual meeting of the National Conference of Catholic Charities, held in Cincinnati, October 7-10, 1934, the delegates heard the Reverend Luigi Ligutti of Granger, Iowa, make an impassioned plea for the small farmers of the country. Ligutti insisted that the preponderance of large corporate farms over small family-owned farms was one of the major problems facing American agriculture. The large farms permitted too much waste, said Ligutti, who called for a return to small farm ownership. How

---

[42]Ryan to Rev. Urban Baer, Feb. 23, 1934, Ryan Papers.
[43]*Catholic Farmer* (supplement to the *Catholic Herald*), June 14, 1934, p. 1, and Dec. 13, 1934, p. 2.
[44]*Catholic Action,* Dec. 1934, p. 19.

this would curtail the problem of overproduction, he did not say. But he wanted more people on farms and felt that the breakup of large farms and extension of long-term federal loans at low interest rates to young independent homesteaders would accomplish this goal. This theme of the need to return to the small family farm was one of the recurring ideas of Catholic agrarianism.[45] Earlier a Catholic editor had called the subsistence homestead movement "one of the sanest plans in our national reconstruction."[46]

President Roosevelt had always favored the idea of subsistence homesteads as a means of relieving the farm problem. With FDR's support, Senator John Bankhead of Alabama inserted an amendment for the execution of such a scheme into the National Industrial Recovery Act.[47] Father Ryan had been an early supporter of the Bankhead proposal. "It seems to me," he wrote, "that this [subsistence homestead idea] is a very meritorious project and deserving of the support of all who would like to see some of the unemployed become self-supporting as farmers."[48] Indeed, Bankhead's early proposal fitted perfectly with the Catholic idea of a back-to-the-land movement and the advantages of rural life over urban. In fact, President Roosevelt also shared this idea of the advantages of rural living.[49]

By 1935 Senator Bankhead had formulated an independent bill designed to aid tenant farmers and farm laborers in becoming genuine landowners. The bill, in the opinion of one historian, "reflected the reformer's faith in

[45]NCCC Proceedings, Oct. 7–10, 1934, pp. 265-66. Father Ligutti's interesting story is told in Conkin, Tomorrow, 296-301. He was a leader in CRLC and "one of the most influential of American agrarians and distributists." See ibid., 294.
[46]Denver Catholic Register, April 22, 1934, p. 1.
[47]Leuchtenburg, Franklin D. Roosevelt, 136.
[48]Ryan to Rev. Howard W. Bishop, May 3, 1933, Ryan Papers.
[49]Leuchtenburg, Franklin D. Roosevelt, 136.

the Jeffersonian dream of the yeoman farmer."[50] If this is true, then many American Catholics were enamored by this dream. The National Catholic Rural Life Conference, meeting in Rochester, New York, October 27-30, 1935, was quick to support the bill. This organization spoke up for the New Deal's attempt at rural resettlement and for anything that would encourage an urban to rural movement. The NCRL spelled out the advantages of the Bankhead bill as "enabling tenant farmers, their sons, and farm-minded city people to become independent proprietors."[51]

Father Schmiedeler also spoke in favor of the bill. "We find," said Schmiedeler, "that the general principles underlying the Bankhead bill are in thorough accord with the Catholic attitude toward land ownership." He then went on to quote from the writings of Leo XIII, who favored as large a diffusion of land ownership as possible. The priest felt that if more laborers could gain a share in the land, the gulf between vast wealth and deep poverty would be narrowed.[52]

Members attending the twenty-first annual meeting of the NCCC at Peoria, Illinois, September 29-October 2, 1935, heard a number of speakers endorse the Bankhead bill. The Reverend James M. Campbell, president of the National Catholic Rural Life Conference, called for an immediate program of land resettlement as an alternative to the dole system for combating chronic unemployment. He pointed out that "a land resettlement program . . . that would provide reasonable terms of repayment and low rates of interest, and that would assist the people to develop cooperative undertaking, would not fall very far short of a self-liquidating program." Campbell concluded

[50]*Ibid.*, 140.
[51]Quoted in *Catholic Action*, Dec. 1935, p. 25.
[52]*NCWC News Service*, April 13, 1935.

by warning the Church that she could not afford to neglect the land resettlement program.[53]

The Roosevelt administration had its own advocate at this meeting in the person of Brooks Hays, special assistant to the Rural Resettlement Administration. The RRA, headed by Rexford Tugwell, had been set up in April 1935 to promote rural rehabilitation by loans to farmers for tools and machinery and by resettlement and retraining of farmers.[54] Before his audience at the NCCC meeting, Hays pushed the idea of resettlement by citing the work of Luigi Ligutti. Father Ligutti had formed a sponsor group for resettlement in his area and had succeeded admirably. Hays used this example to make his point about the need of "enlightened religious leaders" in the fight for better opportunity for "economic exiles" such as tenant farmers.[55]

Important elements of the Catholic press also came to the support of the Bankhead bill. *Commonweal* thought it merited "the strongest support of all Americans" because it would guarantee liberty, which was dependent upon "the possession of really personal property in land by great numbers of individuals." The editor also quoted the statement of Leo XIII on the need for wide ownership of land and the statement by Pius XI on the right of the state to "adjust ownership [of property] to meet the needs of the public good."[56] The Jesuit magazine *America* echoed these sentiments and called for support of the efforts of the Catholic Rural Life Conference in its campaign for a wider distribution of land ownership.[57] The Catholic *Interracial Review* also found support for the

[53]*NCCC Proceedings*, Sept. 29–Oct. 2, 1935, pp. 98-102.
[54]Arthur M. Schlesinger, Jr., *The Coming of the New Deal* (Boston, 1959), 370.
[55]*NCCC Proceedings*, Sept. 29–Oct. 2, 1935, p. 96.
[56]April 26, 1935, pp. 719-20.
[57]Cited favorably by the *Catholic Messenger*, May 2, 1935, p. 2.

Bankhead bill in the teachings of Leo XIII. The idea of spreading private ownership of land widely among the people was clearly in line with Catholic teaching. The magazine recommended that Catholics give active support to the bill.[58]

Many Catholics supported the agricultural policies of the New Deal in 1935 because these policies seemed to agree with the Church's teaching on the benefits of the family farm and on wide distribution of land. While many regretted the tight crop control and destruction of surplus, they also realized that it was impossible for the home market to absorb production. Some agreed with F. P. Kenkel, editor of *Central-Blatt and Social Justice,* who said, "We are living in a new world; we must take into account the economic dislocation the world has experienced and the need for economic reorientation, such as many nations have been repeatedly forced in the course of centuries to adapt themselves to."[59]

During 1936, the year in which the AAA was struck down by the courts, Father Ryan and Father Schmiedeler continued to support the New Deal agrarian measures. Ryan was appointed by President Roosevelt to a special committee on farm tenancy. The president wrote to Ryan outlining his hopes of "developing a land tenure system which will bring an increased measure of security, opportunity, and well-being to the great group of present and prospective farm tenants." Ryan replied by expressing his great interest in the problem and his hope for corrective legislation.[60] At the same time, Schmiedeler was urging farmers to cooperate with and support both rural resettle-

[58]*Interracial Review,* VIII (May 1935), 68. When finally passed in 1937, the Bankhead-Jones Farm Tenancy Act created a Farm Security Administration, replacing Tugwell's RRA, to grant loans at low interest for the purchase of small family farms. It also created aid camps for migratory workers.

[59]*Central-Blatt and Social Justice,* XXVIII (April 1935), 7.

[60]*Catholic Action,* Dec. 1936, p. 16.

ment and rural electrification. But he realized that the cure of the agricultural problem was inexorably bound up with the industrial problem. Indeed, he felt that both areas demanded the same remedy—"the organization of society into occupation groups, . . . a minimum of active help on the part of the government, . . . the moral reformation of the individual." The ideas were based largely on the philosophy expressed in *Quadragesimo Anno*.[61] Applying his ideas to the situation in the United States, he was forced to recommend support for New Deal agricultural agencies and specifically to ask the support of the CRLC for the Bankhead-Jones Bill.[62]

[61]E. Schmiedeler, "Concern of the Encyclicals for Welfare of Agriculture," *Catholic Action*, May 1936, p. 12, and Aug. 1936, p. 5.
[62]*Ibid.*, Nov. 1936, p. 24.

5

NRA and
American Catholics

TO cope with the problems of industrial recession, the
Roosevelt administration fashioned the National Industrial Recovery Act, passed on June 16, 1933. A complex measure based on self-regulation of industry, the act
created the National Recovery Administration, which was
to supervise the drawing of codes to govern each industrial and trade association. These codes were to regulate
all phases of an industry's operation, from production to
market. Federal courts could issue injunctions against
violators of the codes. As NRA administrator, Roosevelt
chose General Hugh S. Johnson.

Across the United States, Catholics reacted with genuine enthusiasm to NRA. The hierarchy set a tone of praise
which was echoed by Catholic periodicals, newspapers,
religious organizations, and finally by influential individuals. Many members of the eastern hierarchy made public
statements in favor of NRA. Cardinal O'Connell of Boston, the first churchman in America by seniority, gave his

full backing to NRA by declaring that, in order to push the president's plan, August 27, 1933, would be observed as "Rally Sunday" in every Catholic church in the Boston archdiocese. He directed the parish priests to enlist the support of their parishioners for the NRA. The cardinal also wrote a personal letter to Victor M. Cutting, chairman of the NRA for the Boston area, pledging his full cooperation with an endeavor that he felt closely resembled the plan outlined in the papal encyclicals of Leo XIII and Pius XI. O'Connell also promised to urge his people to patronize stores that displayed the "blue eagle" sign.[1]

Joining in Cardinal O'Connell's sentiments was Cardinal Hayes of New York, who issued a statement that FDR had instituted NRA "to banish the want of recent years and to insure wider employment." The cardinal went on to say that, "because the welfare of the entire country is involved, the National Recovery Act merits the unqualified and wholehearted support of every American."[2] In Brooklyn, Bishop Thomas E. Molloy followed Cardinal Hayes's lead. On September 11, 1933, in an address to religious teachers of his diocese, Molloy called NRA "one of the greatest acts toward the restoration of the economic well-being of a sorely tried people."[3]

Elsewhere in the East, the response was equally enthusiastic. In northern New York, Bishop John A. Duffy of Syracuse went even further than Cardinal Hayes in support of NRA. In an interview the bishop said that FDR "has put into effect the principle announced by Pope Leo XIII forty-odd years ago, that government has not only the right but the duty to assist in the formation of economic units." He called NRA the most Christianlike plan

---

[1]Boston *Pilot*, Aug. 26, 1933, p. 1. The blue eagle was the symbol adopted by Johnson to signify that a particular company was cooperating with the NRA and operating under a government-approved code.

[2]Quoted in *Commonweal*, Sept. 29, 1933, p. 499.

[3]Quoted in *Columbia*, Oct. 1933, p. 13.

of recovery yet devised.[4] John J. Nilan, bishop of Hartford, Connecticut, and Bishop John Mark Gannon of Erie, Pennsylvania, also made public statements urging support of NRA.[5]

In the Middle West, the Catholic hierarchy preached the same theme of full cooperation for, and support of, the NRA. Archbishop John T. McNicholas of Cincinnati sent a pastoral letter to his flock urging them to buy from the "blue eagle." He wrote to Charles F. Williams, local director of NRA, and pledged the support of the Church.[6] One year later the bishop's ardor had not cooled. He admitted there were weak spots in the NRA but felt these were inherent in such an experiment. He prayed that the "old order" would never return, called for local responsibility as the key to success for NRA, and hoped it could be preserved in improved form.[7]

Other midwestern bishops who supported NRA in public statements included Bishop Joseph Schlarman of Peoria, Illinois; Archbishop Samuel A. Stritch of Milwaukee, Wisconsin; and Bishop James Griffin of Springfield, Illinois. Schlarman called NRA the "Industrial Charter of 1933" and compared it to the Magna Charta of thirteenth-century England, because it broke the privileged chains of capitalism. He felt the measure would prepare the way for an improved social order.[8] Griffin, speaking at the installation of Ralph L. Hayes as bishop of Helena, Montana, said: "The NRA does not go as far as Pope Pius XI leads in his encyclical . . . but the NRA is an effort to do for the American people what the Catholic Guilds did for the people of the Middle Ages." While lamenting the

[4]*NCWC News Service*, Aug. 11, 1933; see also *Catholic Transcript*, Aug. 17, 1933, p. 1.

[5]*NCWC News Service*, Sept. 15, 1933.

[6]Brooklyn *Tablet*, Aug. 26, 1933, p. 1, and Oct. 14, 1933, p. 3.

[7]Speech of Archbishop McNicholas, *NCCC Proceedings*, Cincinnati, Ohio, Oct. 10, 1934, pp. 65-66.

[8]Brooklyn *Tablet*, Sept. 9, 1933, p. 10.

fact that Catholic social teaching was so neglected in the United States, the bishop ended with: "Thank God our God-sent President Roosevelt has studied the encyclicals of Pope Leo XIII and Pope Pius XI." He felt that the NRA reflected this study in its rejection of rugged individualism and adoption of the spirit of cooperation.[9]

Further west, American bishops expounded the same theme as did their eastern colleagues—full support of NRA as the incarnation of the papal encyclicals. Among the western bishops expressing public support for NRA were Francis Johannes of Leavenworth, Kansas; Bernard Mahoney of Sioux Falls, South Dakota; Philip G. Scher of Monterey-Fresno, California; and Daniel J. Geroke, of Tucson, Arizona.[10] Bishop Johannes said that NRA was an attempt to "reconstruct the social order largely along the lines advocated in the great encyclicals of Pope Leo XIII and . . . Pius XI."[11] Bishop Scher also supported NRA because "in its broad outlines it follows the principles laid down by . . . Leo XIII and Pius XI on industrial relations." He urged his priests to promote cooperation with the "blue eagle," because it was aimed at "curbing greed, eliminating sweatshops," and at eliminating "that national disgrace, child labor."[12] Following the script, Bishop Geroke expressed full confidence in President Roosevelt and called NRA a wonderful opportunity to spread the economic program of the papal encyclicals. He requested his parish priests to devote a Sunday sermon to NRA and to set up local committees to cooperate.[13] At the same time Bishop Mahoney felt sure that President

[9]*NCWC News Service,* Helena, Mont., Oct. 5, 1933.

[10]*Catholic Transcript,* Oct. 5, 1933, p. 1; *NCWC News Service,* Sept. 16 and 30, and Oct. 5, 1933; clipping of *Michigan Catholic,* Sept. 28, 1933, in *Sel. Mat.*

[11]Quoted in *NCWC News Service,* Leavenworth, Kans., Sept. 30, 1933.

[12]Quoted in the Brooklyn *Tablet,* Sept. 23, 1933, p. 6.

[13]*NCWC News Service,* Tucson, Ariz., Sept. 15, 1933.

Roosevelt's approach to the depression would be success-ful.[14]

Editorial opinion in the Catholic press was also heavily weighted in favor of NRA. Many diocesan papers simply printed the canned editorials sent out by the *News Service* of the NCWC, which reflected the bishops' idea that NRA was the embodiment of Catholic social teaching.[15] The editor of *Extension* magazine expressed grave doubts about the principles of NRA but concluded by saying, "Let us brush aside whatever doubts and misgivings we may have, and repose our faith, our hope and confidence, in the one man the nation has chosen as its leader. . . ."[16] The *Catholic Telegraph* of Cincinnati called the critics of NRA the same "money-changers and industrial barons whose greed and selfishness have been the main causes of the depression."[17] The Milwaukee *Catholic Herald* cited favorably an article that had appeared in *L'Illustrazione Vaticana* stressing the great similarity between the NRA and the papal encyclicals.[18] The Brooklyn *Tablet* urged Roman Catholics to buy from stores displaying the "blue eagle" emblem.[19] For their interpretation of NRA, many Catholic papers relied heavily on the comments of Father John Ryan, who always stressed the fact that the measure was in harmony with the principles of *Quadragesimo Anno*.

Many Catholic organizations and lay groups supported the president's recovery program. The two major lay affiliates of the National Catholic Welfare Conference— the National Council of Catholic Men and the National

[14]Clipping of the *Michigan Catholic,* Sept. 28, 1933, in *Sel. Mat.*

[15]*Commonweal* remarked that "so far as we are aware, the whole weight of the Catholic press has been thrown to the President." See Aug. 11, 1933, p. 355.

[16]Sept. 1933, p. 20.

[17]Nov. 30, 1933, p. 4.

[18]June 14, 1934, p. 4.

[19]Nov. 4, 1933, p. 8.

Council of Catholic Women—were enthusiastic in their support of NRA. At its annual convention in St. Paul, Minnesota, on October 7-11, 1933, the NCCW passed a resolution expressing joy and satisfaction at the achievements of NRA and "pledging fullest support and cooperation to the government, to the end that social justice be established throughout the land."[20] Ten days later their male counterparts, the NCCM, met in annual convention in Chicago and passed a similar resolution. The NCCM noted that the crisis in the United States was the result of a neglect of Christian social justice and that the NRA was an attempt to reassert this justice. Because NRA conformed "in part" with Catholic teaching, the NCCM pledged support and urged "upon all Catholics, employers and wage earners alike, active cooperation in accomplishing the success of the act."[21] Such public support did not go unrecognized by the federal government. Louis J. Alber, chief of the Speakers Division of NRA, wrote Father John J. Burke, general secretary of NCWC, that the latter's organization and its affiliates were giving the NRA splendid cooperation.[22]

Another powerful organization of Catholic laymen, the Knights of Columbus, also threw its support behind NRA. At their annual convention in Chicago, August 15-17, 1933, the Knights heard their supreme secretary, William J. McGinley, move that the organization take a pledge to cooperate and support President Roosevelt in carrying out the plans of NRA. The motion was seconded by Mayor Edward Kelly of Chicago and was passed by the convention amid numerous speeches praising Roosevelt's leadership as "unparalleled and courageous."[23]

Local chapters of the Knights swung their weight be-

[20]Quoted in *Catholic Action,* Nov. 1933, p. 18.
[21]Quoted in *ibid.,* 27.
[22]*Ibid.,* Oct. 1933, p. 16.
[23]*Columbia,* Oct. 1933, p. 10.

hind the president. The editor of the *Knights of Columbus Journal,* Philadelphia chapter, praised the concern of the New Deal with insuring a living wage to labor. The paper rejected the charge that NRA was regimentation, pointing out that the government must act vigorously or face revolution.[24] In Augusta, Georgia, the local Knights sponsored a radio speech by the Reverend Harold J. Barr, who drew parallels between NRA and the encyclicals of Leo XIII and Pius XI. Barr said that Catholics should support a plan so obviously patterned after the encyclicals. "There is no group of citizens more confident of the success of the NRA or more enthusiastic about its possibilities than we Catholics," he went on, "for there is none more convinced of the soundness of the principles upon which it is based."[25]

Another important source of support for NRA was the Catholic Conference on Industrial Problems. This organization was started early in the 1920's by the NCWC as an attempt to bring Catholic principles to bear on society at the diocesan level under the auspices of the local bishop. Regional conferences were held under the auspices of this organization and nationally known speakers were supplied by NCWC. During the depression these regional conferences adopted a radical outlook on what should be done to save the country. Father John Ryan, Father Raymond A. McGowan, and other reformers usually held the spotlight. All during the depression these conferences called for national action to combat the crisis. It was only natural that they should support the NRA.[26] To cite one instance, Arthur D. Maguire, chairman

[24]*Knights of Columbus Journal* clipping, Sept. 1933, OF 28, Roosevelt Papers; the Roosevelt Papers contain many copies of resolutions pledging support from local chapters of the Knights of Columbus throughout the United States.

[25]Quoted in *NCWC News Service,* Aug. 11, 1933.

[26]Francis L. Broderick, *The Right Reverend New Dealer: John A. Ryan* (New York, 1963), 200.

of the Detroit regional meeting of the Catholic Conference on Industrial Problems, held December 4-5, 1933,
was happy to write to the White House that "the whole
trend of the conference was favorable to NRA, and this
moral support of the President and his policies, and the
publicity given to this support has had a tremendous and
beneficial effect . . . throughout the country."[27]

This organizational support for Roosevelt's industrial
recovery program was augmented by the efforts of many
distinguished individual Catholics, whose public support
could only enhance the attractiveness of the plan to their
coreligionists. NRA was, of course, supported by the social reformers connected with the NCWC. Father Ryan
went about the country making speeches in which he
praised NRA, presented its major features in laymen's
terms, and dispelled many fears.[28] Ryan's colleague and
assistant in the Social Action Department of NCWC,
Father McGowan, wrote and spoke to the same effect. He
declared NRA to be "in line with the program of Catholic
Action" and pointed out that Catholics were proud of the
similarity.[29] The Reverend Francis J. Haas, who was
working for NRA, called the principles behind the program correct in their approach. Haas spoke along these
lines before a mass meeting of the Amalgamated Clothing
Workers of America. At a later date he also urged American Negroes to support NRA because it offered better
conditions for all labor.[30]

Other distinguished leaders of American Catholicism
also supported NRA. At South Bend, Indiana, the Reverend John F. O'Hara, acting president of Notre Dame, came

[27]Maguire to Marvin McIntyre, Dec. 7, 1933, Reel 1, *Sel. Mat.*

[28]Washington I. Cleveland to Ryan, Oct. 26, 1933; Ryan to P. H.
Burkett, S.J., Nov. 28, 1933, Ryan Papers.

[29]McGowan, "Legislative Trends and Effects on Industrial Life,"
NCCC Proceedings, New York City, Oct. 1–4, 1933, p. 561.

[30]*NCWC News Service,* Troy, N.Y., May 3, 1935; Brooklyn *Tablet,*
Sept. 16, 1933, p. 5.

to the defense of NRA after it had been attacked by the United States Chamber of Commerce. O'Hara pointed out that business could not go its merry way unregulated, for that policy had produced the depression. "There must be invoked a power that will free business from its own defiance of economic and moral laws," he added.[31] Mary G. Hawks, president of the NCCW, addressed the thirteenth annual convention of that organization on the duty of Catholics to support NRA. She urged the NCCW to use its farflung organization to explain the provisions of NRA and to invite cooperation with the "blue eagle."[32] At the same time, members of the Commonwealth Club of California heard Roy A. Bronson, vice president of the National Catholic Alumni Federation, say that the philosophy behind NRA was the same as that behind *Quadragesimo Anno.*[33]

Members of the clergy across the country expressed a deep commitment to the industrial recovery program. Edmund A. Walsh, S.J., vice president of Georgetown University, spoke over the radio and called NRA the last stand of democracy in the United States. Father Walsh, who led the Catholic opposition to FDR's plan to recognize Russia, felt that it was the duty of all citizens to support NRA.[34] The Reverend Jones I. Corrigan, speaking from a Boston radio station, called NRA "the most progressive and skillfully devised plan for national recovery enacted in any nation."[35] In Denver, participants in the annual Catholic Action Week, March 11-17, heard Monsignor William O'Ryan praise FDR as one who would lead

[31]Quoted in the *Catholic Transcript,* Nov. 30, 1933.

[32]Mary G. Hawks, "The Catholic Duty in the Present Crisis," *Catholic Action,* Oct. 1933, p. 7.

[33]*NCWC News Service,* San Francisco, Aug. 10, 1933; see also *Catholic Transcript,* Aug. 10, 1933, p. 1.

[34]Quoted in the Brooklyn *Tablet,* Nov. 18, 1933, p. 11.

[35]Quoted in the Boston *Pilot,* Oct. 21, 1933, p. 6.

the nation out of the present crisis and compare NRA
with the papal encyclicals.[36] In Chicago, radio listeners
heard the Reverend J. W. R. Maguire attack the Chicago
Tribune and the *Daily News* for their attempts to "black-
jack the NIRA."[37]

Clearly the NRA had strong support among all elements of American Catholicism. Less clear, however, are
the reasons for this support. Certainly, in seeking motives, one should give much weight to the very despera-
tion of the times. Many people were willing to accept any
scheme that gave hope of ending the depression. It is
conceivable that Catholics would have been just as sympathetic to a program radically different from NRA. Another motive to be considered, and one that was expressed
at the time, was that there was really no alternative to
NRA except a return to the "devil take-the-hindmost,
every-man-for-himself type of industrialism, the failure of
which has brought the nation to its present frightful condition."[38]

Yet as Catholic thinkers appraised the NRA in more
depth, certain other themes seemed to predominate their
interpretation. There were those who liked the plan on its
own terms. Others saw in it a recognition of Catholic
social teaching; some felt that the proposal was based
squarely on the papal encyclicals.

In August 1933 the National Catholic Alumni Federation passed a resolution in which they heartily endorsed
the NRA's plan to set up trade associations and to organize the economy. They did stress, however, that labor, the

[36]*Catholic Action*, April 1934, p. 19.
[37]Maguire, "Blackjacking the NIRA," Nov. 8, 1933, Box 88, F. P.
Walsh Papers. Considerable additional evidence of grassroots Catholic support for Roosevelt exists in the form of telegrams and letters
from pastors of small parishes in such places as Fort Smith, Ark.;
Bridgeville, Pa.; Aurora, Ill.; and Grand Rapids, Mich.; see *Sel. Mat.*
[38]*Commonweal*, Aug. 4, 1933, p. 335.

consumer, and the government should share with business in controlling these associations. The federation did not favor a system promoting monopoly unless concrete gains for all society were forthcoming.[39]

Visitors to the Catholic Industrial Conference held in Detroit during December 1933 were surprised to hear the Reverend Frederic Siedenburg, ex-dean of Detroit University, praise President Roosevelt as "still a champion of capitalism." Siedenburg felt that NRA revealed Roosevelt as a man who was trying to control and humanize capitalism to meet the needs of the people during the depression. To this priest, NRA represented a conservative attempt to save capitalism from failure and real regimentation. This same idea—that the NRA was an attempt to help capitalism rid itself of its vices—was also expressed by William F. Montavon, secretary of the Legal Division of NCWC.[40]

Meanwhile, in Boston, Father Corrigan was telling his radio audience on "The Catholic Truth Hour" that NRA was good because it prevented ruinous competition. Regulated cooperation had replaced competition in industry; the results, he believed, would be more economic stability and fuller employment. Both labor and capital would benefit from NRA because "it will remove the ruthless antagonism between them." Corrigan concluded that "the only way that men can be set free is by imposing restraints on the abuse of freedom," and he felt that "the Recovery Act must be read in the light of this principle."[41] The editor of the *Catholic World* applauded the ideas expressed by Corrigan and went further in condemning capitalism. The Roman Catholic Church, insisted

[39]National Catholic Alumni Federation, "A Program of Social Justice," *Catholic Mind*, XXXI (Aug. 8, 1933), 281-88.

[40]Brooklyn *Tablet*, Dec. 16, 1933, p. 4; William F. Montavon, "73rd Congress," *Catholic Action*, Aug. 1933, pp. 7-10.

[41]Quoted in the Boston *Pilot*, Oct. 21, 1933, p. 6.

the editor, has a "definite socialistic bias," and no one should try to lay the albatross of capitalism on the Church's shoulders. "If the National Recovery Act means anything," he continued, "it is an announcement to the world that in the U. S. . . . unregulated competition is henceforth taboo."[42] Another commentator viewed the codes in NRA as "hastening the day when we shall see a new spirit of social justice in accord with Pope Leo XIII's encyclical on labor and Pope Pius XI's encyclical on the reconstruction of the social order."[43]

On a superficial level, we find many Catholics continually stressing that NRA was the most concrete example of the New Deal's attempt to apply Christian social teaching to the depression. Father Haas felt that NRA was a start in applying the remedy of *Rerum Novarum* and *Quadragesimo Anno* to the crisis.[44] Michael O'Shaughnessy, in his *Social Justice Bulletin*, remarked that the encyclicals of Pius XI had a determining influence on the president and his advisers. The *St. Francis Home Journal* of Pittsburgh also expressed the idea that NRA meant the government had finally recognized the wisdom of Catholic social principles.[45] According to *America* NRA recognized the excellence of the ideas of Leo XIII and Pius XI. The editor pointed out that for years Catholic social teaching had been ignored in America, but suddenly, both Catholics and non-Catholics were turning to these principles. He concluded that "the scene has been set for the recognition of many of its [*Quadragesimo Anno*] principles by the new American administration."[46]

These vague generalizations linking NRA with the

[42]*Catholic World*, CXXXVIII (Oct. 1933), 1, 3.
[43]*Pax*, Sept. 1933, p. 199.
[44]*Catholic Action*, May 1935, p. 3.
[45]Clipping of *Social Justice Bulletin*, No. 8 [n.d.]; *St. Francis Home Journal* [n.d.], in OF, 76-B, Box 4, Roosevelt Papers.
[46]*America*, Sept. 16, 1933, p. 553; Sept. 23, 1933, p. 278.

papal encyclicals received considerable support in more scholarly analyses. Father Raymond A. McGowan of NCWC set out to test the particular aspects of NRA against Catholic teaching. First, seeking points of similarity between NRA and the pope's program, McGowan noted that both schemes defended the idea that government should act to relieve the country of economic disaster; that is, both rejected the laissez faire theory of the state and would substitute industrial order in place of unlimited competition. Both plans condemned the old system of cutthroat competition and disregard of the common good. Likewise, the idea that industrial groups should be formed and directed by the government was a common goal.[47] McGowan also pointed to the similar approach to labor by the papacy and by Roosevelt. The NRA, in section 7a, recognized labor's right to organize and bargain collectively. These same rights were stressed in *Quadragesimo Anno*.[48] There was a congruence also in that both the pope and the president advocated a minimum wage and maximum hour law for labor.[49]

Father John Ryan was another to see points of similarity between NRA and the pope's plan. For one thing, Ryan felt that the system of industrial codes being drawn up, forming what Roosevelt called modern guilds, were quite similar to the "vocational groups" called for in *Quadragesimo Anno*.[50] Ryan felt that "in so far as all the participants in each industry are brought under a code of fair practice and in so far as each association exercises a considerable measure of industrial self-government,"

[47]*NCWC News Service*, Denver, March 23, 1934; R. A. McGowan, "Testing the NRA by Catholic Teaching—I," *Catholic Action*, Oct. 1933, p. 23.
    [48]R. A. McGowan, "The National Industrial Recovery Act," *Catholic Action*, July 1933, p. 6.
    [49]*Ibid.*, 13.
    [50]Ryan to P. J. Connelly, S.J., June 30, 1933, Ryan Papers.

there was a convergence of intent between *Quadragesimo Anno* and NRA.[51]

A student of Catholic social thought has remarked that few Catholic leaders denied the NRA's resemblance, superficially at least, to the vocational group system outlined in the pope's encyclical.[52] Certainly the remarks of Father Haas and Father John LaFarge help to substantiate this observation. Haas saw NRA as essentially a bargain between government and employers, in which the latter received immunity from antitrust and price-fixing laws in return for accepting the government's ideas on minimum wages and maximum hours. The idea of a worker-employer-government partnership was, he felt, in close harmony with the theme of *Quadragesimo Anno*.[53] La-Farge was especially interested in the similarity between the pope's call for the formation of "vocational groups" and the president's desire that the industrial codes form "modern guilds." He also pointed out that both the pope and the president called for a minimum wage for labor.[54]

According to the Brooklyn *Tablet*, there were three areas in which NRA ran parallel to the papal encyclicals. The president's insistence that the formation and cooperation of industrial groups was fundamental to recovery found an echo in *Quadragesimo Anno* that "the aim of social legislation must be the re-establishment of occupational groups." Second, both NRA and the papal encyclicals stressed the fact that membership in these groups or guilds should be strictly voluntary. Finally, the pope's emphasis on the need for a living wage for labor had

[51]John A. Ryan, "Pope Pius XI and a New Social Order," *Catholic Action*, June 1934, pp. 14, 15.
[52]Aaron I. Abell, *American Catholicism and Social Action* (New York, 1960), 248.
[53]Brooklyn *Tablet*, Aug. 5, 1933, p. 1.
[54]John LaFarge, "Doing the Truth," *Interracial Review*, VI (Aug. 1933), 151.

received due consideration in section 7a of NRA. It seemed clear that FDR had patterned NRA after principles he had quoted from *Quadragesimo Anno* in his Detroit speech during the election campaign. The editor concluded that NRA "deserves the hearty endorsement and loyal support of all Catholics."[55]

Other Catholic newspapers joined the chorus linking NRA with the papal encyclicals. The *Catholic Messenger* told its readers that NRA would not destroy individualism but only curb its excesses. Both the pope and the president wanted industry and labor to cooperate to produce a better standard of living for society.[56] While admitting that the NRA was not entirely parallel with *Quadragesimo Anno,* the Denver *Catholic Register* did comment on the "remarkable similarity" in the two programs. The pope called for the control of business and industry for promotion of the common good, and this was also the guiding spirit of NRA.[57]

The editor of the *Register* was so convinced of the soundness of NRA that he even criticized Al Smith when that Catholic hero came out against the measure. Smith thought that government control of industry was a dangerous trend, thereby disagreeing with Pope Pius XI who wrote that "free competition and still more economic domination must be kept within just and definite limits, and must be brought under the effective control of the public authority."[58] Rather than being dangerous, NRA was, said the Denver editor, in many ways parallel to the pope's program. Both Roosevelt and Pius would protect private property while at the same time trying to distribute the goods of the earth more equally.[59] Finally, in

[55]June 24, 1933, p. 8.
[56]June 22, 1933, p. 2.
[57]May 2, 1933, p. 1.
[58]Quoted in *ibid.,* Aug. 10, 1933, p. 1.
[59]*Ibid.*

Washington, the NCWC *News Service* spread the word that "under the direction of General Hugh Johnson . . . the far-reaching experiment of molding national economic policy to social requirements, foreshadowed in the encyclicals of Pope Leo XIII and his successors, is gradually being put to the test."[60]

A few perceptive prelates even argued that the papal program was more radical than President Roosevelt's scheme. The most pronounced difference, which was pointed out by Ryan and McGowan and others, was that the NRA did not provide for as much active participation by labor as Pius XI desired. Labor was not given an active role in constructing and executing the various industrial codes; and the fact that business was not interpreting section 7a of the law as permitting the closed union shop meant that labor's right to organize and bargain collectively was jeopardized. This also meant there was little hope of achieving under NRA Pius' goal of labor sharing ownership with the employer.[61] While both the president's and the pope's programs sought increased purchasing power for the masses, NRA would rely on high wages to achieve this, while Pius asked for profit-sharing and a wider ownership of property to gain the same result.[62] Another discrepancy, which made clear that the pope's plan was more radical than NRA, was that the occupational groups called for in the encyclical posited a much closer association of labor and management than that provided for under the industrial codes of FDR's plan.[63]

[60]*NCWC News Service*, June 19, 1933.

[61]All the following argued that the pope was more radical than FDR: Ryan, "Pope Pius," 14, 15; Ryan, *Social Doctrine in Action: A Personal History* (New York, 1941), 249; Joseph F. Thorning, S.J., "Principles and Practices of NRA," *Catholic Mind,* XXXII (Oct. 8, 1934), 361-68; McGowan, "The National Industrial Recovery Act," 13.

[62]R. A. McGowan, "Testing the NRA by Catholic Teaching—II," *Catholic Action,* Nov. 1933, pp. 28-29.

[63]Address of Father John Ryan before Catholic Conference on In-

Perhaps the most cogent presentation of the differences between NRA and the papal plan was that given by Father McGowan, who found three major areas of divergence. First, in NRA only employers directed an industry while labor remained a separate bargaining body. In the pope's plan for vocational groups, all aspects of industry were in joint control. Second, under NRA "each industry stands separate from every other industry" and from the government. The vision of the encyclical was the joining together of all industry to promote the common good, "separate, but not independent, of government." Third, in the encyclical all occupations and professions, including agriculture, were considered groups to be organized, whereas NRA was interested only in urban industry, banking, and trade.[64]

Admitting these deficiencies in NRA, Ryan and Mc-Gowan, who were the two most consistent students of the act, still saw it as a progressive piece of legislation. While the minimum wage might be too low, it was still established as a principle. While cooperation of all elements of the economy could have been closer, NRA was still the first step toward a more radical national planning of the economy. While labor could have had more power allotted to it, still the right to organize and bargain collectively was on the statute books even if weakened by the open-shop interpretation of section 7a. Both Ryan and McGowan were optimistic about NRA. Ryan felt that it could easily evolve "into the kind of industrial order recommended by Pope Pius XI."[65] McGowan likewise viewed NRA as a first step "towards the social order of

dustrial Problems, Detroit, in New York Times, Dec. 5, 1933, p. 8; America, March 17, 1934, p. 557.

[64]R. A. McGowan, "Testing the NRA by Catholic Teaching—III," Catholic Action, Jan. 1934, pp. 12, 31.

[65]Ryan, Social Doctrine, 249.

'vocational groups,' . . . of Guilds, which the encyclical of Pius XI advocates."[66] To many Catholic social thinkers NRA clearly marked the beginning of a period of fulfillment for the Church's social teaching in the United States.

As usual, however, there was a vocal minority in the Church who took a more critical view. An extreme position is represented by F. P. Kenkel, editor of *Central-Blatt and Social Justice,* who labeled NRA as the beginning of "State Socialism." Kenkel felt that the measure would surely destroy the middle class in America: "It [NRA] gives great power to big companies and will drive the little fellow to the wall." As for the idea that NRA was similar to the guild system advocated by the popes, Kenkel felt there was little basis for such comparison. The liberals behind NRA looked toward socialism rather than toward any eighteenth-century guild system for their model.[67]

Another author who disliked NRA was L. S. Herron. Writing in *Central-Blatt and Social Justice,* Herron remarked that NRA would surely "strengthen the position of capitalistic industry and still further intrench monopoly." The codes gave big business an unfair advantage over small. The NRA, according to Herron, was "essentially the national-planning scheme, seized upon by big business and pushed through Congress in the guise of an emergency measure." Herron felt that NRA was a roadblock to social cooperation and real economic reform because it legalized "the unfair and monopolistic practices of big business."[68]

On the West Coast, disenchantment with NRA was also

[66]McGowan, "Testing NRA—III," p. 11.
[67]F. P. Kenkel, "New Deals, Past and Present," *Central-Blatt and Social Justice,* XXVII (July-Aug. 1934), 112, 117, 241.
[68]L. S. Herron, "Codes Threaten Growth of Cooperation," *ibid.,* XXVI (March 1934), 385-88.

expressed by the *Monitor* of San Francisco, whose editor felt that certain Catholics were only fooling themselves by praising NRA as being based on the papal encyclicals. He pointed out that the Roosevelt plan contained as many parallels with Marxism and Kantism as with Catholicism. "The NRA," he insisted, "can very deftly be turned into an American brand of Communistic state." To this editor, the brain trusters who conceived the bill were advocating an alien philosophy and should be watched carefully.[69]

Other Catholics criticized NRA not because they thought it was leading to state socialism but because it was failing in its job. Many recognized that one of the main weaknesses of NRA was the failure of business to live up to the codes. Employers, they believed, were reluctant to make any sacrifices for the common good.[70] Others regretted that NRA lacked the power to force the rugged individualist to conform.[71] In Detroit, Father Coughlin agreed that the NRA would fail because only a minority of American industrialists had subscribed to the codes of NRA.[72] Even pro-NRA men such as McGowan and Ryan insisted that in order to work properly, NRA had to give more power to labor. Ryan further feared that NRA was "placing too much faith in automatic methods of recovery."[73] The fact that the American Negro had not received much benefit from the act was another shortcoming mentioned.[74]

Despite these criticisms, the majority of American Catholics probably agreed with Father Ryan when he praised the program as a step in the right direction. He

[69]July 29, 1933, p. 1; Aug. 19, 1933, p. 1.

[70]*Columbia*, Nov. 1933, p. 13.

[71]*Catholic Herald*, March 1, 1934, p. 4.

[72]Peter Morris, "Father Coughlin and the New Deal" (unpublished M.A. thesis, Columbia University, 1938), 29.

[73]*Columbia*, Aug. 1933, p. 13; Quoted in New York *Times*, March 26, 1935, p. 8.

[74]Justin McAghon, "The Negro Under the New Deal," *Interracial Review*, VIII (March 1935), 38-39.

felt that the only alternatives to NRA were socialism, communism, or fascism. He told his audience at the annual meeting of the NCCC that by backing the NRA, Catholics had a great opportunity for "putting into effect the Catholic conception of a social order reconstructed upon the principles of social justice."[75]

Public criticism of the NRA reached its apex with the publication of the Darrow Report in 1934. After many charges by small businessmen that they were being discriminated against because of NRA's tendency to favor monopoly, Roosevelt decided to investigate. In March 1934 he created the National Recovery Review Board, headed by Clarence Darrow, the famous defense attorney, to study these charges. After a brief investigation, Darrow reported that "giant corporations dominated the NRA code authorities and squeezed small business, labor, and the public."[76]

Catholic reaction to the report was mixed. *America* felt that if the report was correct, the basic purpose of NRA was being defeated. The solutions offered by Darrow, however, would probably lead to even worse results.[77] F. P. Kenkel felt that the review board's findings justified his complaint that NRA was strangling the American middle class.[78] Other Catholics viewed the report with skepticism. Some felt that Darrow was exaggerating in order to attract attention, and that such a large undertaking as NRA was bound to have some weaknesses.[79]

The members of the National Catholic Alumni Federation applauded Hugh Johnson, head of NRA, who spoke to them on May 31, 1934, denouncing the Darrow Report.

[75]John A. Ryan, "Shall the NRA Be Scrapped?" *Catholic Action*, Nov. 1934, p. 4.
[76]William E. Leuchtenburg, *Franklin D. Roosevelt and the New Deal* (New York, 1963), 67.
[77]June 2, 1934, p. 169.
[78]*Central-Blatt and Social Justice*, May 1935, p. 48.
[79]Denver *Catholic Register*, June 3, 1934, p. 4.

Johnson, with characteristic exaggeration, said the NRA was the personification of the golden rule in business and called its opponents "scribes and pharisees."[80] When talk arose of forming a small review board to hear the specific complaints of small businessmen, the Reverend Maurice S. Sheehy told General Johnson that "since we had the biggest communist and atheist in the country at the head of the other board," it would be wise to put someone like Father Ryan in charge of the new board.[81]

The strong Catholic support for NRA which did exist was not limited to mere written and spoken praise. Many Catholic priests and laymen played an active role in administering the various facets of NRA. The two most prominent of such priests were Father Haas, director of the National Catholic School of Social Service, and Father Ryan. Haas had been asked by Roosevelt to serve on the Labor Advisory Committee of NRA, was later appointed to the National Labor Board, and finally served as labor representative on the new General Code Authority of NRA.[82]

Father Ryan played his most active role as one of the three members of the Industrial Appeals Board, formed to hear complaints of small businessmen against NRA. Precipitated by the Darrow Report, the appeals board lasted ten months and heard approximately seventy cases. Ryan later remarked that few businessmen claimed discrimination by NRA. Rather, the majority requested that they be exempted from the requirement to pay the minimum wage rates fixed by the codes. Ryan had little sympathy for these petitions.[83]

Other Catholics played minor roles in the functioning of

[80]Quoted by the New York *Times,* June 1, 1934, p. 6.

[81]Sheehy to Ryan, June 28, 1934, Ryan Papers.

[82]Boston *Pilot,* Oct. 14, 1933, p. 1; Oct. 13, 1934, p. 1; Frances Perkins, *The Roosevelt I Knew* (New York, 1946), 216.

[83]Broderick, *Right Reverend,* 217-18; Ryan, *Social Doctrine,* 249-50.

industrial reform. The Reverend George Johnson, director
of the NCWC Educational Department, was appointed to
the four-man NRA committee of the American Council of
Education. Miss Mary G. Hawks, national president of the
NCCW and Mrs. Nicholas F. Brady, distinguished New
York Catholic, were members of the Committee for Mobilization for Human Needs and the National Committee for
Child Health. The Most Reverend Thomas K. Gorman,
bishop of Reno, Nevada, served on a regional recovery
board for the rehabilitation of the industrial system. William G. Bruce, prominent Catholic publisher, was named to
the Wisconsin State Advisory Board of the Federal Emergency Administration of Public Works. Monsignor C. J.
Donohoe served as chairman of the Davenport, Iowa, Adjustment Board of the NRA. The Reverend Frederick Siedenburg was named director of the Detroit Regional Labor
Relations Board by President Roosevelt. In the deep
South, the Reverend Peter M. H. Wynhoven of New Orleans, Louisiana, was chairman of one of the twelve
regional United States Labor Boards. Elsewhere in the
country, prominent Catholics served on NRA boards and
on various labor dispute boards. Altogether, the involvement of American Catholics with the industrial recovery
program of the New Deal was extensive.[84]

This involvement helps explain the rather keen reaction
produced among American Catholics when the NRA was
declared invalid by the Supreme Court on May 27, 1935.
In 1933 the Legal Committee of the National Catholic
Alumni Federation said that NRA was constitutional and
would, at least in its broad outlines, probably be upheld
during the period of emergency.[85]

[84]*Catholic Action,* Jan. 1934, p. 13; Oct. 1933, p. 14; Brooklyn
Tablet, Aug. 12, 1933, p. 1; *NCWC News Service,* Davenport, July 31,
1934, and Detroit, Sept. 17, 1934; *Catholic Messenger,* Dec. 28, 1933,
p. 1.
[85]*Catholic Herald,* July 20, 1933, p. 4.

When the measure was struck down by the Supreme Court, many Catholics attempted to rationalize the decision. In Chicago, the *New World* admitted that there was little hope of resurrecting the project because of the unanimity of the decision. Trying to look on the bright side, however, the editor pointed out that NRA had made certain definite gains, such as eliminating sweatshops, restricting child labor, and, most important, stirring the people to the possibilities of a better social order. Certainly such a project was not to be condemned because it did not fit the Supreme Court's view of the constitution. The constitution was not, the editor insisted, "intended to handicap Americans in the pursuit of life, liberty and happiness, which, in the present instance, means a fearless . . . effort to bring about a better social order." The constitution, he concluded, is "the bulwark of our liberties," not, "a millstone on our necks." The editor of *America* was just as disturbed but more optimistic about the decision. He felt that all was not lost by the Court's decision because the NRA had already served a noble purpose. It had educated the people of the United States to the doctrines of social justice that were preached by Popes Leo XIII and Pius XI, and this gain could not be erased by the Court's action. *Commonweal* likewise regretted the passing of NRA and took issue with those who applauded the Court's decision. The editor felt that the industrial codes were definite achievements as moving toward a cooperative organization of industrial society.[86]

Individual Catholics also spoke out on the Court's decision. Father McGowan regretted both the decision and the Court's tendency toward a strict interpretation of the constitution. He felt it essential that the Court change its

[86]*New World*, Oct. 5, 1934, p. 4; June 7, 1934, p. 4; *America*, June 8, 1935, p. 194; *Commonweal*, June 7, 1935, p. 142; June 14, 1935, p. 169.

viewpoint if the federal government was to be responsible for the economic welfare of the people. More attention should be paid, said the priest, to the constitutional clause calling on the government to promote the general welfare.[87] In Denver, Hubert A. Smith, editor of the diocesan newspaper, felt the Court's decision was a calamity. He advised the Roosevelt administration to continue the fight by passing a constitutional amendment giving the government the powers outlined in NRA. Smith felt that NRA had prevented revolution in America, but feared what would happen after it had been declared void.[88] To the Reverend James Gillis, editor of the *Catholic World,* the issue was simple. The removal of NRA meant that all hope of social and economic reform was gone, and that revolution would result.[89] These sentiments were shared by Father Ryan. Upon hearing of the invalidation of NRA, Ryan issued a public statement urging that another way be found to subordinate wealth and business for the general good of the country. Ryan feared, with NRA gone, that the standard of living would drop, wages would be cut, and hours would be lengthened.[90]

In order to unite Catholic opinion against any such reactionary trend, Ryan and McGowan composed a statement of Catholic principles relevant to the economic crisis. McGowan had been working on such a statement before NRA had been struck down. The text was now revised by Ryan to incorporate the latest development. In its final form the statement, "Organized Social Justice," called for a new NRA, under a constitutional amendment, to include farmers and professional men in a system of occupational group organizations providing freedom of economic behavior and collaboration with the federal government. Any

[87]Quoted in *Commonweal,* June 13, 1935, p. 4.
[88]Denver *Catholic Register,* May 30, 1935, p. 1; June 9, 1935, p. 1.
[89]*Catholic World,* CXLI (July 1935), 385-86.
[90]Broderick, *Right Reverend,* 219.

return to the old system or failure to construct a new NRA would mean communism or fascism for the United States. The statement declared that the NRA could have developed into the kind of industrial order that was recommended by the pope.[91]

Father Ryan worked assiduously to get a cross section of Catholic businessmen and industrialists to sign the statement. Many of his correspondents refused because they feared an increase in the power of the federal government which would follow a constitutional amendment as suggested in the Ryan statement. Although Ryan's correspondence indicates his discouraging experience, the priest still insisted that at least 80 percent of those to whom the document was sent were willing to sign it. Altogether, 131 distinguished Catholics signed the manifesto, most of them outspoken liberals. Among the signers, besides McGowan and Ryan, were Frank P. Walsh, assistant secretary of labor; Edward F. McGrady; Father Haas; Father Gillis; and Dorothy Day, editor of the *Catholic Worker*. No member of the hierarchy signed. Originally, two bishops—Robert E. Lucey of Amarillo, Texas, and Aloysius J. Muench of Fargo, North Dakota—signed the statement, but their names were blocked out of the published edition in order to avoid embarrassing them by their uniqueness. It seems clear that "Organized Social Justice" failed in its purpose to present a truly representative statement of Catholic social teaching because its support was limited to that element already fully committed to the New Deal.[92]

[91]Quoted by the New York *Times*, Dec. 5, 1935, p. 28; Broderick, *Right Reverend*, 220-21.

[92]Broderick, *Right Reverend*, 221; Clipping of Baltimore *Sun*, Dec. 5, 1935, Ryan Papers; Abell, *American Catholicism*, 251. David O'Brien, "American Catholic Social Thought in the 1930's" (unpublished Ph.D. dissertation, University of Rochester, 1965), 387-90, argues that Catholics, because of their minority status, feared an extension of federal power.

6

Labor and Social Security

FROM what has been written concerning the major provisions of NRA, it should be apparent that for the most part American Catholic spokesmen were prolabor. This support of labor had historic roots in a church made up primarily of the lower classes and immigrants. Father Ryan, a longtime advocate of a living wage for labor, had been praised by Secretary of Labor Frances Perkins for his forward-looking ideas. Besides being a public advocate of labor's rights, Ryan was constantly writing fellow priests and laymen on the advantage of good labor legislation.[1]

In his struggle for better labor laws, Ryan was joined by the Reverend Francis J. Haas. When Haas was appointed to the Labor Policies Board of the Works Progress Administration, many Catholics saw the action as a vindication of the Church's stand for a living wage, for labor's right to organize, and for shorter hours. He gave strong support to Secretary of Labor Perkins' program of improving working conditions.[2] Haas was radical enough to declare it the duty of every worker to join a union and actively to assist Sidney Hillman's attempt to recruit members for the Amalgamated Clothing Workers of America.[3]

Elsewhere, Father McGowan of NCWC also commended the work of Secretary Perkins as being in accord with Pius XI's encyclicals. In 1932 Dorothy Day founded the Catholic Worker Movement in New York City. In 1937 the Reverend John P. Monaghan established the Association of Catholic Trade Unionists. Both of these movements were attempts to keep the loyalty of the Catholic laborer who might be attracted to Marxism.[4]

How some Catholics felt about the labor problems facing America during the depression is indicated by their reaction to the 1933 proposal of Senator Hugo Black of Alabama for a thirty-hour workweek. The Black bill, which Roosevelt refused to support because he felt it was unconstitutional and negative in its approach, was endorsed by many Catholics.[5] Father Ryan was enthusiastically in favor of the proposal. He wrote to Frances Perkins in April 1933 that he was glad it had passed the Senate and felt that its quick passage augured well for the president's program.[6] He also wrote to Senator Black,

[1]John A. Ryan, *Social Doctrine in Action: A Personal History* (New York, 1941), 279; Bishop Francis C. Kelley of Oklahoma City to Ryan, Jan. 7, 1933; Ryan to Rev. Phillip H. Burkett, Nov. 9, 1935, and other letters in the Ryan Papers. David O'Brien, "American Catholics and Organized Labor in the 1930's," *Catholic Historical Review*, LII (Oct. 1966), 323-24, 349, points out that support of labor was always qualified by fear of violence or strikes and respect for private property. O'Brien concludes that Catholic social thought had little longrun influence on the development of American unionism.

[2]Haas to Perkins, March 14, 1934, Correspondence-general, 1933, Haas Papers; Brooklyn *Tablet*, Aug. 3, 1935, p. 9.

[3]Haas to Rev. William C. Keane, director of Catholic Charities of Albany, N.Y., May 8, 1934, Haas Papers; John Ryan to Edward Keating, Nov. 9, 1933, Ryan Papers.

[4]John Tracy Ellis, *American Catholicism* (Chicago, 1956), 144; Dorothy Day, *The Long Loneliness* (New York, 1952), 219; NCWC *News Service*, June 29, 1935.

[5]*Catholic Action*, June 1933, p. 26.

[6]Ryan to Perkins, April 7, 1933, Ryan Papers.

remarking that some six months earlier he had made a speech in support of the thirty-hour workweek in the Town Hall meeting in New York City. He referred to the senator's bill as able and comprehensive, and was surprised at the good argument that could be made by using the powers in the interstate commerce clause to establish minimum hours for labor.[7] Indeed, Ryan even requested an opportunity to testify in favor of the bill before the House Committee on Labor. He wrote to Congressman W. P. Connery, chairman of the committee, expressing his great disappointment that he was denied the chance to help prevent the bill's death.[8]

Catholic priests took an active part in securing labor's rights under NRA. Ryan's role has already been mentioned. A few of the more prominent prelates who served as mediators in the labor disputes in 1933 and 1934 include Archbishop Edward J. Hanna, chairman of the National Longshoreman's Board; Father Haas, as federal mediator in the Minneapolis truck drivers' strike; and the Very Reverend John W. R. Maguire, Chicago Regional Board and mediator in the Kohler Wisconsin strike. Other priests served on local and regional NRA boards—John O'Grady on the NRA National Sheltered Workshop Committee; James F. Cunningham, Los Angeles Advisory Board, Dress Code Authority; Monsignor P. M. H. Wynhoven, chairman of the New Orleans Regional Labor Board; John P. Boland, chairman of Buffalo Regional Labor Board; and Frederick Siedenburg, chairman of the Detroit Regional Labor Board.

Not only were Catholics involved in the labor policies of the New Deal, but many even criticized these policies because they were not radical enough. As already noted, some regretted the negligible part labor had played in

[7]Ryan to Black, April 7, 1933, Ryan Papers.
[8]Ryan to Connery, May 3, 1933, Ryan Papers.

formulating the NRA codes. There was also dissatisfaction with the contents of section 7a. One Catholic spokesman, Ernest F. Dubrul, told the annual meeting of the NCCC in October 1934 that it was against Catholic teaching to force a man to join a union.[9] But voluntary unionism was not what Father Haas and other Catholic liberals wanted. In fact, section 7a was criticized by more progressive Catholics precisely because it seemed to support such rights as Dubrul argued were necessary according to the teachings of the Church. One editor felt that labor had been shortchanged by NRA because "this administration does not support, and never did, an interpretation of Section 7a which would have helped labor."[10] Another critic of the collectivist tendencies of NRA complained that it was setting up company unions and thereby leading to disaster for the workingman.[11] In Brooklyn an editor expressed fear that the right of collective bargaining spelled out in section 7a would be undermined by a weak interpretation or by simply ignoring it in practice.[12] Father Haas publicly called for the establishing of independent unions over the company unions. He wrote to William Green, president of the A. F. of L., expressing hope that the administration would not act rashly on the labor provisions of NRA, for this was an all-important matter.[13] Another source felt that section 7a was too weak because the interpretations of it by government and industry "have been turning collecting bargaining and the right to organize into an insulting delusion."[14]

Such Catholic impatience with NRA's labor policy was

---

[9]Ernest F. Dubrul, "NRA and Collective Bargaining," *NCCC Proceedings,* Cincinnati, Oct. 7–10, 1934, pp. 287-93.

[10]*America,* May 11, 1935, p. 97.

[11]*Monitor,* Sept. 9, 1933, p. 1.

[12]Brooklyn *Tablet,* Sept. 2, 1933, p. 6.

[13]*Ibid.,* Aug. 26, 1933, p. 1; Haas to Green, Nov. 11, 1933, Haas Papers.

[14]*America,* March 24, 1934, p. 582.

well founded. It is clear that neither FDR nor other New
Dealers like Johnson and Richberg looked upon section 7*a*
and the NRA as a means of building up industrial unionism in the United States.[15] Yet when NRA was invalidated
by the Supreme Court, Roosevelt was already supporting
the Wagner Labor Bill.[16] Senator Robert Wagner of New
York had been trying to get his bill through Congress
since 1934 but had failed to receive administration support. As passed in July 1935, the act set up a National
Labor Relations Board as "a permanent independent
agency empowered not only to conduct elections to determine the appropriate bargaining units and agents but to
restrain business from committing 'unfair labor practices'
such as discharging workers for union membership or
fostering employer-dominated company unions."[17]

Many Catholics were attracted by the proposals outlined in the Wagner bill. When it was being debated in
the Senate Committee on Education and Labor in 1934,
the Bishops' Administrative Committee of the NCWC
drafted a statement for presentation before this body. The
statement was a vigorous defense of labor's right to organize freely of its own accord. Portions of Pius XI's
encyclical *Quadragesimo Anno* were placed in evidence
in support of the bill. In a letter to David I. Walsh, chairman of the House committee and a prominent Massachusetts Catholic, the Reverend John J. Burke, general secretary of NCWC, urged that the bishops' statement be given
strong consideration.[18]

[15]William E. Leuchtenburg, *Franklin D. Roosevelt and the New
Deal* (New York, 1963), 108.

[16]James M. Burns, *Roosevelt: The Lion and the Fox* (New York,
1956), 226, points out that FDR supported the Wagner Act before
NRA was declared invalid.

[17]Leuchtenburg, *Franklin D. Roosevelt*, 151.

[18]Raphael M. Huber, ed., *Our Bishops Speak: National Pastorals
and Annual Statements of the Hierarchy of the United States, 1919–
1951* (Milwaukee, 1952) 305.

This statement stressed that the Wagner bill would protect the worker's right to self-organization. The prelates also liked the idea of establishing an industrial tribunal for the mediation of labor disputes. They remarked that both of these ideas "are in complete accord with and are required by the Catholic social program enunciated by Pope Leo XIII in 1891 and by the present Holy Father, Pope Pius XI in 1931." Inherent was labor's right to organize unions and to bargain collectively. A tribunal of adjudication was necessary to resolve conflicts between labor and management.[19]

Father Ryan, actively supporting the Wagner bill, felt it was "probably the most just, beneficent, and far-reaching piece of labor legislation ever enacted in the United States."[20] He made public statements endorsing the bill and sent many letters to congressmen urging their help in its passage. He wrote to Senator David I. Walsh, giving his full backing to Wagner's proposals. Ryan himself favored the bill because, like the bishops, he thought it was in accord with the wishes of both Pope Leo XIII and Pope Pius XI. He pointed out that the act was needed to make the NRA codes effective.[21] Ryan's stand was echoed by the Denver *Catholic Register*, which felt that the bill, if constitutional, would put labor and capital on a more equal footing.[22]

From the foregoing, it would appear that a significant element of the Catholic Church was vigorous in supporting the more radical labor policies of the New Deal. Yet when one approaches the question of child labor, the eradication of which was a goal sought by the New Deal, a striking amount of opposition is revealed on the part of the Church. Federal child-labor legislation had begun as

[19]Quoted in *Commonweal*, April 27, 1934, p. 701.
[20]Quoted in Frederick L. Broderick, *The Right Reverend New Dealer: John A. Ryan* (New York, 1963), 220.
[21]*Catholic Action*, May 1935, p. 17.
[22]June 20, 1935, p. 4.

early as 1916, with the Keating-Owen Act, but the Supreme Court had seen fit to declare invalid this and subsequent acts. In 1924 a child labor amendment to the constitution was submitted to the states by Congress, but by 1932 it still lacked the needed support of at least ten states. It was against this amendment that much of the Catholic opposition was directed. The amendment provided, first, that "Congress shall have power to limit, regulate, and prohibit the labor of persons under eighteen years of age"; second, that "the power of the several states is unimpaired by this article except that the operation of state laws shall be suspended to the extent necessary to give effect to legislation enacted by Congress." Altogether it did not seem a radical proposal; yet Catholic opposition to the measure was widespread.

Michael J. Ahern, S.J., one of Cardinal O'Connell's bright young men, gave the most elaborate explanation of Catholic opposition. Speaking over the Boston radio, Ahern pointed out that he, of course, did not approve of child labor, but this had nothing to do with Catholic opposition to the amendment. Catholics were opposed to the amendment because it invested too much power in Congress. Because it gave Congress such unlimited power, Catholics thought it dangerous and un-American. Limitations to the measure had been suggested to Congress before its submission to the states, but all were rejected. Friends of the measure urged that the people depend upon a reasonable interpretation by Congress of its responsibilities under the amendment. Ahern stressed that "we much prefer to have this reasonableness written into the Constitution, than to have it left to the vagaries of political opinion." As it stood, he said, Congress could use the power granted to "regulate, limit, and even prohibit the education of these young people." This was not expected, but why not make such things clear in the amendment? "It seems to us," he continued, "that under this amendment as it now stands Congress could regiment all children and youths under eighteen years of age, as they have been regimented in some communistic and fascist countries." The priest went on to note that the amendment had other weaknesses of omission, such as the failure to distinguish between harmful and nonharmful child labor. Furthermore, he insisted, child labor was no longer a major problem and President Roosevelt had already admitted that he needed no amendment to eradicate what was left.[23]

Much of this argument appears incredible now, but it should be made clear that a number of Catholic bishops and much of the Catholic press expressed opposition to the amendment along the lines mentioned by Ahern. The Catholic Daughters of America (CDA) and various local Holy Name Societies also came out against the proposal. The CDA argued that the amendment would "substitute for the authority of the parent, the authority of Congress."[24]

In Massachusetts the amendment ran into the opposition of Cardinal O'Connell. The cardinal's representative at the Massachusetts legislative committee dealing with ratification of the amendment, the Reverend Jones I. Corrigan, surprised his congressional audience by asserting that the amendment was communistic. He argued that the ratification of the amendment would be to "Russianize American parents and nationalize American children."[25] This remarkable outburst prompted a reply by John J. Cummings of Boston, a Catholic and former legislator, who insisted that the cardinal was really too old to know what the amendment said. He also pointed to such prominent Catholics as Ryan, Haas, and P. H. Callahan, who

[23]Quoted in the Boston *Pilot,* Feb. 27, 1937, p. 6.
[24]Quoted in the New York *Times,* Feb. 23, 1936, II, 1; Feb. 8, 1937, p. 5.
[25]Quoted in the Boston *Pilot,* Feb. 23, 1935, p. 1.

favored the amendment, as evidence that it was not communistic in nature.

The cardinal, however, was to have his way; the Massachusetts legislature failed to ratify the amendment both
in 1936 and 1937, despite a personal plea broadcast by
President Roosevelt. Roosevelt was assisted in the preparation of his plea by Bishop Francis Spellman of Boston,
who was a former assistant to Cardinal O'Connell. The
Massachusetts action caused Michael Flaherty, secretary
of the Boston Painters Union, to charge that the Church
obviously must own some sweatshops and that the cardinal was running the legislature.[26]

Other states also witnessed Catholic opposition to the
amendment. In Connecticut, Bishop McAuliffe of Hartford sent a representative to oppose the amendment before the state legislature.[27] In Texas one state senator
remarked that ratification of the proposal was being hin-
dered by pressure from the Catholic Church "which has
been pouring letters and telegrams into the Senate."[28] At
the same time, however, Texas was the home of the most
outspoken friend of the child labor amendment in the
American hierarchy. Robert E. Lucey, bishop of Amarillo,
did his best to promote ratification. He wrote to the governor endorsing the latter's stand for the amendment.
Lucey also quelled the opposition organized by the state
council of the Knights of Columbus.[29] But the bishop
seems to have been alone among the hierarchy in publicly
supporting the amendment.

In New York State the opposition reached its apogee.

[26]Robert I. Gannon, The Cardinal Spellman Story (New York,
1962), 154; New York Times, Feb. 20, 1937, p. 18.

[27]Columbia, April 1937, p. 3.

[28]Claude C. Westerfeld to Marvin McIntyre, Feb. 22, 1937, OF 58-A,
Box 5, Roosevelt Papers.

[29]Lucey to Frank P. Walsh, Jan. 23, 1937, Box 136, F. P. Walsh
Papers. The Walsh Papers in the New York Public Library are a
rich source of information on this whole question.

All eight New York bishops came out in opposition to ratification by the state legislature. Bishop Gibbons of Albany appeared in person before the legislative committee to oppose the amendment. Cardinal Hayes of New York City asserted that "authority over the lives of children rests in their parents" and not in any removed governmental agency. Bishop William Turner of Buffalo also spoke out against the amendment.[30]

Throughout the struggle for ratification, which occurred off and on from 1935 through 1937, President Roosevelt was aware of the opposition of the Catholic Church to the amendment. Charles C. Burlingham wrote to him, asking him to intercede in New York to overcome the hierarchy's resistance.[31] Roosevelt himself remarked to Harold Ickes that the Catholic opposition to the amendment could prove very harmful to the Church because it might provoke Protestant reaction.[32] This same thought was expressed to Father Ryan by Irving Brant, editor of the St. Louis *Star-Times*. Brant felt that the hierarchy's action would lead to a renewal of anti-Catholicism and anticlericalism. In his reply, Ryan emphasized that only a small minority of bishops were involved in the controversy while most were silent.[33]

Yet in the words of the Reverend Wilfrid Parsons, editor of *America*, the Catholic press was "overwhelmingly against the amendment."[34] The Jesuit weekly did indeed oppose the measure.[35] Other Catholic sources also came out against it, but none more strongly than the Boston

[30]*Commonweal*, March 5, 1937, p. 509; *Catholic Action*, Feb. 1935, p. 21.

[31]Burlingham to Roosevelt, Jan. 24, 1935, OF 58-A, Box 5, Roosevelt Papers.

[32]Harold Ickes, *The Secret Diary of Harold Ickes* (New York, 1954), II, 86.

[33]Brant to Ryan, April 22, 1937, Ryan Papers.

[34]Parsons to Mrs. G. F. Zimand [n.d.], copy in Ryan Papers, 1937.

[35]March 10, 1934, p. 535.

Pilot and the Brooklyn *Tablet.* The Boston paper supported Cardinal O'Connell's opposition with editorials, pointing out that "it is the solemn duty of [the Cardinal] to safeguard these children from any menace to their sacred and essential inheritance as Americans and as Catholics." The amendment under consideration was an invasion of the individual's private rights. The editor regretted the president's support of the measure which so endangered parents' rights over their children.[36] The Brooklyn *Tablet* opposed the measure for various reasons, one of which was the fear it "would result in new Federal snooping and a million-dollar enforcement bureau with all the graft that went with national prohibition." The editor felt the amendment was designed to regiment adolescents and argued that boys fifteen and over should be allowed to work if their family needed the additional income.[37] The official publication of the Knights of Columbus also came out against the proposal because it meant a further encroachment upon local self-government. The Catholic Central Verein concurred in this judgment that the measure would mean the federal government would assume more state power.[38]

Against this formidable array of opposition was pitted a group of influential Catholics determined to see the amendment ratified. As might be expected, foremost in this group was Father John Ryan. His early support took the form of letters addressed to members of state legislatures where the amendment was being considered. In this vein, on November 3, 1933, he wrote to W. W. Burke, chairman of the Missouri Child Labor Committee, who had requested the priest's assistance in promoting the

[36]Boston *Pilot,* Feb. 17, 1934, p. 4; Jan. 23, 1937, p. 4; Feb. 27, 1937, p. 6.
[37]Brooklyn *Tablet,* Feb. 24, 1934, p. 8; Dec. 1, 1934, p. 8; Jan. 19, 1935, p. 8.
[38]*Columbia,* April 1935, p. 12; Boston *Pilot,* Feb. 17, 1934, p. 4.

passage of the amendment in that state. Ryan was glad to write that he supported the amendment and wished it were law.[39] A similar statement went to Victor A. Olander, secretary of the Illinois State Federation of Labor, who was pushing ratification of the amendment in his state.[40] Ryan sent his endorsement to the Illinois legislature, as well as to those in Nebraska, Idaho, Massachusetts, and Indiana. In many of his letters Ryan quoted the late Senator Thomas J. Walsh of Montana, who had said that the amendment was subjected to "selfish and pernicious propaganda." The priest felt that Catholics had fallen prey to this propaganda and were misguided in their opposition.[41] The fears that Congress would set the minimum age for working at eighteen were, he believed, unfounded. Furthermore, the amendment did not give Congress any exhaustive power in education. Indeed, the states already had more power over children's education than did the federal government. Why, asked Ryan, were the states so much safer than the federal government?[42] In all his correspondence concerning the measure, Father Ryan was careful to point out that the National Catholic Welfare Conference had made no official pronouncement either for or against the Federal Child Labor Amendment, but that he personally supported it.[43]

One group dedicated to the ratification of the constitutional amendment, and one attracted by Ryan's statement, was the National Child Labor Committee (NCLC). The committee secretary, Courtenay Dinwiddie, was desirous of enlisting some prominent Catholics for his group, in view

[39]Ryan to Burke, Nov. 3, 1933, Ryan Papers.
[40]Ryan to Olander, June 14, 1933, Ryan Papers.
[41]Francis Downing, "American Catholicism and the Socio-economic Evolution in the United States," in *Church and Society: Catholic Social and Political Thought and Movements, 1789–1950*, ed. Joseph N. Moody (New York, 1953), 875.
[42]Ryan to Ethel Van Benthuysen, Jan. 20, 1934, Ryan Papers.
[43]Ryan to Cranston Brenton, Aug. 23, 1935, Ryan Papers.

of the outspoken opposition of some of the bishops. With this in mind he wrote to Father Haas asking him for a public statement in favor of the amendment. Haas replied that he was in complete agreement with NCLC's position and felt that some Catholic criticisms of the amendment were "positively stupid." He regretfully declined, however, to make a public statement in favor of the amendment because he feared it might affect his opportunity to serve the National Labor Board.[44]

Some time later, Dinwiddie tried again. He telephoned to Father Ryan, suggesting that the priest organize a committee of Catholics in favor of ratification. After discussing the matter with Father McGowan, who also favored the amendment, Ryan replied that a committee was a good idea but that it could not be connected with the NCWC or the Catholic Conference on Industrial Problems. Furthermore, he would privately support the organization but could not officially sponsor it.[45]

While Ryan was reluctant to sponsor such an organization, Frank P. Walsh, New York attorney, was not. On February 17, 1936, Walsh announced the formation of a Catholic Committee for Ratification of the Child Labor Amendment. Walsh made a public statement that he was distressed by the opposition of many Catholics to the amendment. This opposition was, in Walsh's opinion, "influential in blocking the ratification of the amendment in certain of the state legislatures."[46] He went on to stress that his committee felt the amendment was necessary for the elimination of child labor in the United States. He listed as charter members such prominent Catholics as Father Ryan, Father McGowan, the Reverend J. W. R. Maguire, Professor Carlton J. H. Hayes, Professor David

[44]Haas to Dinwiddie, Feb. 12, 1934, Correspondence-general, 1934, Haas Papers.
[45]Ryan to Dinwiddie, Nov. 5, 1935, Ryan Papers.
[46]Quoted in Commonweal, Feb. 28, 1936, p. 495.

A. McCabe, Grover Whalen, Rose J. McHugh, Dorothy Day, and Theodore A. Thomas.[47] Walsh later added the name of Michael O'Shaughnessy to his list of supporters. O'Shaughnessy was convinced of the need for the amendment by FDR's statement that child labor had increased since the invalidation of NRA. He wrote, "The present evil overshadows the possible evil of congressional interference with education to the detriment of religion."[48]

Naturally the Walsh committee came in for some criticism from Catholic sources. The Brooklyn *Tablet* assailed both the leader and the cause for going against the wishes of the hierarchy.[49] The Boston *Pilot* also felt that Walsh's efforts were misguided and pointed out that ratification was not really a Catholic issue but touched all men who did not want to surrender control over the education of their children to Congress.[50] S. A. Baldus, editor of *Extension* magazine, criticized the Walsh group because they had failed to consult proper ecclesiastical authority before dragging the Church into politics. He felt that the group should not be supported by Catholics.[51]

This discussion of the debate on the child labor amendment reveals a definite paradox in Catholic labor thought during the first term of President Roosevelt. During Roosevelt's first term, most Catholic spokesmen argued for a wider role of labor under the NRA, and later supported the benefits of the Wagner Labor Relations Act, because they felt that both the freedom to join a union and collective bargaining were part of the papal program. At the same time, however, elements of the hierarchy vigorously opposed the ratification of the amendment. While

[47]New York *Times*, Feb. 16, 1936, II, 2.
[48]O'Shaughnessy to Walsh, Jan. 4, 1937, Box 136, F. P. Walsh Papers. The Walsh Papers have material dealing with the work of this committee.
[49]New York *Times*, Feb. 17, 1936, p. 19.
[50]Feb. 29, 1936, p. 4.
[51]May 1936, clipping in Box 136, F. P. Walsh Papers.

some Catholics called for a more radical interpretation of
NRA to permit the growth of occupational groups, others
opposed the child labor movement because it would
mean an increase in state power. How clergymen, who in
1933 could call for a strong assertion of federal power in
combating the depression, could only a few months later
work against the child labor amendment because they
feared that under its provisions this same federal government would bolshevize their children is a paradox.[52]

If American Catholic opinion on labor had its ambiguous aspects, no such division was evident in its attitude
toward social security. The Wagner-Lewis or Social Security Act, signed by President Roosevelt on August 15,
1935, was one of the most important relief measures fostered during the New Deal. As enacted, the law created a
cooperative federal-state system of unemployment compensation. It levied a tax on employers and authorized
grants to the states to finance the administration of unemployment insurance. It provided a tax for old-age and
survivor's insurance to be levied in equal amounts upon
employers and employees. It further provided cash grants
to states to subsidize old-age pensions allowed under
state laws and various other forms of relief to the desti-
tute and infirm.

In connection with the administration of the new law,
President Roosevelt addressed a personal letter to the
clergymen of America. In this note of September 23, 1935,
he stressed that he was "particularly anxious that the
new social security legislation . . . shall be carried out in

[52]David O'Brien, "American Catholic Social Thought in the 1930's"
(unpublished Ph.D. dissertation, University of Rochester, 1965), 387-
90, argues that early Catholic support for the New Deal was a
reflection of Christian concern for suffering rather than a commitment to reform ideas involved in particular actions. Yet there is
abundant evidence that many Catholics—bishops and priests—both
understood and welcomed the powers implicit in New Deal legislation.

keeping with the high purpose with which this law was enacted." He wanted the clergymen in America to write to him about the conditions in their communities and suggest to him how the government could help.[53]

Catholic support for the new law was swiftly evident. Harry Hopkins, federal relief administrator, spoke in support of the law to the members of the New York Catholic Committee of the Laity. He was followed to the platform by Cardinal Hayes who also endorsed the measure. The cardinal said, "The security program of our President is . . . taking into consideration the preservation and conservation of those principles of action so vital to man's liberty and man's happiness here on earth."[54]

At the annual meeting of the National Conference of Catholic Charities, Katherine F. Lenroot, chief of the Department of Labor's Children's Bureau, hailed the Social Security Act as an important step toward protecting the family. She further stated that the foundation for the act could be found in both Pope Pius XI's encyclical and the statements of the American bishops. President Roosevelt honored the meeting with a personal letter in which he stressed that the NCCC and similar organizations were necessary to complete the structure of the national security.[55]

Other leaders of Catholic welfare work joined in the support of the social security measure. Mary L. Gibbons, a director of the New York Catholic Charities Bureau, called it only a first step but a good beginning. She warned, however, against an optimism which might lead to the belief that passage of the act would remove the necessity for a continuation of direct federal relief. After

[53]Samuel Rosenman, ed., *The Public Papers and Addresses of Franklin D. Roosevelt* (New York, 1938-1950), IV, 370.

[54]*NCWC News Service*, New York City, May 6, 1935.

[55]Quoted in New York *Times*, Sept. 30, 1935, p. 15; *Catholic Action*, Nov. 1935, p. 14.

all, she pointed out, the federal government only entered the field when it became obvious that local resources were inadequate to meet the needs of the depression.[56]

At the Cincinnati meeting of the Catholic Conference on Industrial Problems, Edwin E. Witte, ex-director of the President's Committee on Economic Security, urged the promotion of social insurance laws. He made a point of thanking Church leaders for their support of the social security program. After praising the encyclical *Quadragesimo Anno*, he called President Roosevelt's economic program "a major step in achieving for Americans the ideals of social justice set forth in that document."[57]

At the 1936 meeting of the NCCC, a formal statement was made on social security. The executive committee, which drew up the statement, endorsed the idea that the federal government was responsible for promoting social security. The statement submitted to the conference, which was largely the inspiration of the Right Reverend John O'Grady, secretary, accepted the government's role as protector of the industrial economy.[58] At the same meeting, the Right Reverend Thomas J. O'Dwyer, ex-director of the Los Angeles Catholic Welfare Bureau, pointed out that there was much room for expansion in the Roosevelt social security program. It was, however, "a very substantial beginning and is one of the most significant governmental actions in history."[59]

The 1935 convention of the National Council of Catholic Women also went on record as favoring the new social security law. A resolution was passed which called for vigorous state action along the same lines to provide

[56]Mary L. Gibbons, "The Future of Public Relief," *NCCC Proceedings,* Peoria, Ill., Sept. 29–Oct. 2, 1935, p. 80; see also Donald P. Gavin, *The National Conference of Catholic Charities, 1910–1960* (Milwaukee, 1962), 130-31.

[57]*NCWC News Service,* Cincinnati, March 25, 1935.

[58]Boston *Pilot,* May 23, 1936, p. 7.

[59]*NCCC Proceedings,* Seattle, Wash., Aug. 2–5, 1936, pp. 126-31.

assistance for unemployment insurance and pensions for the aged.[60]

Many distinguished individual Catholics also threw their support behind the social security measure. Father Ryan was wholeheartedly in favor of the measure. He called it a great document which "brings the United States up to date with Europe on the question of social insurance in one bold stroke."[61] As a matter of fact, Ryan played a part in constructing the legislation. He worked as a member of Frank P. Graham's general advisory council on social security.[62] Joining Ryan in support of the new law was the influential Jesuit author John LaFarge. LaFarge was "entirely in sympathy" with the measure and feared that without it "we should be facing chaos."[63]

Significant elements of the Catholic press also gave their endorsement to social security. The Brooklyn *Tablet* felt that the act followed in the direction of the papal encyclicals and was a major accomplishment.[64] The Boston *Pilot* called the principles behind the bill commendable. The editor liked the idea of both state and federal governments sharing this responsibility. His only criticism was that the act did not provide enough funds for the aged and unemployed. The Denver *Catholic Register* supported the new law and applauded the decision of the Supreme Court which upheld its constitutionality. The editor felt that the law was in accord with the spirit of *Quadragesimo Anno*. The editors of the two influential Catholic periodicals *Commonweal* and *America* were not as head-

[60]*Catholic Action*, Dec. 1935, p. 24. The annual convention was held in Fort Wayne, Ind., Nov. 17–20.

[61]John A. Ryan, "Social Justice in the 1935 Congress," *Catholic Action*, Sept. 1935, pp. 7-9. In this same article Ryan endorsed the Labor Disputes Act.

[62]Broderick, *Right Reverend*, 219.

[63]Quoted in New York *Times*, Sept. 26, 1935, p. 2.

[64]Aug. 24, 1935, p. 10, but one year later, July 18, 1936, the same editor felt the bill had been "poorly drawn."

long in their endorsement as was the editor of the Denver
Catholic Register, but both agreed with the bill's general
goals. The editors of *Commonweal* felt that almost everyone was in sympathy with the aims of the measure but
lamented that inefficient government pump priming was
leading the president nowhere. The editor of *America*
also was behind the aims of the bill, but remarked that
"social insurance is not a goal itself but only the indication of a deeper evil in our society." He also felt that the
law would have a difficult time passing the test of constitutionality. "From the standpoint of constitutional law,"
he remarked, "the . . . act seems to be an example of
doing the right thing in a wrong way."[65]

[65]Boston *Pilot*, April 27, 1934, p. 4; Jan. 26, 1935, p. 4; Denver
Catholic Register, June 6, 1937, p. 4; *Commonweal*, Dec. 13, 1935, p.
171; *America*, March 30, 1935, p. 582; Aug. 31, 1935, p. 482.

7

Ill Feeling over Russia

DURING Roosevelt's first term in office, foreign affairs took a backseat to the more pressing domestic economic problems. When Catholics took any interest in the foreign policy of this period, they were generally in complete harmony with the feelings of the majority of their fellow citizens. Most Americans were primarily interested in keeping the United States out of European affairs and neutral in any international quarrel.[1] The Catholic attitude was just as disinterested in foreign affairs with two notable exceptions. The first dealt with the question of the United States recognizing the Soviet Union. The second concerned the United States diplomatic dealings with Mexico during a period of anticlericalism there. These two questions produced some uniquely Catholic reactions.

Probably the first major question of foreign policy Roosevelt had to face upon assuming office was whether or not the United States should adopt an international spirit in attempting to solve the problems of the depression. One popular view of the depression in the United

States was that, since it was worldwide, an international effort would be needed to solve it. To these people the stabilization of international currency was a prerequisite for recovery. More prevalent, however, was the argument of such people as Raymond Moley and Rexford Tugwell —that the problems of the depression were to be found and solved inside the United States.[2]

Roosevelt himself had supported the idea of an international economic conference and had agreed to participate in one that had been arranged during Hoover's administration and scheduled to meet in London in 1933. But he soon became convinced that he should not tie his hands in domestic recovery by any international agreements. Specifically, he refused to endorse the London Conference's plan for monetary stabilization because he feared that "stabilization would jeopardize his attempts to raise domestic prices."[3]

While Father Ryan, Father McGowan, and others called for international cooperation for economic reasons, it became readily apparent that this spirit of internationalism did not extend, in Catholic opinion, to United States dealings with the Soviet Union. Woodrow Wilson had severed diplomatic dealings with Russia after the overthrow of the Kerensky provisional government in 1917. The Republicans who followed Wilson in power during the 1920's looked askance at Russia's attempts to confiscate all private property, her repudiation of international debts, and her emphasis on world revolution. Although the Soviet Union sought on a number of occasions to

[1]James M. Burns, Roosevelt: The Lion and the Fox (New York, 1956), 247-49; see also Robert A. Devine, The Illusions of Neutrality (Chicago, 1962), 57-81.

[2]Arthur M. Schlesinger, Jr., The Coming of the New Deal (Boston, 1959), 184-88.

[3]William E. Leuchtenburg, Franklin D. Roosevelt and the New Deal (New York, 1963), 200.

discuss the points of dispute with the United States, Communist propaganda in the form of diatribes on the evils of capitalism did not help to promote understanding between the two countries.[4]

During the 1932 presidential campaign, the question of the recognition of Russia was hardly the most topical one. Yet it did arise. In an interview published in the October issue of *Soviet Russia Today,* Roosevelt was asked his position on the question of recognition. His answer was adroit but noninformative. He pleaded that domestic affairs were so pressing that he had taken little time to inform himself in this matter. Actually there is evidence to indicate that Roosevelt did oppose the current nonrecognition policy as being a mere "futile gesture." But there was little political sense in pushing a topic that could only alienate some Catholic voters and really did not relate to the major issue of 1932—the economic crisis.[5]

Roosevelt's equivocation, however, failed to satisfy Edmund A. Walsh, vice president of Georgetown University and a leading Catholic authority on communism. Father Walsh, who opposed recognition, demanded that Roosevelt make his position as clear as Hoover had, when the latter stated that he would continue the policy of nonrecognition. The excuse of being uninformed on the subject was hardly adequate to Walsh, who warned, in an address to the New York Civic Federation, that Russia desperately needed United States recognition because of her floundering economy.[6]

After Roosevelt's victory in November, however, it became increasingly clear that the administration was seri-

[4]Robert Browder, *The Origins of Soviet-American Diplomacy* (Princeton, 1953), 18, 22.

[5]Travis Jacobs, "America Recognizes Russia: A Conspiracy?" (unpublished M.A. thesis, Columbia University, 1960), 70-71.

[6]New York *Times,* Oct. 15, 1932, p. 9.

ously contemplating a revision in American policy toward
the Soviet Union. There were various rumors as to why
Roosevelt should sponsor recognition. Some commenta-
tors pointed out that the United States could hardly assume world leadership—a position that seemed to be
thrust upon her by the worldwide depression—and ignore
the existence of Russia.[7] Others speculated that the
recognition would be only part of a new foreign policy
aimed at curtailing the power of Germany in Europe and
halting the Manchurian penetration of the Japanese. Even
more popular was the theory, held by Al Smith and William Borah, that Russian trade would help lift the United
States out of the depression. Finally, there was the belief
that recognition would do much to help restore international good will.[8]

Yet members of Roosevelt's official family were by no
means united on the question. In the cabinet, Secretary of
State Cordell Hull, Secretary of Agriculture Henry Wallace, and Postmaster General James Farley opposed recognition. Hull's reasons for opposition are not clear. According to Henry Morgenthau, Hull wanted the Russians to
permit religious freedom for American nationals, but he
also believed that recognition would only antagonize
large elements of Catholic Democrats because of the anti-
Christian attitude of Moscow.[9] Yet other factors entered
into Hull's decision. He was also concerned with the
Communist repudiation of the Czarist debt and the subversive activities of the Third International. Wallace
opposed recognition because of the harsh policies of collectivization then being practiced under Stalin. He ex-

[7]NCWC News Service, May 22, 1933.

[8]Ibid., Jan. 9, 1933; Jacobs, "America Recognizes," 71, 83.

[9]John M. Blum, ed., From the Morgenthau Diaries: Years of Crisis,
1928–1938 (New York, 1959), 56; Robert E. Bowers, "Hull, Russian
Subversion in Cuba, and Recognition of the U.S.S.R.," Journal of
American History, LIII (Dec. 1966), 542, 553-54.

pressed his opposition to both Hull and Roosevelt.[10] Farley, on the other hand, agreed with Hull and disliked the anti-Christian tendencies of the Bolsheviks. He was skeptical of any promise of religious freedom by the Russians, and tried to convey this skepticism to Roosevelt, but without success.[11]

This internal opposition was not all that Roosevelt had to cope with on the recognition question. The Catholic Church had been expressing vigorous opposition to communism and Russia long before the 1932 campaign. Recognizing the militant atheism of the Russian leaders as a direct assault on the very foundations of the Church, priests and laymen united in resisting the advance of bolshevism. This opposition was directed primarily at the philosophical basis of communism, but as the Russian state practiced a vigorous anti-Christian campaign, the antagonism naturally shifted to the existential exponents of the philosophy, namely, Soviet leaders and their government.

The rumors that President Roosevelt was planning to recognize Russia soon after taking office produced a significant reaction from American Catholic spokesmen. The Catholic press was virtually unanimous in its opposition to such a move. The Brooklyn *Tablet* started campaigning against recognition as early as December 1932 and carried on right up to November 16, 1933, when official recognition was extended. In 1932 the editor expressed shock that Roosevelt was even considering such a course and pointed out that recognition would be approval of "the godless policy" of Russia. A few months later the paper printed front-page headlines calling for Catholics to awaken to the insidious campaign afoot to promote recognition. The writer warned the administration that such recognition would be looked upon as treason by twenty-million Catholics. A few months later, after Roosevelt

[10]Wallace, Letter to author, South Salem, N.Y., Jan. 23, 1964.
[11]Farley, Interview with author, March 20, 1965.

sold some surplus cotton to Russia, the managing editor warned that "dealing with Russia . . . is a blunder materially, morally, and patriotically."[12]

In New England, the Boston *Pilot* kept up a continuous barrage against any proposals to deal with the Soviets. Attacking the argument that recognition would be good for trade, the editor reminded his readers that England had not experienced any increased trade after extending recognition. Furthermore, commerce should be secondary when discussing a nation that not only denied every human right but also persecuted the church.[13]

Many other Catholic diocesan papers also came out against any dealings with Russia. The San Francisco *Monitor* compared the American offer of friendship to Russia to a man that "has clasped to his bosom a viper more deadly than death." The *Catholic Telegraph* of Cincinnati, Ohio, admitted Roosevelt's "sincerity and honesty of purpose," but said that "only insatiable greed" could prompt such a mistaken course as Russian recognition. The *Catholic Herald* of Milwaukee was against any dealings with Russia. The editor insisted that the Russian attempt to destroy democracy should be the main consideration in this debate, and not trade advantages. In Chicago, the *New World*, which was usually liberal, asserted that the United States would lose face by dealing with the Russians and gain nothing in the way of commerce. The *Catholic Messenger* of Davenport, Iowa, argued that recognition of Russia would only stimulate Communist agents in the United States to greater acts of subversion. The editor warned that Roosevelt, by treating with the Soviets, might lose all the good will he had gained. Even before sitting down with the Russians, said the editor, Roosevelt should insist upon Soviet recognition of the

[12]Brooklyn *Tablet,* Dec. 10, 1932, p. 10; March 25, 1933, p. 1; July 8, 1933, p. 9.
[13]March 4, 1933, p. 1.

Czarist debt and an end to subversion by the current masters of Russia. The hatred of religion exhibited by the Soviet leaders was the main factor in turning the editor of the Denver *Catholic Register* against attempted negotiations. He insisted that "many will ask whether the price we must pay by closing our eyes to moral filth is not too great."[14]

Catholic periodicals joined the diocesan papers in their campaign against dealing with Russia. The *Central-Blatt and Social Justice* magazine felt that recognition would only strengthen a monster and push forward "the day when the resurrected hordes of Genghis Khan will put an end to European civilization." *Commonweal* attacked the ideas that recognition would mean more trade with Russia and that she was an honest customer. Russia's presumed repudiation of international law, her opposition to religious freedom, and her ignorance of basic human rights were, in this magazine's eyes, enough cause for refusing recognition. *America* was also against recognition, chiefly because of Russian persecution of the church. *Columbia*, the official journal of the Knights of Columbus, insisted that the Russian government "does not merit the recognition of any civilized people." The question of trade benefits could not possibly make up for the loss of national honor that would follow any dealings with "such atheists."[15] In the *Sign*, a national Catholic magazine, the Reverend Harold Purcell, editor, published articles condemning the recognition of Russia. Purcell

[14]*Monitor*, Aug. 12, 1933, p. 8 (this editorial view was endorsed by the *Western Catholic*); *Catholic Telegraph*, Aug. 3, 1933, p. 4; Nov. 2, 1933, p. 4; *Catholic Herald*, May 11, 1933, p. 4; *New World*, April 21, 1933, p. 4; *Catholic Messenger*, Oct. 5, 1933, p. 2; June 8, 1933, p. 2; *Catholic Register*, Oct. 29, 1933, p. 4; *Michigan Catholic* and *Our Sunday Visitor* (Huntington, Ind.) were other Catholic papers opposed to recognition.

[15]*Central-Blatt and Social Justice*, XXVI (April 1933), 11; *Commonweal*, April 12, 1933, pp. 646-47; Aug. 4, 1933, p. 337; *America*, Nov. 4, 1933, p. 97; *Columbia*, Jan. 1933, p. 17; April 1933, p. 11.

wrote "in the hopes of doing the little within our power to give a true picture of Soviet Russia and do what we can to prevent our Christian Government from entering into diplomatic or trade relations with the anti-Christ and anti-God Bolsheviks.[16]

The opposition of the Catholic press was augmented by the efforts of various distinguished individual Catholics and by religious organizations. Prominent Catholic priests who expressed public opposition to the idea of the United States dealing with Russia included Charles Coughlin, John LaFarge, James Gillis, Jones I. Corrigan, and Bishop Joseph Schrembs. But undoubtedly the most vigorous voice in opposition belonged to Edmund A. Walsh.[17]

A number of Catholic organizations also came out publicly against any change in relations with the Soviet Union. The National Council of Catholic Men passed a resolution stressing the fact that a nation which denied the existence of God could hardly be expected to abide by an international agreement.[18] In Detroit, two hundred representatives from the Holy Name Societies of the city started a campaign to oppose recognition on the grounds that the Soviets were opposed to both democracy and religion.[19] The Long Island Chapter of the Knights of Columbus, stressing religious persecution in Russia, denounced any dealings with that nation. This group also pointed to the Communist attempt to spread world revolution as another factor that should prevent the United States from dealing with them.[20] In Massachusetts a petition against recognition gained over 600,000 signatures

[16]Quoted in NCWC News Service, March 31, 1933.
[17]John LaFarge, "Shall We Recognize Russia?" America, Feb. 18, 1933, pp. 472-73; Brooklyn Tablet, Feb. 25, 1933, p. 3; May 20, 1933, p. 1; Jacobs, "America Recognizes," 16; Commonweal, Nov. 10, 1933, p. 29.
[18]Catholic World, CXXXVIII (Dec. 1933), 357.
[19]Michigan Catholic, May 18, 1933, p. 1; also NCWC News Service, Detroit, Feb. 11, 1933.
[20]Brooklyn Tablet, April 1, 1933, p. 1.

and was presented to the Roosevelt administration by Senators David Walsh and Marcus A. Coolidge. The petition seems to have attracted little notice in the press, and there is every indication that it did not reach President Roosevelt.[21] From Vatican City came unofficial comments expressing hope that recognition of Russia by the United States could be prevented.[22]

Not all Catholics, however, were so certain that the United States should ignore the Soviet Union. The Catholic Association for International Peace, during its annual convention in 1933, attempted to draw up a comprehensive report on Russia, but was unable to make much headway because of the varied opinions represented in the organization. Nevertheless, a tentative report was drawn up which embodied all the different views expressed at the convention. One statement said that Russia was so important from an economic, political, cultural, and religious standpoint that dealings with her, if possible, should be undertaken. Another comment was that Russia's communistic system made her a threat to world peace and impossible to deal with; thus, rather than recognition, action short of war should be taken to assist the Russian people in overthrowing the Bolsheviks. Finally, one group proposed that after recognition, the United States should undertake by propaganda and diplomatic action to secure a change in the Russian attitude toward religion. This preliminary report, which revealed both an awareness of the complexity of the problem of recognition and a divided mind on the solution, was signed by Father McGowan and other prominent prelates.[23]

[21]When queried on it, Stephen Early wrote that it probably went to the State Department; he had not shown it to FDR. Early to Mrs. J. C. Gray, Aug. 2, 1933, OF 220-A, Russia miscellaneous, Box 4, Roosevelt Papers.

[22]Clipping of Washington Post, Oct. 22, 1933, in Russia, 1933, Box 18, Papers of R. Walton Moore at Roosevelt Library, Hyde Park, N.Y.

[23]Report of Catholic Association for International Peace, Washington, D.C., in Box 88, F. P. Walsh Papers.

Elsewhere Catholics were shocked to read that Al Smith, in an appearance before the Senate Finance Committee, had advocated recognition of Russia. Smith expressed the opinion that he did not know any reason for refusing recognition. He pointed out that, although the Czars owed the United States money, this country had kept troops in Russia while technically at peace with her and that this occupation had caused some damage. More importantly, Smith stressed the fact that America already had clandestine trade with Russia, so why not bring it out in the open? He did not personally like the Soviet system, but felt that communism was no threat to the United States.[24] These comments were enough to cause *America* to wonder if there was not "a dent in the brown derby."[25]

Another prominent Catholic layman who supported the idea of recognition was Frank P. Walsh of New York City. Walsh received a letter from Albert Coyle in which the latter sought assistance in his campaign to become American ambassador to Russia. Coyle wrote to Walsh, saying, "Your office should logically get a very substantial amount of the legal business that is certain to follow recognition of the Soviet Union."[26] While this does not mean that Walsh was motivated by material gains, it is true that he favored recognition. When relations were finally established with Russia, Roosevelt received a telegram from Walsh assuring him that the deed would receive "a high place in the record of your splendid achievements."[27]

Smith and Walsh, however, represented a distinct minority in Catholic opinion. Most Catholics agreed with Father Gillis, Father Walsh, and others who vigorously op-

[24]Paul Boller, Jr., "The Great Conspiracy of 1933," *Southwest Review*, XXXIX (1954), 99.

[25]March 11, 1933, p. 543.

[26]Coyle to Walsh, Nov. 9, 1933, Box 88, F. P. Walsh Papers.

[27]Mr. and Mrs. F. P. Walsh to Roosevelt, telegram, Nov. 18, 1933, OF 220-A, Russia miscellaneous, Box 4, Roosevelt Papers.

posed recognition. There was some optimism generated during 1933 that Roosevelt would back off from recognizing Russia. In the invitation to an international conference in Washington during April to discuss the worldwide depression, the president ignored the Soviet Union—a fact looked upon by some as a sign that all plans of recognition had been shelved. Roosevelt's remarks to the National Conference of Catholic Charities in early October promoted a similar conclusion. At the conference, Roosevelt had made the remark that a nation could not ignore God and survive. This was interpreted as a direct slap at the Soviet Union. Yet other Catholics realized that recognition of the Russian government really had little to do with the president's feeling on communism. It was reported that the whole question was being weighed as a practical one. Neither approval nor disapproval of the regime was associated with diplomatic recognition, which merely indicated "a working arrangement with a de facto authority which will facilitate commercial intercourse."[28]

In October, however, Roosevelt took a step that dispelled much of the false optimism occasioned in Catholic circles by his speech to the NCCC. On October 10, 1933, the president made public a letter that he had addressed to Mikhail Kalinin, president of Russia. In the letter Roosevelt requested that the Soviet government send a representative to the United States to discuss all outstanding differences between the two countries in hopes of settling them. In response to this invitation, Maxim Litvinov, commissar for foreign affairs, left Russia for the United States.

With this development, many Catholics turned to Edmund Walsh for advice. Walsh was the first and foremost critic of recognition. Right after the 1932 election, Walsh addressed a women's club of Holyoke, Massachusetts, on

[28]*NCWC News Service*, April 10, 1933, and "Washington Letter" of Oct. 9, 1933.

the eternal conflict between the Russian and the American views of life. Soviet dedication to world revolution was the one thing that made Russia unique and made dealing with it different from dealing with any other nation.[29] A few days later, in Brockton, Massachusetts, Walsh continued his campaign against Russia, but said hopefully, "I doubt very much that a Democratic administration will repudiate a national policy initiated by Woodrow Wilson and continued by three Republican administrations."[30]

As rumors of impending recognition grew stronger in 1933, Walsh increased the pace of his campaign. He saw Russia's withdrawal from the League of Nations as a diplomatic move to promote United States recognition in exchange for Soviet pressure against Germany and Japan.[31] In reply to Smith's statement favoring recognition, Walsh asserted that the New Yorker was really missing the main point of the dispute. The questions of trade and repudiation of debts were really secondary to the fact that the two civilizations were "diametrically opposed in their principles, their practices, and their objectives."[32] *Commonweal* added that Father Walsh was opposed to recognition primarily because "he is bitterly and justly opposed to the war upon religion, to the suppression of fundamental rights of the Christian conscience, which prevails there."[33]

Walsh himself presented the most detailed statement of his argument against recognition before a mass meeting held in Washington on April 18, 1933, and attended by representatives from the A.F. of L., the American Legion, and other groups opposed to dealing with the Soviet Union. Once again the priest stressed the ideological aspects of

[29]Boston *Pilot,* Nov. 19, 1932, p. 5.
[30]Quoted in Brooklyn *Tablet,* Nov. 26, 1932, p. 6.
[31]*Ibid.,* March 18, 1933, p. 1.
[32]Boston *Pilot,* April 29, 1933, p. 12.
[33]May 5, 1933, p. 4.

the problem. His basic premise was that Russia was trying to destroy democracy via the Third International. Furthermore, the Communist ethic recognized no legal or moral law. Also the Bolsheviks could not even lay claim to complete sovereignty of Russian territory because of daily revolts by her enslaved people. Walsh concluded that only by abandoning the Third International and the aim of world revolution could Russia demonstrate a sincere desire to live in the community of nations. Strangely, Walsh made no mention in his speech of Russia's persecution of the church or of the militant atheism of the Communist party.[34]

While Father Walsh was the most persistent opponent of recognition, he had valuable support from other sources. The Most Reverend Joseph Schrembs, bishop of Cleveland and episcopal chairman of the Department of Lay Organization of the NCWC, gave a public interview on October 23, 1933. In his statement the bishop expressed the hope that the administration would demand as one prerequisite of recognition that "Russia promise liberty of conscience and of religious worship to its citizens and that it cease its active communistic propaganda."[35] In Rome, Bishop Michele d'Herbigny, president of the Pontifical Commission for Russia at the Vatican, called on President Roosevelt to demand religious liberty as a requirement for United States recognition of Russia.[36] Other sources indicate that even the pope wished Roosevelt would use recognition as a lever to get some guarantee from Russia of religious freedom.[37]

Behind the scenes it appears that President Roosevelt

[34]Copy of address by Edmund Walsh in *Congressional Record*, 73rd Cong., 1st Sess., in OF 220-A, Russia miscellaneous, Box 4, Roosevelt Papers; Browder, *Origins*, 39.

[35]*NCWC News Service*, Cleveland, Oct. 23, 1933.

[36]Jacobs, "America Recognizes," 13.

[37]Robert I. Gannon, *The Cardinal Spellman Story* (New York, 1962), 98.

was noting this Catholic opposition and taking steps to ameliorate it. On the very day that he sent his letter to President Kalinin inviting discussion of the outstanding differences between the two countries, Roosevelt met with Father Walsh to discuss the whole question at the White House. Walsh was later convinced that recognition was already a fait accompli and that Roosevelt suggested the talk simply to find out the priest's reaction. Afterward the Jesuit stated that the president seemed to have a rather cavalier attitude toward the issue. Said Walsh, "In reply . . . to certain observations I had made respecting the difficulty of negotiating with the Soviets, he answered with that disarming assurance so characteristic of his technique in dealing with visitors. 'Leave it to me, Father; I am a good horse dealer.' "[38] Perhaps to impress Walsh with the importance he had attached to religious freedom, the president asked him to prepare a report on the state of religion in Russia, which could be used when serious discussions were undertaken. Despite Walsh's later misgivings, it appears that he was sufficiently convinced of Roosevelt's sincerity to promise not to make any public statements that would embarrass the president in his talks with the Russians. This was a rather substantial concession for a man who had taken a strong public stand against recognition.[39]

Indeed, other sources exist which seem to indicate that Roosevelt had succeeded in converting Walsh into an ally after their talk of October 10. On October 15, 1933, Walter G. Hooke of New York City wrote to say that "he [Walsh] was prepared to place the AFL, the American Legion, the Bishop Freeman Committee [Protestants], and the Catholics squarely behind the administration's program for Russia, solely on economic grounds, and

[38]Louis J. Gallagher, S.J., Edmund A. Walsh, S.J.: A Biography (New York, 1962), 93.
[39]Jacobs, "America Recognizes," 89.

with reasonable protection of our own interest." Admitting that this was an exaggerated view of Walsh's influence, it still represents a rather startling new position for the priest. In the same letter, Hooke requested that McIntyre arrange a conference for Walsh with the president because the priest was "anxious to furnish certain information."[40]

After the meeting, which occurred on October 20, 1933, Walsh wrote to McIntyre to thank him for arranging it. The priest also said that he was preparing the memo requested by the president. He enclosed a copy of a press release he had made on October 21, "which I trust," he said, "will contribute something to the tranquility of mind needed for the forthcoming negotiations." The priest also mentioned that he had canceled a scheduled lecture on Russia in Providence, Rhode Island, and was substituting one on capitalism instead.[41]

The October 21 press release that Walsh referred to is a revealing document. In it the priest declared that President Roosevelt should not be restricted in his dealings with Russian diplomats by public debate among American citizens. "The President," said Walsh, "should not be hampered, or annoyed, or embarrassed, as he undertakes to fulfill his constitutional duty and exercise his constitutional prerogative in the conduct of our international relations." This seemed a rather remarkable statement for someone who had engaged in vigorous public debate on the question of recognition for almost twelve months. Now when the issue reached its most critical stage, Walsh called for silence. Elsewhere in the statement, Walsh said he was not convinced that the president's letter to Kalinin insured that recognition would take place. According to

[40]Hooke to Marvin McIntyre, Oct. 15, 1933, OF 220-A, Russia, miscellaneous, Box 4, Roosevelt Papers.
[41]Walsh to McIntyre, Oct. 21, 1933, OF 220-A, Russia, miscellaneous, Box 4, Roosevelt Papers.

the priest, FDR simply wanted to discuss the outstanding problems between the two countries. Walsh said that if these difficulties could be resolved, he would be first to support recognition. He promised to refrain from making public comments until the conference between Roosevelt and Maxim Litvinov was over.[42]

How can this remarkable turnabout in Walsh's outlook be explained? It should be recalled that Walsh had constantly attacked the inherent conflict between the Russian or communistic philosophy of life and American democracy. Another subject of his attack was the subversion practiced by the Third International.[43] He had given little discussion to the question of religious freedom in Russia or to the persecution of the church. Instead, he had concentrated on the conflict of systems of governments and philosophy. How he expected a conference of diplomats to resolve this conflict is difficult to understand. Probably he did not expect any resolution to the problems he had raised in his speeches, but now realized that, in Walter Hooke's words, "the President has the cards in his hands and he knows it."[44]

It seems clear, however, that the president had convinced Walsh that his best course of action, if he really wanted to assist his country in the forthcoming negotiations, would be to submit a private memorandum specifying in detail the particular grievances of the Church against Russia, citing cases and individual names. This would be worth more than public speeches filled with bitter generalities which could only weaken Roosevelt's hand in his talks with the Russians.

Before Walsh could present his memorandum, how-

[42]New York Times, Oct. 22, 1933, p. 25; this press release seems to contradict Gallagher's observation that Walsh had already accepted recognition as an accomplished fact.

[43]Jacobs, "America Recognizes," 89.

[44]Hooke to McIntyre, Oct. 15, 1933, OF 220-A, Russia, miscellaneous, Box 4, Roosevelt Papers.

ever, there were other developments. The priest had called Marvin McIntyre on October 30 and promised delivery of his memo on the following day. At the same time, he requested another private conference with President Roosevelt. In McIntyre's words, "certain embarrassing complications had come up" and Walsh felt that "we were going to run into opposition but that it could be straightened out."[45] What complications he referred to were not stated, but it should be noted that Bishop Schrembs of Cleveland had recently made a public statement in which he listed certain demands that the United States should make as a prerequisite to recognition of Russia. Naturally, religious freedom was one of the bishop's demands. Furthermore, the Catholic press had not ceased discussing the question. Wilfrid Parsons, editor of *America,* wrote an open letter to Litvinov, in which he stressed the point of religious liberty.[46]

The memorandum that Walsh sent to President Roosevelt on October 31 discussed the entire question of religious liberty in Russia. The priest began by asserting that "the attitude of the Soviet Government toward Religion is entirely different from any other government in the world." To prove his thesis, he used illustrations from the pages of history and concluded by saying: "Communism, which is the political, social and economic force controlling the Soviet Government, undertakes to abolish religion itself, the 'God idea,' in its every form and manifestation." Walsh then went on to sketch the history of religion under the Communist party in Russia. Atheism was, said Walsh, an integral part of a movement both international in design and militant in attitude. This being the case, "the anti-religious content of Soviet foreign

[45]McIntyre to Roosevelt, confidential memo, Oct. 30, 1933, OF 220, Russia, miscellaneous, Box 1, Roosevelt Papers.
[46]Nov. 4, 1933, p. 107.

policy, inasmuch as it visualizes the entire world, is as inadmissible by other foreign states as is the Third International. One is directed against our political sovereignty, the other against our religious institutions. Both are sponsored by the Soviet Government, no matter what the evasions or pretexts may be." Once having said this, Walsh went on to make clear that he did not favor extending diplomatic recognition to Russia. If, however, recognition was extended, he hoped that the following objectives might be supported by the United States: "1. Complete liberty of conscience for all, whether citizens of Russia or nationals of a foreign jurisdiction residing on Soviet territory, be they Catholics, Orthodox, Protestants, Jews or Mussulmans. 2. Private and public exercise of their religious beliefs for all by such external forms as appertain to their respective worship without discrimination arising from adherence to such religious beliefs. 3. Release of prisoners—Bishops, priests, other ministers of religion, and laymen—now in confinement under charges connected with religion."

Walsh admitted that conventional guarantees were useless. This made it even more imperative that Roosevelt take a strong stand, because the United States was the last government that was able effectively to implement any guarantees. This could be done "by requiring appropriate and explicit clauses to be inserted in any proposed agreement—and published before recognition or at least simultaneously." Walsh insisted that "the unusual circumstances and the extraordinary importance of the issue justify unusual and extraordinary measures." Certainly the priest realized that if the United States did recognize the Soviet government without the aforementioned guarantees, such action could not be interpreted as meaning that Roosevelt or his administration favored the religious policies of the Communists. Nevertheless, he insisted that "recognition without [such guarantees] would have the practical effect of helping to perpetuate conditions that are a matter of public record." Although pessimistic, Walsh could only hope that Russia might "now be pre-pared to do something concrete in amelioration of reli-gious persecution in order to secure what they most need from the United States."[47]

A few days later, Walsh sent in a supplement to his original document. In this letter, dated November 7, the priest pointed out that in several conferences he had with ex-Senator S. W. Brookhart of Iowa on Soviet recogni-tion, a certain Boris Skvirsky, the unofficial Soviet repre-sentative in the United States, had entered into the talks and had relayed their substance to Moscow. According to Walsh, Moscow's reply was "Let Walsh specify who is in prison on account of religion and where. We will con-sider his proposition." Father Walsh suggested to Roose-velt that this answer was "valuable as indicating at least a tendency on the part of the Soviets to listen to the recommendations outlined in the memorandum—and which we all devoutly hope you can persuade Mr. Litvinov to accept." Walsh also included for Roosevelt copies of editorials from *Commonweal* and *America*. He described the views expressed therein as representing the feelings of the majority of American Catholics.[48]

A list of Catholic demands as preconditions for any dealings with the Soviet Union holds few surprises. Cer-tainly a cessation of religious persecution was high on the list of priorities. Other sources spelled out the precondi-tions in more detail. The Vatican, it seems, had asked

[47]Edmund A. Walsh, "Memorandum on Religion in Soviet Russia," presented to Roosevelt, Oct. 31, 1933, Washington, D.C. Copy in Edmund Walsh Papers at Georgetown University, Washington, D.C.

[48]Edmund A. Walsh to Roosevelt, Nov. 4, 1933, OF 220-A, Russia, miscellaneous, Box 4, Roosevelt Papers. The editorials will be dis-cussed below.

Cardinal Hayes of New York to express to Roosevelt its desires that he raise the question of religious persecution in his forthcoming talks with Litvinov. Cardinal Hayes sent Monsignor Robert F. Keegan to the White House to transmit this desire. On November 1 Keegan presented to President Roosevelt a memorandum on four topics: freedom of conscience for Russians and foreigners; freedom of worship, public and private; liberation of those imprisoned for their faith; and cessation of propaganda against God.[49]

Keegan must have been very eloquent in his presentation, for on November 2 Cardinal Hayes wrote a confidential note saying: "The President conferred with the Monsignor for more than one hour . . . and substantially [accepted] the points of the memorandum."[50]

During this same period, Bishop Francis Spellman of Boston also got into the act. He received a letter from Count Enrico Galeazzi which told of the pope's desire to have the president insist upon religious freedom as a prerequisite for recognition of Russia. After recognition was extended to Russia, Bishop Spellman wrote in his diary, "Jack Kelly and Mr. Galeazzi, whose names will never appear in history, did much to get President Roosevelt to insist that American citizens at least should worship God as they wished in Russia."[51] Count Enrico Galeazzi was the official Vatican architect and Pius XI's "closest lay adviser." According to the Reverend Robert I. Gannon, Galeazzi and John C. Kelly gave FDR a picture of the religious situation in Russia "and the deep concern of all religious people outside of Russia."[52]

[49]Gannon, *Cardinal Spellman,* 425 n.2, who cites the Spellman Papers, a source open only to a few individuals.
[50]*Ibid.*
[51]Excerpts from Cardinal Spellman's diary, Nov. 7, 1933, and Nov. 10, 1933, cited in Gannon, *Cardinal Spellman,* 98.
[52]Gannon, Letter to author, May 6, 1965.

While these oblique negotiations between Catholics and the administration over the terms of Russian recognition were going on, an incident occurred which indicates that Walsh, Keegan, and Spellman did not represent all American Catholics in this matter. The bishops of the Administrative Council of the NCWC were scheduled to meet in Washington on November 15, 1933, with Bishop James Ryan of Catholic University as host. Before the meeting opened, the Reverend Maurice S. Sheehy of Catholic University wrote a letter to Marvin McIntyre, presumably with the knowledge and concurrence of Bishop Ryan, in which he made a number of interesting proposals. Sheehy felt that the meeting of the bishops during the turmoil of debate on the recognition of Russia presented an opportunity to "render some service to the President, to whom we are unutterably indebted." One must speculate that this indebtedness was due to Roosevelt's appearance at Catholic University earlier in the year to receive an honorary degree. The question of Russian recognition, Sheehy continued, had disturbed many American bishops and they had, in turn, asked Bishop Ryan for guidance. Sheehy suggested that the president might want to address the bishops on the way religion could serve the government during the crisis. If this were not feasible, the priest recommended a formal statement by FDR that "the interests of religion were properly safeguarded in all international dealings." Sheehy's purpose was obvious—he wanted to forestall any statement by the bishops that might, as Walsh had earlier warned, hamper the president in his negotiations with Litvinov. It is strange that Sheehy was not aware of the negotiations already in progress between Walsh and Roosevelt, but there is no indication that he was. Sheehy ended his letter with a revealing statement: "The press and the educational institutions of the Catholic Church have been solidly behind President Roosevelt in his every move. We are concerned to insure that there be not the slightest break in this united front back of the President's program." The priest feared that the negotiations with Russia might produce such a break and desperately wanted to head it off. He need not have had any fears, for, as has been seen, other sources were already making arrangements with the administration. Sheehy's own efforts, however, came to naught, primarily because McIntyre felt the proposal too explosive and did not even acknowledge receipt of the letter.[53]

It appears that only certain elements of the Church were aware of the administration's willingness to listen to Catholic objections to recognition. These elements included Walsh and Cardinal Hayes. Despite this limited awareness, the Catholic press shifted its stand on the entire question soon after Roosevelt sent his letter to President Kalinin of Russia on October 10. Editors no longer completely ruled out recognition, but insisted, instead, that the negotiations consider the question of religious freedom and persecution.[54] Most editors agreed that Roosevelt himself was dedicated to such principles and would press for them more vigorously if public manifestations were made. The *Monitor* of San Francisco now agreed to recognition "if Russia is willing to recognize free religious organization in Russia." The *Michigan Catholic* urged a joint statement by all Catholic organizations demanding, as a prerequisite to diplomatic relations, "definite guarantees against religious persecution and war on our government." The Brooklyn *Tablet* made similar demands, as did *America*.[55] In the latter publication,

[53]Sheehy to Marvin McIntyre, Nov. 3, 1933, OF 220-A, Russia miscellaneous, Box 4, Roosevelt Papers. McIntyre sent the letter to Miss LeHand with a memo saying, "Maybe I am unduly cautious, but I am not even acknowledging this letter."

[54]*Pax*, Nov. 1933, p. 55.

[55]*Monitor*, Oct. 28, 1933, p. 1; *Michigan Catholic*, Nov. 2, 1933, p. 4; Brooklyn *Tablet*, Oct. 28, 1933, p. 1; *America*, Nov. 4, 1933, p. 97.

Father Parsons wrote an article entitled "Open Letter to M. Litvinov" in which he demanded religious freedom for Russia, but significantly stated that Catholics should stand behind the president in the discussions. Addressing himself to Litvinov, Parsons warned, "You may be sure at the outset that the President has our confidence and support in these discussions."[56] *Commonweal* echoed the sentiments of Bishop Joseph Schrembs that Roosevelt should make Russia "promise liberty of conscience and of religious worship." *Extension* magazine realized that the United States could not conduct international diplomacy on moral platitudes, but was still against recognition of Russia because in doing so it would just give the Communist an opportunity to buy American goods on worthless credit.[57]

In this atmosphere, after nine days of discussion, Roosevelt and Litvinov formally exchanged notes on their conversation on November 16. The notes contained a number of salient features. First, Russia promised to curtail subversive activity in the United States. Second, the Soviets agreed to permit to American citizens in Russia free exercise of their religion. Third, both nations promised to negotiate a settlement of mutual financial claims. This exchange of notes represented the extension of full diplomatic recognition to the Soviet Union by the United States. Clearly the question dealing with religious freedom played a significant part in the negotiations. William Bullitt, special assistant to Hull, even described Litvinov as becoming exasperated with Roosevelt's preoccupation with religion while important trade matters were yet to be discussed.[58]

This emphasis on religion, however, was not due solely

[56]*America*, Nov. 4, 1933, p. 107.
[57]*Commonweal*, Nov. 10, 1933, p. 30; *Extension*, Dec. 1933, p. 17.
[58]Gannon, *Cardinal Spellman*, 175.

to the pressure of American Catholics. It should be recalled that Roosevelt himself had a high regard for the role of religion in any society. His remark to the NCCC that nations must recognize God in order to survive was not mere political window dressing. Frances Perkins, secretary of labor under Roosevelt, was convinced that it was the president's personal convictions, rather than Roman Catholic pressure, which caused him to stress the religious guarantees in the talks with Litvinov. "It seemed to him," she wrote, "a natural moral guarantee."[59] Furthermore, Roosevelt frequently took pleasure in describing how he lectured Litvinov on the importance of religion, even going so far as to predict that the Russian would himself return to God before he died. Roosevelt related that at this, "Max got red and fumbled and seemed embarrassed and just didn't know quite what to say."[60] Of course, recognition of Roosevelt's religious sincerity does not preclude recognition of his political sensitivity. Here was one occasion when by serving one he also "served the additional purpose of placating some of the vigorous opposition to recognition . . . by the Catholic Church."[61]

As other observers have pointed out, most Americans were quite satisfied with the terms of recognition worked out by Roosevelt and Litvinov. Before Litvinov sailed for home, he was given a farewell dinner in New York City. Many prominent American businessmen attended, but it was noted that "no Cardinal or other Catholic official was present."[62] This did not mean, however, that American Catholics were displeased with President Roosevelt's ac-

[59]Frances Perkins, The Roosevelt I Knew (New York, 1946), 142-43.
[60]Quoted in ibid., 143.
[61]Rexford G. Tugwell, The Democratic Roosevelt (Garden City, N.Y., 1957), 346. Tugwell observes that FDR "felt very strongly" about freedom of religious worship.
[62]Boller, "Great Conspiracy," 111.

tions. Indeed, evidence indicated that the president emerged from the affair with an even higher reputation among Catholics than he had possessed before it started. Monsignor Robert F. Keegan, Cardinal Hayes's secretary, congratulated Roosevelt on his achievement. "The masterly fashion," wrote Keegan, "in which you championed the vitally sacred principles which we Americans hold so dear is clear." Keegan also spoke of the cardinal's satisfaction over the terms of recognition.[63] The president replied that "we have really accomplished much in regard to the difficult question of religion in Russia," and asked for official Catholic sentiment on the terms.[64]

Official Catholic sentiment on the terms of recognition was not difficult to discover. Individual Catholics did not hesitate to comment on the proceedings. Father Walsh issued a statement in Washington on November 23. He felt the agreement meant the end of the Third International. Acceptance of the president's terms, said Walsh, meant "a significant abandonment of the previous Soviet policy." But he was careful to point out that much depended upon the honest fulfillment of the terms by the Soviet Union.[65] Joseph F. Thorning, S.J., one of *America's* editors, emphasized that the chief aspect of the entire agreement was that the inherent spiritual nature of man had been recognized by Russia. The talks were a lesson in morality for the Soviet Union and could possibly open the door for a change in her godless policy.[66] Another Jesuit, John LaFarge, was skeptical of Russia's sincerity but not of FDR's. No one who had seen President Roosevelt's "profoundly religious and patriotic attitude," said LaFarge, could doubt that he would insist upon the fulfill-

[63]Keegan to FDR, Nov. 18, 1933, PPF, Box 628, Roosevelt Papers.
[64]FDR to Keegan, Nov. 22, 1933, *ibid.*
[65]Quoted in the Boston *Pilot,* Nov. 25, 1933, p. 12.
[66]Joseph F. Thorning, "What Russian Recognition Means," *America,* Dec. 2, 1933, p. 200.

ment of the terms of the agreement.[67] Bishop Henry P. Rohiman of Davenport, Iowa, reported that Pope Pius XI was gratified with Roosevelt's work in securing freedom of worship for Americans in Russia.[68]

The Catholic press, while divided on the merits and terms of recognizing Russia, was unanimous in its praise of President Roosevelt's personal behavior. The Brooklyn *Tablet* did not want recognition at any time, but felt that FDR's handling of the entire matter was splendid. The *Catholic News* of New York was skeptical about Russia's sincerity, but hoped that recognition might mark the beginning of a change in that country. The Baltimore *Catholic Review* was not satisfied with religious freedom solely for Americans, but wanted it extended to Russians as well. The Denver *Catholic Register* felt that "President Roosevelt acted in the best of conscience," but that "recognition was granted because of secret international fears." Both the *Intermountain Catholic* of Salt Lake City and the *Witness* of Dubuque, Iowa, called recognition a mistake. The *Catholic Universe Bulletin* of Cleveland felt obliged to support FDR's action because he apparently knew more of the entire situation than did the general public, and the paper trusted his judgment. In Rochester, New York, the *Catholic Courier* congratulated President Roosevelt for winning concessions on freedom of religion. The *Western Catholic* of Quincy, Illinois, speculated that Litvinov must have been shocked by Roosevelt's great stress on religion. FDR's action, according to the *Catholic Herald* of St. Louis, Missouri, served "official notice that religion means something to the American people."[69]

[67]Quoted in the Brooklyn *Tablet,* Jan. 6, 1934, p. 4.
[68]New York *Times,* March 27, 1934, p. 9.
[69]A review of these editorial opinions is presented in *NCWC News Service,* Dec. 4, 1933.

Throughout its coverage of the negotiations, the Catholic press seemed certain of two facts: that recognition of Russia was a bad policy no matter how interpreted; and second, that President Roosevelt was a hero for defending the value of religion in society against communistic propaganda.[70] The overall reaction was best summarized by *Commonweal,* which said that FDR "accomplished as much for religious freedom in Russia as . . . was possible." A few sources even credited Catholic pressure with being the decisive factor in winning for the issue of religious liberty a place at the bargaining table. It was, asserted the Brooklyn *Tablet,* the united action of Catholic and Protestant groups which caused FDR to move slowly in the negotiations and to demand religious freedom as one of the conditions for recognition. The *Michigan Catholic* felt that Roosevelt obviously "kept uppermost in his mind" the demands by Catholics that he request guarantees of religious liberty from the Russians. *America* was satisfied with the terms because its call for religious freedom had been acknowledged.[71]

What remains unexplained amid all this editorial comment is how the Catholic Church could change from a position that expressed outright hatred for a godless regime, whose basic principles precluded international agreements or any dealings with democracies, to a position, while still skeptical, that could view the terms of recognition as a real achievement, provided Russia kept its word. After constantly hammering away at the untrustworthiness of the Russians, "suddenly, the hierarchy seemed to believe that Moscow, with equal suddenness, would faithfully adhere to the paper pledges."[72] After de-

[70]*Pax,* Dec. 1933, p. 91.

[71]*Commonweal,* Dec. 1, 1933, p. 117; Brooklyn *Tablet,* Nov. 18, 1933, p. 1; *Michigan Catholic,* Nov. 30, 1933, p. 4; *America,* Dec. 2, 1933, p. 193.

[72]Jacobs, "America Recognizes," 90.

bating the question of relations on a level that took note
of such historic and philosophical principles of communism as world revolution, the class struggle, and ethical
pragmatism, Catholics seemed greatly reassured over paper pledges of religious liberty for Americans—a condition that Litvinov insisted already existed in Russia.[73] A
final explanation for this shift in position is impossible,
but one may hypothesize that perhaps the Church and
most Catholic spokesmen never really expected to prevent Roosevelt's negotiations with Russia, but felt duty-
bound to make their opinions known on the subject. Then
when the administration seemed to take cognizance of
their views, they became flattered by the unexpected
hearing. Thrown slightly off balance by the president's
interest, they accepted his largely meaningless demand
for religious liberty of Americans in Russia with little
critical analysis. How else can we explain the attitude of
Father Walsh, who at one time stressed the untrustworthiness of Russia and afterward said that the only thing
that remained short of normal relations was the "honest
. . . fulfillment of Moscow's public pledge"? Surely all
his prior comments indicated to him that such an honest
fulfillment from the Soviets was impossible.

[73]*Ibid.*, 19.

8

The Mexican Affair

THE Roosevelt administration has been praised by historians for its development of a "good neighbor" policy toward Latin America. The merits and justice of this title are beyond the scope of this book. Any final assessment of Roosevelt's Latin American policy would, however, be incomplete without an evaluation of his dealings with Mexico during the height of that country's troubles with the Catholic Church. Such a commentary may also throw additional light on the relationship between the American Catholic Church and the Roosevelt administration, for the antagonism aroused over the "Mexican question" was the most severe strain imposed on the generally harmonious relationship between Roosevelt and American Catholics.

For anyone to appreciate the sensitivity of the Mexican situation, it should be recalled that the question of the Roman Catholic Church's role in Mexico, following the epic period of the revolution, had not been settled satisfactorily. As a close ally of the old established regimes preceding the revolution, the Church was viewed by many

Mexicans as being opposed to the revolution and the ideas behind it. The Church's influence in education was considered to be a serious hindrance to the social goals of the revolution. During the 1920's, much antiecclesiastical legislation had been passed and actual physical conflict had broken out between the followers of the government and the Church. American Catholics had shown a lively interest in the fate of their coreligionists south of the border and, through the good offices of Ambassador Dwight W. Morrow, had participated in negotiations to bring about a truce between church and state in 1929. This unofficial arrangement, however, was a precarious one at best and soon the Mexican government was once more challenging the Church's prerogative in education.[1]

It was with a keen awareness of this situation that American Catholics viewed the appointment of Josephus Daniels as the Roosevelt ambassador to Mexico. Daniels, as secretary of the navy under President Wilson, had been the chief of the young Franklin D. Roosevelt, who was serving as assistant secretary. Daniels' selection as ambassador in 1933 meant, as the NCWC viewed it, that "FDR would have a personal representative in this extra sensitive post."[2]

American Catholics lost little time in informing Daniels of the importance of his new post. The Reverend Wilfrid Parsons wrote an open letter to the new ambassador calling upon him to use his position to pressure the Mexican government into curtailing its persecution of the Church. Parsons assured Daniels that he had the authority to do this based upon the precedents established by Ambassador Morrow. Thus from the very outset Daniels was

[1] E. David Cronon, *Josephus Daniels in Mexico* (Madison, Wis., 1960), 83; E. David Cronon, "American Catholics and Mexican Anticlericalism, 1933–1936," *Mississippi Valley Historical Review*, XLV (Sept. 1958), 202.
[2] *NCWC News Service*, March 20, 1933.

called upon by American Catholics to become embroiled in the church-state question.[3] While not directly calling for Daniels to meddle in the internal affairs of a foreign nation, the Reverend John Burke, secretary of the NCWC, wrote a confidential letter to the ambassador cautioning him about the explosiveness of the church-state question in his new post.[4] As news of the murder of priests and nuns and the burning of churches was played up in the American press, local Catholic feeling became heated. Many American Catholics needed little excuse in order to protest against what they considered to be unjust treatment of their coreligionists in Mexico. On January 12, 1933, the Bishops' Administrative Committee of the NCWC issued a statement protesting the anticlerical practices of the Mexican government. They asked American citizens "to interest themselves in the restoration in Mexico of religious freedom for its citizens."[5] Despite Burke's warning, Ambassador Daniels was about to become a scapegoat for an attempt to pressure the Roosevelt administration into helping the Church in Mexico.

Daniels soon realized that it was virtually impossible to avoid the critical eyes of American Catholics. When presenting his credentials to President Abelardo L. Rodriguez upon arrival in Mexico, the new ambassador expressed admiration for the great social advances made by the Mexican people. The statement was a mere platitude, almost universal among diplomats at largely ceremonial meetings. Yet Daniel's remarks provoked condemnation by the Baltimore *Catholic Review* and a few other Catholic publications. This, to Catholics, inauspicious beginning

[3]Parsons, "An Open Letter to Ambassador Daniels," *America*, April 1, 1933, pp. 618-19; *NCWC News Service*, April 1, 1933.

[4]Cronon, *Josephus Daniels*, 85.

[5]Raphael M. Huber, ed., *Our Bishops Speak: National Pastorals and Annual Statements of the Hierarchy of the United States, 1919–1951* (Milwaukee, 1952), 201.

was mitigated some by the effect of the ambassador's call for freedom of religion in his address in Mexico City on July 14, 1933. This address was given wide coverage by American Catholic papers.[6]

In the meantime, events occurred in Mexico which gave Daniels reason to hope that his conduct could win the support of American Catholics. Archbishop Diaz of Mexico City, one of the leading churchmen in the country, had seen fit to praise Daniels for his "high conception and conduct . . . on religious matters." The archbishop remarked in private conversation that the ambassador's public statements and actions "had gained the friendship, respect and confidence of many people in and out of government circles."[7]

Daniels' hopes were short lived, for soon American Catholics were demanding his recall. In retrospect, the cause célèbre that was the reason American Catholics called for Daniels' dismissal and pressured President Roosevelt to intervene in Mexican affairs seems embarrassingly innocent. On July 26, 1934, Ambassador Daniels addressed the members of a seminar on education in Mexico City. In the course of his speech, he quoted the remarks of General Plutarco Elias Calles on the importance of education to the future of Mexico. Calles had said, "We must enter and take possession of the mind of childhood, the mind of youth." Daniels, considering this phrase innocent enough, had remarked, "To the carrying out of that aim, which alone can give to Mexico the high place envisioned by its statesmen, the Government is making the rural school a social institution."[8]

---

[6]Brooklyn Tablet, July 22, 1933, p. 1; Cronon, "Mexican Anticlericalism," 203-204.

[7]Memorandum of a conversation between Colonel Moreno and Archbishop Diaz, Mexico City, Aug. 28, 1933, Box 777, Josephus Daniels Papers, Manuscript Division, Library of Congress.

[8]Copy of address by Daniels, Box 777, Daniels Papers.

What appeared innocent to Ambassador Daniels, however, was not viewed in the same light by American
Catholics. A few Catholic publications immediately criticized the speech. Seeking to head off an unpleasant situation, the *News Service* of NCWC sought out Daniels' own
interpretation of the affair and published a fair account.
It stated that the ambassador was only endorsing the type
of public school system used in the United States.[9] But
many Catholic editors had a different interpretation of
the speech. *Commonweal* wrote that Daniels' action in
"upholding the destructive central policy of the absolute
state, will have a profound effect upon the New Deal in
the U. S." It would cause Americans "to ask themselves
how soon they are to meet the same fate here as their
fellow religionists are suffering in Russia, Germany, and
Mexico."[10] The *Catholic World,* through the editorial
comments of the Reverend James Gillis, said that the education praised by Daniels was socialized and atheistic.
Gillis felt that Daniels should keep quiet or else resign his
post.[11] *America* agreed that Daniels should resign. If the
ambassador did not know the context of Calles' remarks
that he had quoted, his ignorance could not be excused.
Later the same magazine claimed that the entire good-
neighbor policy developed by Roosevelt was being jeopardized by an antireligious government fostered by the
State Department.[12]

The protest soon spread to Catholic organizations. In
New York City, delegations of Catholic students picketed
the Mexican consulate and called for the resignation of

[9]Cronon, "Mexican Anticlericalism," 208.
[10]Oct. 26, 1934, p. 600.
[11]*Catholic World,* CXL (Dec. 1934), 259-60.
[12]*America,* Sept. 1, 1934, p. 484; Dec. 1, 1934, p. 169. Catholic diocesan papers also joined the general condemnation of Daniels; see
Denver *Catholic Register,* Baltimore *Catholic Review,* and Brooklyn
Tablet, which all expressed disapproval of Daniels' remarks and
suggested his removal. Cronon, "Mexican Anticlericalism," 208;
Brooklyn *Tablet,* Nov. 3, 1934, p. 9.

Ambassador Daniels. The Catholic Evidence Guild sent letters of indignation to President Roosevelt and Secretary Hull. Even the Ancient Order of Hibernians got into the act.[13] Mary C. Duffy, regent of the Catholic Daughters of America, wrote to the president protesting Daniels' endorsement of the pagan education of Mexico.[14] The Holy Name Societies of Cleveland, Ohio, and Richmond, Virginia, passed similar resolutions rebuking Daniels and asking for his recall.[15] Both the National Council of Catholic Women and the Massachusetts League of Catholic Foresters sent resolutions to the White House expressing very much the same theme.[16]

Other signs appeared which indicated the growing seriousness with which American Catholics viewed the situation. A public meeting was called in New York City to protest the anticlerical policy of the Mexican government. Father Wilfrid Parsons made the major speech of the evening and criticized Ambassador Daniels. Parsons also sounded a note that was to recur during the whole episode. He called on the United States to stop intervening in Mexican affairs as it was doing through its support for the current anticlerical government. Here was a nice bit of doublethink. Realizing the futility of calling for Roosevelt to intervene to help the church in Mexico, Parsons avoided this difficulty by calling for a cessation of intervention, both a possible and a popular move. The priest pointed to Daniels' endorsement of Calles' speech as evidence that the United States was, in fact, intervening in Mexico.[17] The priest's assertion received support from the Reverend Charles C. Coughlin, the radio priest

[13]Boston *Pilot,* Dec. 22, 1934, p. 1.

[14]Duffy to Roosevelt, Nov. 8, 1934, Reel 1, *Sel. Mat.*

[15]Cronon, "Mexican Anticlericalism," 209; *NCWC News Service,* Cleveland, Oct. 20, 1934.

[16]Cronon, "Mexican Anticlericalism," 209; Boston *Pilot,* Jan. 12, 1935, p. 3.

[17]New York *Times,* Nov. 19, 1934, p. 14.

of Detroit. Coughlin told his listeners that the United States government "from Wilson down to our President Roosevelt, has aided and abetted the rape of Mexico."[18]

What explains the scope and rapidity of protest following Daniels' action? The fact that such a storm of protest followed so quickly the remarks of the ambassador makes one speculate that American Catholics were anxiously looking for some reason to voice their growing concern over the persecution of the Church in Mexico. If Daniels had not made his statement, some other excuse would no doubt have been found to release the frustrated feelings of American Catholics. Indeed, as events developed, Daniels himself soon faded into the background; Catholics directed their pressure toward the president, demanding that he intervene in Mexico to arrest the persecution of the Church. It was perhaps inevitable that Roosevelt would be dragged into the dispute that arose over Daniels. The ambassador was a personal friend of the president. Furthermore, as the scope of criticism widened, it was essential to Catholics that the president become the focal point for pressure, since he alone could dictate the policy they sought.

A great volume of mail poured into Washington from Catholic sources. Most of these letters asked for Daniels' removal and for an end to Mexican anticlericalism. The list of senators and representatives asked to take action in this matter is a lengthy one. It included such disparate individuals as Senator Francis T. Maloney of Connecticut, Representatives James M. Meade of New York and Ernest Lundeen of Minnesota. In fact, few senators and representatives were neglected in the surge of protest mail, which came both from individuals and from groups such as the Knights of Columbus. Of course, the fact that a senator or a representative presented a petition to Con-

---

[18]Quoted in the Brooklyn *Tablet*, Dec. 29, 1934, p. 3.

gress did not mean that he was personally committed to the ideas expressed in the petition. Senator Robert Wagner of New York, for one, simply put forward petitions sent to him by his constituents without any supporting remarks. Although some Catholic papers attempted to leave the impression that Wagner was in sympathy with the resolutions, such was not the case.[19]

Catholic attempts to exert congressional pressure on the administration to take action against Mexico received unexpected support from widely respected Senator William E. Borah of Idaho. Borah introduced a resolution in the Senate in late January, calling for an investigation by the foreign relations committee "into the persecution of Christians . . . now being practiced in Mexico." The measure also called for Senate resolutions protesting the "anti-religious campaign" in Mexico.[20] Why Senator Borah, an avid isolationist and non-Catholic, should sponsor a measure so inconsistent with his career is difficult to analyze. When asked to explain his action, Borah said he had evidence that American citizens were being maltreated in Mexico. If American citizens were not involved, he said, "the situation would be different."[21]

Evidence exists that the idea of a resolution originated with Martin H. Carmody, supreme knight of the Knights of Columbus. The Knights had visited Congress in early January 1935 to help put pressure on the Roosevelt administration. A delegation had met with Representative Higgins and Senator David I. Walsh of Massachusetts.

[19]Clipping of the Catholic Telegraph, Jan. 24, 1935, in Box 778, Daniels Papers; Boston Pilot, Jan. 26, 1935, p. 1; see OF 28, Roosevelt Papers, for letters of protest. E. David Cronon, in Josephus Daniels, calls Wagner "an influential Catholic Democrat." As a matter of fact, Senator Wagner did not become a Catholic until the 1940's. Cronon is also mistaken about the religious affiliation of Rep. John Higgins of Massachusetts, whom he also discusses under the topic of Catholic congressmen.
[20]Quoted in the Catholic World, CXL (March 1935), 746.
[21]Quoted in the Boston Pilot, Feb. 16, 1935, p. 3.

Judge John E. Swift, Massachusetts director of the Knights, reported later that both men promised to be helpful.[22] Walsh, who was in contact with the apostolic delegate regarding the Vatican's attitude toward Mexico, apparently agreed to approach Borah and ask him to present the resolution. Walsh and Carmody probably felt that the petition would gain more weight if introduced by a widely respected non-Catholic.[23] In any event, Carmody wired to Borah on January 31, 1935, that Walsh had informed him of Borah's willingness to sponsor the resolution.[24] The question still remains, however, as to why Borah should be susceptible to Walsh's pressure. One scholar has speculated that this was a payoff for the strong Catholic support Borah had earlier received in defeating the World Court resolution.[25] Whatever his motive, it was soon apparent that Borah was not enthusiastic about the resolution. He failed to defend it vigorously and even refrained from voting for it when it later came up before the committee.

The Catholic press, on the other hand, strongly supported the Borah resolution. *Commonweal,* generally temperate in its statements, supported the congressional attacks on Daniels. The editor of *America* answered the objection that the Borah resolution would be intervention in Mexico's internal affairs by asserting that "the Mexican question is an American question of the most domestic kind." His reasoning was based on the premise that the United States had put the existing "atheistic" Mexican

[22]Newspaper clipping, Jan. 21, 1935, in Scrapbook No. 49, David I. Walsh Papers, Holy Cross College Library, Worcester, Mass.

[23]Clipping of Boston *Globe,* Jan. 27, 1935, Scrapbook No. 49, David I. Walsh Papers.

[24]Robert E. Quigley to Rev. W. L. Lucey, Sept. 13, 1960, in Letter File, 1935, David I. Walsh Papers. Quigley, professor of history at La Salle College, wrote Lucey, Holy Cross librarian, and cited Carmody's telegram to Borah of Jan. 31, 1935, in the Borah Papers.

[25]Cronon, "Mexican Anticlericalism," 214.

government in power originally. "An inquiry into religious persecution in Mexico," wrote the editor, "is an inquiry into our own dealings with Mexico." When it appeared that Roosevelt was not supporting the Borah resolution, the *Catholic World* wrote that the administration would be more sympathetic "if Methodists or Baptists were suffering in Mexico."[26] Diocesan newspapers also clamored for the passage of the Borah resolution. They generally insisted that Americans had a right to know what was going on in Mexico. The idea that President Roosevelt might be out to kill the resolution led some of these papers to warn that the consequences of such an action might be political alienation.[27]

These newspapers were right in their assessment of President Roosevelt's attitude. The administration viewed the Borah resolution as a gigantic mistake. R. Walton Moore, assistant secretary of state, wrote to Senator Pittman that the measure was "a premature indictment of a friendly neighboring Government." More importantly, Moore said the measure had the effect of permitting the Senate to shape foreign policy "without the aid or advice of the President."[28] Actually there was little danger of the measure being adopted once the president and Cordell Hull let their desires be known.

This setback, however, did not distract some of the more vitriolic critics of Roosevelt's Mexican policy. Representatives Clare G. Fenerty of Pennsylvania, Hamilton Fish of New York, and John P. Higgins of Massachusetts kept the drums beating in the House. By June, Higgins was circulating a petition among his colleagues asking for an inquiry into the religious persecution in Mexico. This

[26]*Commonweal*, Jan. 18, 1935, p. 329; *America*, Feb. 16, 1935, p. 437; March 2, 1935, p. 487; *Catholic World*, CXL (Feb. 1935), 523.
[27]Brooklyn *Tablet*, April 13, 1935, p. 10; *Catholic Herald*, April 4, 1935, p. 4; Boston *Pilot*, Aug. 31, 1935, p. 6.
[28]Moore to Pittman [n.d.], Box 10, Mexico, Moore Papers.

was the Borah resolution minus Borah. Higgins succeeded in obtaining the signatures of 242 members of the House to his petition. What this meant in terms of real support is unclear because various motives were involved in the response. The names of several Catholic representatives were not on the list. Furthermore, pressure was successfully exerted by some Catholic representatives who did sign the petition to add a footnote saying that the signees were "unalterably opposed to any semblance of . . . intervention in Mexico."[29]

On July 16, 1935, Higgins presented the petition to President Roosevelt at the White House. In its final form, the document deplored the persecution of all Christians and not just the Catholic Church. It asked Roosevelt to inquire about the inability of American citizens to practice their faith in Mexico, but rejected any intervention by the United States into the internal affairs of Mexico. It appeared that the petitioners really wanted a statement by FDR in which he would publicly disassociate himself from Mexico's antireligious policy.[30] Roosevelt, however, was aware that the main question remained the status of the Catholic Church under the current Mexican government. In answer to the petition, he issued a statement saying he was in sympathy with those who "make it clear that the American people and the Government believe in freedom of religious worship not only in the United States, but also in other nations."[31]

The Catholic press was happy to play up the president's remark as a forthright call for a cessation of religious persecution in Mexico. A large number of diocesan papers carried verbatim reports of the president's state-

---

[29]Edward L. Reed to R. Walton Moore, June 21, 1935, Box 10, Moore Papers; Cronon, "Mexican Anticlericalism," 219; New York Times, July 17, 1935, p. 1.

[30]New York Times, June 22, 1935, p. 13; July 17, 1935, p. 1.

[31]Samuel Rosenman, ed., The Public Papers and Addresses of Franklin D. Roosevelt (New York, 1938–1950), IV, 305.

ment.[32] The *News Service* of the NCWC sent out a story with the explanatory note that President Roosevelt's remarks must be construed as a protest against Mexico's antireligious campaign. This protest was, according to this source, the motive behind the petition.[33] The Denver *Catholic Register* thanked FDR "for breaking the silence on the persecution of Catholics in Mexico," and confidently predicted an official protest to Mexico from Washington. Such a protest, the editor felt, would have a telling effect. *Commonweal* applauded the president's statement and suggested that this attitude might lead to a "Kellogg Pact" type of international agreement by all nations "pledging freedom of religious worship." The editors of *America* said that when FDR issued his statement, "a major objective of our campaign on Mexico was achieved."[34] Altogether, the congressional petition seemed to have produced satisfactory results.

Not all Catholics, however, were satisfied with this settlement. Existing concurrently with congressional pressure were the efforts being made by the Knights of Columbus. Indeed, the Knights represented the most serious Catholic effort to have Roosevelt intervene in Mexico. The Knight's activities began in January 13, 1935, when the supreme board met in New York City and adopted a resolution attacking the Mexican government as being "opposed to religion, morality, justice, and liberty." The resolution further declared that the anticlericalism in Mexico meant that this nation had "forfeited its rights to further association with our government." As a consequence of this feeling, the supreme board, in the name of 500,000 Knights, petitioned the Roosevelt administration "to make representations to the government of Mexico,

[32]P. H. Callahan to James A. Farley, Aug. 1, 1935, Box 778, Daniels Papers.
[33]July 22, 1935.
[34]*Catholic Register,* July 18, 1935, p. 1; *Commonweal,* July 26, 1935, p. 316; *America,* July 27, 1935, p. 362.

that unless the evils . . . are ended forthwith, further recognition of the Mexican government will be withdrawn and diplomatic relations will be severed."[35]

These statements were the opening broadside in a campaign by the Knights which would last throughout 1935. The major protagonist in the Knights' effort was Martin H. Carmody of New Haven, Connecticut. Carmody was the supreme knight of the organization and was characterized by one observer as "a life-long Republican."[36] Early in January 1935 Carmody and a committee of Knights sought a private interview with the president to press their case. Their argument at that time, and throughout the dispute, incorporated all the stock phrases used by Catholics to attack the Mexican government and gave little indication of original or personal investigation. Roosevelt demurred from meeting the Knights at this time, claiming the press of public business, and referred them to Cordell Hull and the State Department. After meeting with the secretary for an hour, the Knights emerged, calling the talk "very satisfactory." From there they visited Senators Pittman, Wagner, and David Walsh, undoubtedly to coordinate the congressional petitions on Mexico.[37]

Roosevelt, however, was mistaken if he felt he could placate Carmody and company by having Hull assure them of the United States' continued interest in religious freedom. By April 1935 Carmody was writing Roosevelt again. In his letter, the supreme knight pointed out that no action had been taken on the January resolution passed by the Knights. He reminded the president that conditions in Mexico had grown worse since that time and that women and children were being persecuted for

[35]Quoted in the Boston *Pilot,* Jan. 26, 1935, p. 2.
[36]P. H. Callahan to Stephen B. Gibbons, Aug. 8, 1935, Box 778, Daniels Papers.
[37]*NCWC News Service,* Jan. 22, 1935.

their faith. Carmody requested a private conference with
Roosevelt as soon as possible to discuss the matter. Before FDR had time to reply, another letter, dated May 3,
arrived from Carmody. In this second letter, Carmody
was acting under authorization of the supreme board of
directors who, meeting in Detroit in early May, had apparently been stirred to action by the May 1 statement of
the American bishops on the Mexican situation. Carmody
now complained about Roosevelt's disregard of the
Knights' prior petitions, explained that conditions in
Mexico were getting worse, and deplored the apparent
opposition of the administration to the Borah resolution.
The supreme knight also insisted that there was clear precedent for intervention in such a case of religious
persecution as was now occurring in Mexico.[38]

Roosevelt referred Carmody's second letter to the State
Department for preparation of a suitable reply. By May
11 Assistant Secretary of State Moore had drawn up a
reply for the president's signature. Moore stressed that
the United States had no more right to intervene in the
case of church-state relations than it had in any other
domestic Mexican question. In an attempt to explain
United States policy, he made reference to the "Convention on the Rights and Duties of States" signed at Montevideo, December 26, 1933. At this meeting Secretary
Hull, acting for the United States, had voted for the article forbidding one state from intervening in the affairs of
another. Indeed, concluded Moore, Carmody's proposal
went against the entire tenor of the good-neighbor policy
Roosevelt was attempting to implement toward Latin
America. It was decided by the White House that Hull,
rather than Roosevelt, should sign this reply to Carmody.[39]

[38]*Catholic World*, CXLI (June 1935), 364.
[39]Memorandum of May 11, 1935, by Assistant Secretary of State,
OF 146, Mexico, 1933–1940, Box 1, Roosevelt Papers.

Carmody and the Knights of Columbus were not so easily satisfied. On June 23 Carmody again wrote to the president and stressed his disappointment over Roosevelt's refusal to acknowledge the earlier telegram. Carmody also regretted that he was unable to see the president personally and lamented the fate of the Borah resolution.[40] After this communication, Roosevelt apparently decided that something had to be done to satisfy the Knights. He sent Carmody's latest note to Hull with the following memorandum: "For preparation of reply for my signature as quickly as possible, as I think that speed is essential."[41]

Meanwhile, the State Department was feeling direct pressure over the Mexican question from the Knights and other Catholic groups. This prompted Assistant Secretary Moore to write to Hull that, although they must refrain from any action offensive to Mexico, if they did not make some statement "fairly satisfactory" to the Catholic interest, "the political effect may be injurious in many localities." Moore, modifying his earlier position, felt that there would be no harm in making a reply to indicate that the State Department did "honestly regret the situation in Mexico." With this in mind, he submitted a draft reply to Catholic inquiries which made the following points: There was no treaty between the United States and Mexico covering religion; the United States had always demanded religious freedom for its nationals within its jurisdiction; the United States had no power to act in this case, since it would be an unwarranted intervention in Mexico's domestic affairs.[42]

A few days after receiving this recommendation from his assistant secretary, Cordell Hull also received FDR's

---

[40]Carmody to Roosevelt, June 23, 1935, OF 28, Roosevelt Papers.
[41]*Ibid.,* June 26, 1935.
[42]R. Walton Moore to Hull, June 24, 1935, Mexican Religious Situation, Box 10, Moore Papers.

request for a reply to Martin Carmody's new letter. After consultation with James Farley, who recommended that the Knights be ignored for their discourtesy, Hull submitted a draft reply, which the president on July 3 sent to Carmody. Apparently Hull had decided not to incorporate Moore's recommendations into the reply because, in its final form, the letter simply explained to Carmody that pressing public business had prevented a private audience earlier, but that the president would now be glad to meet and discuss the Mexican situation with him.[43]

After some preliminaries, a meeting was arranged for July 8 between the president and a delegation of Knights, including Carmody; William J. McGinley, secretary; D. J. Callahan, treasurer; Luke E. Hart, advocate; John E. Swift; and James Donahoe. The delegation declared that they represented not merely the 500,000 Knights but all American Catholics. They reiterated their plea that the president protest the persecution of the Church going on in Mexico and brought up many precedents in which the United States had spoken out under similar circumstances. Roosevelt listened with his usual patience and good manners. He made a few remarks about religious conditions in the world and about communism, but was noncommittal regarding the particular subject of the Knights' visit. The group left, reporting to the press that the president was very courteous and generous with his time.[44] It should be noted that it was only eight days after this visit that President Roosevelt met with the congressional delegation on the same topic and issued his statement on religious freedom.

Roosevelt's statement of July 17 to the congressional delegation did little to placate the Knights of Columbus. As reports continued to flow into the United States of

[43]Memorandum of Secretary of State, June 26, 1935, Mexico, 1933–1940, OF, Box 1, Roosevelt Papers.
[44]*Columbia*, Aug. 1935, p. 4; New York *Times*, July 9, 1935, p. 6.

atrocities against Christians in Mexico, the Knights met at
their annual convention in New York City on August 21.
One of their first actions was to authorize Carmody to
send another letter to President Roosevelt concerning
Mexico. In the same unanimous resolution, the Knights
expressed regret at the administration's passivity toward
the question and disappointment that the State Department, with the president's approval, was opposing an investigation.[45] This outburst, however, was only a small
indication of what was to come from the Knights on the
subject of Mexico.

In early October, a quarterly meeting of the supreme
board of directors of the Knights was held in Chicago. At
this meeting it was decided to make another vigorous
representation to the president on the Mexican situation.
A letter of protest was drawn up, but it was not sent until
Roosevelt returned from an extended trip late in the
month. Signed by Carmody and by W. J. McGinley, the
letter traced the events since the July 8 meeting with the
president. At that time, said the Knights, President Roosevelt promised to make a public statement deploring the
Mexican religious situation. It was noted that FDR had
made two statements favoring religious freedom, one on
July 17 and another on October 2 in San Diego, California. At San Diego Roosevelt had said: "Our national determination to keep us free of . . . foreign entanglements
cannot prevent us from feeling deep concern when ideals
and principles that we have cherished are challenged. We
regard it as axiomatic that every person shall enjoy the
free exercise of his religion according to the dictates of
his conscience."[46] Many newspapers suggested that this
statement, because it was made near the Mexican border,

[45]*Columbia,* Oct. 1935, p. 17; New York *Times,* Aug. 22, 1935, p. 15.
[46]Quoted in the Denver *Catholic Register,* Oct. 3, 1935, p. 4, whose
editor praised the statement as an answer to the Knights' charge of
presidential indifference.

was a reply to the Knights' request and was directed
against Mexico. Carmody and company, however, were
more inclined to accept one reporter's opinion that the
speech was "a small sop to the Catholics." Indeed, Carmody not only accepted this interpretation but added that
our good-neighbor policy could not excuse inaction. In a
tone of surprising bitterness, Carmody concluded his letter: "You cannot escape responsibility for throttling the
Borah Resolution. You cannot escape responsibility for
the endorsement given to the Mexican Government . . .
by your Ambassador. You cannot escape responsibility
for nonaction on behalf of bleeding . . . Mexico."[47]

The tone of this latest outburst by the Knights was so
strong that one American bishop felt compelled to reply.
The Most Reverend John J. McNicholas, archbishop of Cincinnati, issued a public statement, read in all churches of
his archdiocese on November 3, that the Knights "in no
sense speak for the priesthood or for the Catholic laity [of
Cincinnati]." This response was made even though the
archbishop himself felt the administration could have done
more to ameliorate the Mexican situation.[48]

Taking note of this episcopal sentiment, the president,
after consultation with Catholics close to the administration such as James Farley and Frank Walker, replied to
the October attack of the Knights. In a letter to Carmody,
dated November 13, Roosevelt flatly refused to interfere
in the domestic affairs of Mexico. As for United States
citizens in Mexico, the administration desired that they
should be permitted freedom of worship. But, Roosevelt
went on, "there has not been brought to this government
during the past year a single complaint by any United
States citizen that such opportunities in Mexico have
been refused him." In light of this, Roosevelt insisted that

[47]Quoted in *Columbia*, Dec. 1935, p. 11; New York *Times*, Oct. 28,
1935, p. 3.
[48]Quoted in the *Catholic World*, CXLII (Dec. 1935), 362.

his policy of nonintervention would continue. This, however, did not mean that he was unsympathetic to the cause of religious tolerance. Roosevelt quoted from his recent speech in San Diego regarding his deep concern for religious freedom. Obviously the president was deeply committed to such freedom, but he did not feel that this was justification for intervening in the domestic affairs of a foreign nation.[49]

For Roosevelt this letter represented the final word in the episode. Catholics had different ideas. The Catholic press was almost unanimous in its criticism of Roosevelt's reply to Carmody. The Brooklyn *Tablet,* predictably critical, pointed out that Catholics had asked Roosevelt to end intervention, not start it.[50] The *Catholic Action of the South,* a New Orleans paper, felt that Roosevelt's attitude could only give comfort to the enemies of religion. The Baltimore *Catholic Review* said that FDR was condoning tyranny. The *Catholic Tribune* of St. Joseph, Missouri, remarked that Catholics should have expected a refusal because of Roosevelt's past actions. The Providence *Visitor* called Roosevelt's reply mere "political hedging" and reiterated the Knights' claim that the president could not escape much of the responsibility for current conditions in Mexico. *Light,* a publication of the International Catholic Truth Society, insisted that FDR should make Mexico honor the pledge of religious freedom given Woodrow Wilson. This paper called Roosevelt's reply to Carmody mere "artful weaving of words."[51] Wilfrid Parsons, editor of *America,* insisted that Roosevelt's letter would give a

[49]Roosevelt to Carmody, Nov. 13, 1935, in Rosenman, *Public Papers,* IV, 450-52; *Commonweal,* Nov. 29, 1935, pp. 113-14.

[50]Nov. 23, 1935, p. 1.

[51]In Albany, N.Y.; Hartford, Conn.; St. Louis, Mo.; Buffalo, N.Y.; Portland, Me.; and Rochester, N.Y., the Catholic diocesan press echoed these criticisms of the president and at times went even further. See *Columbia,* Jan. 1936, p. 18, which published a résumé of Catholic press reaction.

"green light" to those elements in Mexico most antagonistic toward the Church. Unfortunately, the president had intervened even while refusing to do so, said Parsons, and the result was to give "comfort to the enemies of religion."[52]

In retrospect it appears that President Roosevelt had little chance of appeasing these elements of Catholic thought. They insisted that what they wanted was not intervention, but a cessation of the interference taking place. Unfortunately, they could point to no specific action by the Roosevelt administration, save Ambassador Daniels' statement, which could be termed intervention. It is difficult to imagine what more they desired in the way of a public statement by the president. In his reply to the president, Carmody used the same argument—that he had never asked for intervention, only an investigation of charges of oppression. How this investigation was to be accomplished without intervention, he did not specify. Carmody's reply, in the form of a public statement to the press, was made November 17, 1935, in New York City, when the supreme knight insisted that Roosevelt had ignored good precedent for speaking out against foreign religious persecution.[53] After another month had elapsed, Carmody wrote to the president again. On December 16 he accused Roosevelt of distorting history to support his position of nonintervention. The Knights concluded that FDR's reasons for not acting in this case were "based upon a false premise," namely, that the Knights desired actual physical intervention.[54]

This final outburst by the Knights was referred from the White House to Sumner Welles of the State Department. Welles examined the letter and wrote to the presi-

[52]New York *Times,* Nov. 19, 1935, p. 7.
[53]New York *Times,* Nov. 18, 1935, p. 1; *Catholic World,* CXLII (Dec. 1935), 362-63; *Columbia,* Dec. 1935, p. 13.
[54]*Columbia,* Jan. 1936, p. 6.

dent that it did not deserve a reply because it raised no new questions. He further presented a detailed memorandum showing that the supposed incidents of persecution of Americans in Mexico mentioned by Carmody had nothing to do with the religious situation. Roosevelt replied that Welles was correct to assume that Carmody would not be answered and that he and Stephen Early were treating the subject as "a closed incident."[55]

Roosevelt's trouble with the Knights of Columbus, however, was only one aspect of the pressure exerted against his administration in connection with Mexican anticlericalism. Equally important were the feelings of members of the Catholic hierarchy. While all the bishops were not articulate about the Mexican situation, there was enough public criticism to cause some uneasiness in the administration. Ambassador Daniels had been directly rebuked by Bishop William J. Hafey of Raleigh, North Carolina, on October 6, 1934, when the latter publicly regretted the remarks of the former regarding Mexican education and hoped they were unintentional. Yet the bishop felt this "serious error" deserved a public refutation by Roosevelt, so it would not appear that his administration was endorsing Mexican atheism.[56]

Other members of the hierarchy seemed to be in sympathy with Bishop Hafey. At an annual meeting in Washington, D.C., November 14-17, 1934, some seventy-eight members of the American Catholic hierarchy issued a statement on the "Anti-Christian Tyranny in Mexico." "We cannot but deplore," read the statement, "the expressions, unwittingly offered at times, of sympathy with and support of governments and policies which are absolutely at variance with our own American principles." After this jibe at Daniels, the bishops went on to

---

[55]Welles to Roosevelt, Dec. 21, 1935, OF, Box 28, Roosevelt Papers.
[56]Cronon, "Mexican Anticlericalism," 209.

say that they did not believe that the United States favored the actions of Mexico. While the hierarchy praised American principles of toleration and freedom, they did not wish "to impose those principles as political principles upon any other nation," even though they were "as true outside as inside the physical territory of our country." Despite this qualification they called for an end to the indifference with which the United States viewed the Mexican situation and urged citizens to press their representatives to "be guided by true American principles with respect to Mexico."[57]

In February 1935 further episcopal action was forthcoming. An organization called "The Catholic Bishops Commission, Incorporated, for Mexican Relief" was formed under the leadership of such men as Archbishop Michael J. Curley of Baltimore, Bishop Francis C. Kelley of Oklahoma City and Tulsa, and Archbishop Arthur J. Crosserts of San Antonio, Texas. Other prominent prelates who lent their support to the organization included Bishop John M. Gannon of Erie, Pennsylvania, and Bishop James A. Griffin of Springfield, Illinois. This commission was not directed against the administration, but was primarily concerned with soliciting aid and assistance "for the relief and support" of Mexicans suffering under the antireligious laws of their country. Still, a campaign directed toward raising money "for the defense of religious freedom in Mexico" was treading upon international diplomacy and could not help but come under the scrutiny of the United States State Department.[58]

Other members of the hierarchy also spoke out. In February, Cardinal Dougherty of Philadelphia sponsored a mass protest meeting in his diocese against the "anti-

---

[57]"Statement of American Catholic Hierarchy," Nov. 15, 1934, in Huber, *Our Bishops Speak*, 205-208.

[58]*Catholic World*, CXLII (March 1936), 747-48; *Commonweal*, Feb. 7, 1936, p. 411.

God" actions of the Mexican government.[59] In Springfield, Illinois, Bishop James A. Griffin outlined objectives for American Catholics in the controversy, one of which was to awaken public opinion in the United States in favor of an official investigation into Mexican actions.[60]

Unquestionably the most outspoken member of the American hierarchy was Archbishop Michael J. Curley of Baltimore. In an open letter to the Washington *Post*, Curley defended the Borah resolution as a legitimate inquiry that deserved the sponsorship of the Roosevelt administration.[61] A few weeks later, the bishop, addressing a public gathering in Washington, deplored the attitude of the president toward the resolution. "If that resolution is killed," said Curley, "it will be because the Chief Executive of the nation has issued orders that it be killed." These were rather strong words, but Curley was not finished. In a statement that carried overtones of a political threat, the clergyman remarked, "Twenty million American Catholics are getting pretty tired of the indifference shown by the Administration." Despite a further reference to the "Catholic vote," Curley denied he was threatening anyone. He went on to criticize the president for refusing to grant an interview to the delegation of Knights of Columbus which had attempted to call upon him. He castigated the foreign policy of Cordell Hull as being against all American traditions. Finally, he insisted somewhat naïvely, that a mere word from President Roosevelt would suffice to relieve the anticlerical pressure in Mexico.[62] Despite the prominence of the speaker and the proximity of the speech, the Roosevelt administration took no official notice.

[59]*NCWC News Service*, Philadelphia, Feb. 19, 1935.
[60]*Commonweal*, March 29, 1935, p. 625.
[61]*Ibid.*, March 1, 1935, p. 510.
[62]New York *Times*, March 26, 1935, p. 1; Cronon, "Mexican Anticlericalism," 220; W. T. Walsh, "Some Precedents for the Borah Resolution," *Catholic World*, CXLI (Aug. 1935), 555.

The significance of Curley's outburst was that it represented a hardening of episcopal opinion toward the Mexican question. This shift was underlined by the May 1 public statement of the Administrative Committee of the NCWC. These bishops, speaking for the American hierarchy, requested that Washington speak out on Mexican anticlericalism. "The traditional policy of our Government," read the committee's statement, "does not permit it to remain silent at the present moment." They admitted that the government could not "interfere with the internal affairs of another nation," but pointed out that the United States had never been silent regarding such a basic principle as religious freedom. They concluded by promising to continue urging Catholics to petition Congress and the president to restore religious liberty in Mexico.[63] In furtherance of this attitude, Bishop Charles D. White of Spokane, Washington, circulated a petition for signature among the laity of his diocese requesting the president and the secretary of state "to exercise every personal and governmental power possible to relieve the injustices and to avert the threatened dangers of the present antireligious policy of the Mexican Government."[64]

To lend additional emphasis to the bishops' statement on May 1, Bishop John F. Noll of Fort Wayne, Indiana, a member of the Administrative Committee, wrote President Roosevelt a personal letter on Mexico. Noll reminded the president that he had been informed by the Reverend John Burke, general secretary of the NCWC and liaison man to the administration, that "it would be difficult to keep the Catholics quiet" if the Catholic hierarchy was completely ignored. The bishop recalled for Roosevelt that the statement by the American hierarchy had made no mention of the Borah resolution or the petition

[63]Huber, *Our Bishops Speak*, 307; *Catholic World*, CXLI (June 1935), 363-64.
[64]*NCWC News Service*, Spokane, Wash., May 6, 1935.

by the Knights of Columbus. The bishops, said Noll, approved these statements but had refrained from speaking out in order to give the president "an opportunity to do something with less embarrassment." Now Noll asked Roosevelt to make a statement "on the general principles of the rights of all people to religious liberty." Such a statement, he insisted, would be of great help to all oppressed peoples and was certainly within the historical precedents of the United States. Finally, such a statement would also end the rumors of FDR's growing sympathy for communism.[65]

Roosevelt was obviously impressed with the earnestness of Noll's letter. When drafting a reply, he asked Father Burke for advice. Burke composed a letter for the president's examination, and Roosevelt signed it virtually unchanged. In the letter Roosevelt once again asserted his own devotion to religious liberty and promised that the cause of the bishop's letter would receive "earnest, thoughtful attention." The president closed by promising to do all he could "to promote the principle of freedom of conscience and the exercise of religious liberty." Significantly, Mexico was not mentioned in the letter, but Roosevelt did stress the complexity and delicacy of foreign affairs.[66]

Not all members of the Catholic hierarchy, however, were so intent as Noll upon soliciting a statement from President Roosevelt. Indeed, the clergyman closest to the scene of conflict, Archbishop Pascual Diaz of Mexico City, expressed the opinion that nothing could be worse than for the president of the United States to make a statement demanding an investigation of Mexican affairs. "Such an action," said the archbishop, "would be very injurious to the interest of the Church in Mexico" and he

[65]Noll to Roosevelt, May 13, 1935, PPF 2406, Roosevelt Papers; see also Reel 2, *Sel. Mat.*
[66]Roosevelt to Noll, May 23, 1935, Reel 2, *Sel. Mat.*

personally would never condone such a step. The archbishop also expressed the personal opinion that Secretary
of State Hull was doing a great job; the archbishop "thoroughly approved of what he [Hull] had [done] and was
doing to prevent an investigation into Mexican affairs."[67]

In the United States, Bishop Schrembs of Cleveland
was not so much interested in Roosevelt's Mexican policy
as he was in the possibility that the president might con-
sent to appear before the Eucharistic Congress being held
in his diocese. Representative Martin L. Sweeney of
Cleveland, Ohio, was asked by Schrembs to try to convince Roosevelt to do so. Sweeney wrote to the president
that all Catholics were impressed by his July statement
on religious liberty, but that the Eucharistic Congress
would present a perfect forum for a public address on the
same topic.[68] Roosevelt decided to limit his participation
to a message of greeting and good will, which was delivered by his delegate, James Farley. This message was
apparently enough to satisfy Cardinal Hayes of New
York, who, after deploring the religious persecution occurring in other countries, expressed delight over the
president's greeting. Hayes was moved to remark, "We
have a President who believes in religion and wants his
fellow citizens to do likewise." Farley himself remarked
that the United States had set an example of religious
toleration, but that other nations failed to appreciate this
lesson.[69] Bishop Schrembs was also gratified by Roosevelt's contribution and wrote to the president that his
"appeal in the cause of religion" had made a success of
the entire affair.[70]

As one observes overall Catholic opinion at this time, it

[67]Memorandum of private conversation between Mr. Aguirre and
Archbishop Pascual Diaz, Mexico City, April 13, 1935, Box 777,
Daniels Papers.
[68]Sweeney to Roosevelt, Aug. 12, 1935, Reel 3, *Sel. Mat.*
[69]Quoted in the New York *Times*, Sept. 24, 1935, p. 1.
[70]Joseph Schrembs to Roosevelt, Oct. 2, 1935, Reel 3, *Sel. Mat.*

appears that the good feeling manifested over the Eucharistic Congress was a mere lull in the criticism of the administration by Catholic spokesmen. Most public spokesmen for the Church remained angered by the president's failure to take more vigorous action toward Mexico. Some expressed regret that the statements of Hayes and Schrembs, and later the criticism of the Knights by Archbishop McNicholas of Cincinnati, represented a division in the force of Catholic opinion.[71] Large elements of the Catholic press were consistently vitriolic in their criticism of the administration.[72]

Prominent individual Catholics also contributed to the rising clamor against the administration. James Gillis, editor of the *Catholic World*, was disgusted with the procrastination of Roosevelt. Gillis felt that the United States had a mission to "champion the cause of those who suffer persecution for conscience sake."[73] He wanted full-fledged intervention in Mexico. William J. Kenealy, S.J., speaking on "The Catholic Truth Period" over Boston radio, also stressed the responsibility of the United States for anticlericalism in Mexico. According to Kenealy, the Roosevelt administration was keeping the Mexican "atheists" in power by virtue of diplomatic recognition and by financial and moral support.[74] The Reverend G. A. McDonald published an open letter to President Roosevelt in the pages of the *Queen's Work*, in which he criticized the administration's handling of Catholic protest over

[71]*Catholic Transcript*, Dec. 19, 1935, p. 4; Brooklyn *Tablet*, Nov. 23, 1935, p. 8.
[72]For evidence of the position of the Catholic press see *Pax*, Dec. 1935, p. 81; *Extension*, Dec. 1935, p. 17; *Columbia*, May 1935, p. 12; *Commonweal*, Jan. 18, 1935, p. 329; Boston *Pilot*, Nov. 23, 1935, p. 4; *Catholic Transcript*, May 2, 1935, p. 4; *New World*, May 17, 1935, p. 4; *Catholic Messenger*, June 20, 1935, p. 2; and Brooklyn *Tablet*, July 13, 1935, p. 9, all of which attacked either Daniels' incompetence or Roosevelt's timidity.
[73]*Catholic World*, CXLII (March 1936), 641-46.
[74]Boston *Pilot*, Aug. 31, 1935.

Mexico.[75] But perhaps the height of hysteria was reached by Michael Kenny, S.J., author of *No God Next Door*. Kenny wrote that the Supreme Masonic Councils of Mexico and the Supreme Council of the Scottish Rite 33d Degree in Washington were influential in the refusal of President Roosevelt to intervene in Mexico.[76]

Against this seemingly widespread Catholic disillusionment with Roosevelt's Mexican policy was arrayed a minority who attempted to defend both Ambassador Daniels and the president. There were some who sought to counteract the charges made by the Knights of Columbus and the diocesan press. Foremost among these was Colonel P. H. Callahan, an influential Catholic layman and former executive of the Knights of Columbus. Callahan, a native of Louisville, Kentucky, was a prohibitionist and, like Daniels, an old supporter of William Jennings Bryan. He quickly became convinced that the effort by American Catholics to have Daniels removed and to have Roosevelt intervene in Mexico could only hurt the Church's position in that country. Furthermore, Callahan warned, if Catholics succeeded in removing Daniels it would produce a reaction by American Protestants, resentful of this show of political power, that would make the Smith campaign look insignificant.[77]

---

[75]Copy of *Queen's Work*, Dec. 13, 1935, in OF 28, Roosevelt Papers.

[76]Kenny to the editor, *Commonweal*, Dec. 20, 1935, p. 213. These individual protests were supplemented by appeals made by the following Catholic organizations who demanded everything from U.S. intervention to the removal of Daniels: The Ancient Order of Hibernians; National Catholic Women's Union of Hudson County, N.J.; The Supreme Board of the Catholic Daughters of America; St. Louis Council of Catholic Women; and a number of others. Lay Catholics such as Joseph Gurn and Thomas E. Purcell, president of the NCCM, spoke out against recognition of a "communist-dominated" Mexican government and suggested that the good-neighbor policy be used as a pretext for intervention to help Mexican Catholics. See the following: New York *Times*, May 6, 1935, p. 16; Feb. 23, 1936, II, 1; *NCWC News Service*, St. Louis, Mo., May 11, 1935; Washington, D.C., March 8, 1935; Union City, N.J., April 5, 1935.

[77]Callahan to H. L. Mencken, Dec. 21, 1934, Box 778, Daniels Papers.

As soon as Daniels was attacked for his remarks on Mexican education, Callahan began a campaign to defend the ambassador against the charges of the Catholic press. He wrote to such individuals as A. J. Beck, editor of the *Michigan Catholic;* Patrick F. Scanlan, editor of the Brooklyn *Tablet;* Vincent de Paul Fitzpatrick, editor of the Baltimore *Catholic Review;* and Joseph M. Schifferli, editor of the Buffalo *Echo* of New York. Callahan pointed out that Josephus Daniels had no religious prejudice. In fact the ambassador had been extremely generous to Catholics, in the number of chaplains he allotted to each faith when he was secretary of the navy during World War I. Daniels had not, insisted Callahan, endorsed pagan education. As for the ambassador's shaking hands with Calles, what else could be expected from a representative of the United States government? "Some of our co-religious [sic]," wrote Callahan, "expected the Ambassador to conduct himself as if he were representing the Vatican at Rome instead of the U.S.A."[78]

The Colonel constantly sent copies of his correspondence to the White House and the State Department. He also wrote directly to the administration during the height of the pressure campaign by the Knights of Columbus. According to Callahan, Carmody and the supreme council did not represent a majority of the Knights in their opposition to Roosevelt. He also indicated that Carmody and Luke Hart were lifelong Republicans. Callahan suggested to James Farley that Carmody's actions were probably connected with the "plans of Al Smith."[79] It is difficult to determine specifically how this information was used by

[78]Callahan to Patrick F. Scanlan, Feb. 27, 1935; for other letters see "Callahan Correspondence" in Reel 2, *Sel. Mat.* Many of the Callahan letters were published by the diocesan press.

[79]P. H. Callahan to Stephen B. Gibbons, Aug. 8, 1935; Callahan to Farley, Nov. 9, 1935; Callahan to James McGaughey [n.d.], Box 778, Daniels Papers.

the administration, although Secretary of State Hull wrote to Callahan that he had "utilized them [the letters] to good advantage."[80]

Another prominent Catholic layman who assisted the administration in counteracting unfavorable opinion in the Church was Michael Francis Doyle, a Philadelphia lawyer and active Democratic politician. Although in some respects Doyle appears to have been a sycophant of the president, he did strive to counteract Catholic criticism. As soon as it appeared that Daniels was in for a roasting by the Catholic press, Doyle wrote to the administration seeking evidence of the ambassador's pro-Catholic attitude while secretary of the navy.[81] He intended to see that this material was placed in the press. Doyle also wrote of having "conferences" with the NCWC and the Catholic Alumni Sodality, and of stifling their criticism of the administration. Roosevelt and Daniels were both assured that the attitude of the Knights of Columbus and of Archbishop Curley "did not reflect the general attitude of American Catholics" who "fully appreciated [Daniels] splendid qualities and . . . belief in religious toleration."[82] The Philadelphian claimed to be working within various Catholic groups, hoping to moderate their demands for the Borah resolution. One such group was the Catholic Association for International Peace—Doyle succeeded in removing a discussion of Mexico from the agenda of their annual meeting for 1936.[83]

Indeed Doyle appears to have been more concerned over the attitude of American Catholics toward the administration than was Roosevelt himself. After FDR had

[80]Cordell Hull to Callahan, Feb. 15, 1935, Box 778, Daniels Papers.
[81]Doyle to Louis Howe, Dec. 26, 1934, OF 237, Roosevelt Papers.
[82]Doyle to Daniels, Jan. 24, 1935, Box 777, Daniels Papers.
[83]Doyle to Daniels, March 6, 1935; April 17, 1936, Box 778, Daniels Papers.

answered the Knights of Columbus in his November letter, Doyle reported the formation of the Catholic Bishops
Commission for Mexican Relief. He wrote to Marvin Mc-
Intyre, saying, "I fully understand the Administration's
attitude and will do everything in my power to see that
this movement is not used for any political purpose."[84] It
should be noted, however, that President Roosevelt did
not appear unduly affected by the letters Doyle wrote.
The president saw Doyle only once at the beginning of
the Daniels affair, despite the latter's pleading for more
audiences.

Of more importance to Roosevelt was the work done
by John J. Burke, general secretary of the NCWC. Burke
was respected at the White House; Roosevelt often called
upon him to interpret and even answer letters from the
hierarchy. Throughout the Mexican crisis this priest was
sympathetic to both Roosevelt and Daniels.[85] One typical
example of his help came when Cardinal Hayes of New
York, in mid-1935, expressed his disappointment that the
president had not asserted himself in favor of religious
freedom in Mexico. Burke immediately set the record
straight, telling Hayes all that Roosevelt had done and
was attempting to do within the bounds of diplomatic
protocol. The cardinal must have been impressed, for he
wrote to Burke apologizing for his ignorance and expressing appreciation for Roosevelt's efforts. Although Burke
seems to have had little control over the Knights of Columbus, he continually criticized their actions toward the
president.[86]

There were other Catholics who braved the apparent
mainstream of Catholic feeling on Mexico to defend the

[84]Doyle to McIntyre, Nov. 27, 1935, Reel 1, *Sel. Mat.*
[85]Cronon, "Mexican Anticlericalism," 226.
[86]Sumner Welles, assistant secretary of state, to Roosevelt, June
25, 1935, PSF I, Diplomatic Correspondence, Mexico, Box 2, Roosevelt Papers.

administration and Ambassador Daniels. Judge Martin T. Manton of New York City was one. Manton spoke out at the March 1935 annual convention of the Catholic Association for International Peace held in Washington. In his speech he deprecated the Borah resolution as a violation of the Montevideo Convention of 1934 and suggested that the church-state dispute in Mexico be handled by the Permanent Court of International Justice. For implying that American Catholics should stop attacking the administration, Manton was soundly rebuked by such leading prelates as the Reverend John LaFarge, the Reverend J. F. Thorning, and Archbishop Curley. Thorning insisted that Mexico was attacking United States citizens, but the administration was keeping this news from the people. Curley simply called Manton ignorant of both the Mexican situation and the position of American Catholics. One Catholic editor not only applauded Curley's attack but also suggested that Manton get permission of his bishop before making any more public pronouncements on the situation. To some, it seems, the affair had entered the realm of faith and morals.[87]

The Reverend John F. O'Hara, president of the University of Notre Dame, was another prominent Catholic leader who refused to follow the line laid down by Bishop Curley and the Knights of Columbus. In a public interview in December 1934, O'Hara said: "Anything like an attempt at intervention by the U.S. in the internal affairs of Mexico would be distasteful to all Latin American countries, and would result in more harm than good."[88] He also wrote Daniels of the "cherished and affectionate regard" he had for him. Secretary Hull received word from O'Hara on how much the latter re-

---

[87]*Commonweal,* May 10, 1937, p. 44; *Catholic Transcript,* May 9, 1935, p. 4.
[88]Quoted in Cronon, "Mexican Anticlericalism," 227.

gretted "the misunderstanding" between Daniels and American Catholics.[89]

Some elements of the Catholic press actually took a pro-Roosevelt stand. In Chicago, Cardinal Mundelein's *New World* admitted that Daniels was not qualified for his post but also stressed that Catholics had no right to demand his resignation. Indeed, those who did so only succeeded in making themselves appear "rather ridiculous." Daniels was "in no sense anti-Catholic," but the current actions by some misguided souls might turn him against the Church. He was in Mexico to represent the United States, insisted the editor, not to represent the Catholic Church, and his mistakes should be attributed "to ignorance rather than malice."[90]

A significant step toward enlightening public opinion was taken when William Franklin Sands, professor at Georgetown University, toured Mexico to investigate the supposed anticlericalism. Sands reported to the American press that Ambassador Daniels was being unjustly maligned. Daniels had, said the professor, gone out of his way to try to resolve the religious strife in Mexico.[91] Others who helped spread enlightenment included Father

[89]O'Hara to Daniels, Dec. 19, 1934; Jan. 4, 1935, Box 777, Daniels Papers.

[90]*New World,* Oct. 12, 1934, p. 4; Jan. 18, 1935, p. 4. The *Michigan Catholic* attempted to explain the faux pas committed by Daniels by attributing it to his lack of Spanish, which led him to misinterpret Calles' remarks as simply praising popular education (Dec. 6, 1934, p. 1); *Commonweal* pointed out that the ambassador had an excellent record of religious tolerance and that he had supported Al Smith in 1928 against the opposition of many of his North Carolina neighbors (Feb. 15, 1935, p. 441); the Louisville paper *Record* proclaimed: "We stand with President Roosevelt in his commitment . . . of the United States to non-interference in the affairs of Mexico" (clipping, Nov. 21, 1935, Box 778, Daniels Papers); *Central-Blatt and Social Justice* insisted that the entire problem was inherited, not caused, by Roosevelt (XXVII, March 1935, p. 389).

[91]Daniels to Roosevelt, Aug. 2, 1935, PSF I, Diplomatic Correspondence, Mexico, Box 2, Roosevelt Papers.

John A. Ryan, who rejected the overtures of Maurice A. Tobin to become involved in a campaign to pressure President Roosevelt into intervening in Mexico. Ryan felt that the Borah resolution would certainly fail because it was "an undue interference in Mexican affairs."[92] Then there was Joseph P. Tumulty, former secretary to President Wilson, who was barely persuaded by friends not to answer publicly the charges Father Coughlin was making against Ambassador Daniels.[93] Ralph Adams Cram audaciously suggested in the pages of Commonweal that American Catholics place faith in the good intentions of President Cardenas. During a personal visit to Mexico, Cram found Cardenas to be a reasonable man and felt that the Mexican Church could only benefit under his rule.[94]

The most dramatic sign of divided Catholic opinion on the United States' role in Mexico, however, was the decision by the University of Notre Dame to present President Roosevelt with an honorary degree in the midst of his dispute with Martin Carmody. It is not clear who initiated the idea of presenting the degree to the president, but Frank C. Walker, a close adviser of Roosevelt and a graduate of Notre Dame, was deeply involved in the preliminary proceedings. John F. O'Hara, president of the university, was elated over the idea and telegraphed to FDR on November 6, 1935, formally inviting him to receive an honorary Doctor of Laws degree and to speak at a special convocation honoring the Philippine Commonwealth, recently made independent. A week later, O'Hara traveled to Washington for a personal meeting with the president to iron out all the details. The priest even sub-

---

[92]Ryan to Tobin, Feb. 19, 1935, Ryan Papers.
[93]Tumulty to Daniels, Jan. 5, 1935, Box 777, Daniels Papers.
[94]Ralph Adams Cram, "A Note on Mexico," Commonweal, May 22, 1936, pp. 91-92.

mitted to Marvin McIntyre a draft of his welcoming speech, asking for any suggestions on its contents. Quite clearly the university was anxious to have the president appear.[95]

Notre Dame officials were not the only ones elated at the news. The Reverend Maurice S. Sheehy of Catholic University, a close friend of the administration, expressed delight to Marguerite LeHand that Notre Dame was granting a degree to the president. Recalling that Catholic University had acted similarly in 1933, Sheehy said: "When we gave him an honorary degree we made an act of faith in him. That faith has certainly been justified." Sheehy pictured Roosevelt as the man who had saved the country from economic collapse. In an obvious reference to the Mexican situation, the priest regretted the unfortunate "campaign" then being waged against the president. He hoped that Miss LeHand could keep these attacks from the president's view, and he urged her to ignore them herself.[96]

On December 9, 1935, before a large audience at South Bend, Indiana, Notre Dame presented honorary degrees to President Roosevelt and to Señor Carlos P. Romulo, Philippine editor and educator. Presiding at the ceremony was George Cardinal Mundelein of Chicago. Mundelein, an enthusiastic supporter of Roosevelt, used his opening remarks to make his current position clear. The cardinal explained his presence at Notre Dame as a guarantee that Roosevelt would be among friends. He praised the New Deal and FDR's "indomitable persevering courage." As for the current quarrel between the president and the Knights of Columbus, the cardinal made it clear that neither he nor the Church were in politics and that no

[95]Stephen Early to Frank Walker, telegram, Nov. 5, 1935; O'Hara to Roosevelt, Nov. 6, 1935; Nov. 18, 1935; O'Hara to McIntyre, Dec. 5, 1935, Reel 2, *Sel. Mat.*
[96]Sheehy to LeHand, Dec. 2, 1935, Reel 2, *Sel. Mat.*

one had a right to speak for the political allegiance of American Catholics. Despite this disclaimer, the cardinal was in politics whether he liked it or not. The fact that he publicly lavished praise on the president at the same time that the Knights, Bishop Curley, Coughlin, and others were sharply criticizing him was of political significance. Harold Ickes was not alone in interpreting the speech as "a pretty complete endorsement of the President." When informed by reporters on the scene that he had virtually given a nominating speech for the president, the cardinal merely remarked: "I always go all the way for a friend."[97]

Roosevelt, who had hardly expected such an endorsement, was especially pleased with the cardinal's remarks.[98] He prefaced his own speech with an emotional thanks to Mundelein for his praise. The president then went on to speak of the necessity in any "true national life" for the recognition of the right of man. "Supreme among these rights," said FDR, "we . . . hold to be the rights of freedom of education and freedom of religious worship." This was a clear enough endorsement of religious freedom.[99]

Arthur Krock, political editor of the New York *Times*, interpreted the entire affair as a Catholic endorsement of President Roosevelt and a repudiation of the Carmody and Curley campaign. According to Krock, Roosevelt and the New Dealers were especially pleased by the endorsement of Cardinal Mundelein, who usually kept out of politics. His statement had added meaning because, according to Krock, "literally millions look for sociological appraisal as well as spiritual guidance" from the cardinal. There were, thought Krock, three reasons for the cardi-

[97]Robert I. Gannon, *The Cardinal Spellman Story* (New York, 1962), 156; Harold Ickes, *The Secret Diary of Harold Ickes* (New York, 1954), I, 479-80; New York *Times*, Dec. 10, 1935, pp. 12, 13; *Commonweal*, Dec. 20, 1935, p. 216.
[98]Ickes, *Diary*, I, 479.
[99]Rosenman, *Public Papers*, IV, 493-96.

nal's statement. First, Mundelein wanted publicly to rebuke political clergymen like Coughlin who had been attacking the New Deal. Second, he wanted to reprimand laymen like Carmody who had criticized Roosevelt and usurped the prerogative of the bishops to speak for the Church. Finally, he wished "to endorse his conception of the President's efforts to spread the blessing of American prosperity." Krock saw real significance in the fact that a leader in a conservative force like the Church should endorse the New Deal at a time when other so-called conservatives were speaking of Communist influence in government. He concluded: "The unscheduled, fervent praise of the Cardinal made the journey far more notable than any of the White House entourage expected when the trip was arranged."[100]

Other sources did not react as favorably to events at Notre Dame. For certain elements in the Church, it was distinctly embarrassing to have the president granted an honorary degree from the foremost Catholic university in the land and be praised by a leading churchman such as Mundelein. The editor of the Baltimore *Catholic Review,* Bishop Curley's organ, insisted that Catholics were expressing deep regret over the entire affair. Monsignor Albert Smith noted that the honorary degree was only "in gratitude for the independence of the Philippine Islands, a Catholic country."[101] The Brooklyn *Tablet* insisted that Notre Dame would "be years regaining respect" due to its decision to honor Roosevelt. As for the president, he should not expect the Catholic voter to be deceived by his "walking on both sides of the street." Finally, *Commonweal* observed that Catholic opinion of Roosevelt was not significantly affected by the Notre Dame affair. As a

[100]Dec. 13, 1935, p. 24.

[101]Clipping of the New York *Herald Tribune,* Dec. 5, 1935, Reel 1, *Sel. Mat.;* New York *Times,* Dec. 5, 1935, p. 29.

matter of record, the Catholic press did not play up the ceremony.[102]

It is difficult to determine what effect all these Catholic comments had on the internal workings of the Roosevelt administration. It is clear that the president was concerned over the pressure being exerted from various Catholic sources. When Ambassador Daniels first made his remark on the Mexican educational system, the storm of protest that broke loose was enough to cause Undersecretary of State William Phillips to ask Daniels for an explanation. "In view of the political strength of all combined," Phillips wanted to quote Daniels' explanation that he was only praising education in general and that he did not realize there was anything in the Calles speech dealing with religious matters.[103]

The president himself soon felt the pressure of Catholic protest. At his press conference of October 17, 1934, he was asked if Daniels was going to be recalled because of the recent criticism leveled at him by Catholic groups. Roosevelt displayed some irritation and pointed out that most of these charges sounded "fishy."[104]

When it was rumored that Roosevelt intended to visit Mexico in the summer of 1935, some Catholic sources became especially irritated. Daniels was so afraid of the political implications of the Catholic criticism being directed at him that he wanted to avoid having the president involved. Accordingly he suggested to the president that he put off his Mexican trip at this time. Roosevelt apparently agreed with Daniels' analysis, for he wrote, "From present indications . . . the Borah resolution has

[102]Brooklyn *Tablet*, Nov. 23, 1935, p. 9; Dec. 21, 1935, p. 11; *Commonweal*, Dec. 27, 1935, p. 241.
[103]Memorandum of telephone conversation between Ambassador Daniels and Undersecretary Phillips, Oct. 14, 1934, Box 777, Daniels Papers.
[104]Cronon, "Mexican Anticlericalism," 210.

not served to quiet things down and my one great regret is that it may keep me from visiting you . . . this year." The trip was never made.[105]

Meanwhile, Ambassador Daniels did his best to clear up the controversy. He issued a statement through the State Department reaffirming his dedication to "the principles of our country with reference to public schools, the freedom of religion and the freedom of the press."[106] Privately he wrote to Roosevelt expressing bitterness over the criticism being leveled at him. He pointed out that he had supported Smith for the presidency in 1928 and had fought the bigots. His record as secretary of the navy was also evidence of his "disregard of a man's church affiliation in public affairs." In view of this, Daniels said, "it seems strange that they could forget my lifetime devotion to freedom of religion and my freedom from discrimination against Catholics."[107]

In a letter to the *Catholic Columbian,* Daniels presented a detailed defense of his behavior as ambassador. He pointed out that he was a Christian, that he had no sympathy for atheism, and that he felt the American public school system was the best in the world. As for the incident that precipitated Catholic criticism, Daniels insisted that, as he understood it, Calles had "simply made a declaration for universal education." Admitting that he had not seen the entire text of Calles' speech, the ambassador could not understand how anyone could interpret his comments as being against religion. This was, he wrote, especially surprising in view of his "lifelong devotion to the precepts of the Christian religion" and his "unbroken opposition to intolerance in any shape or form."[108]

[105]Daniels to Roosevelt, Feb. 1, 1935; Roosevelt to Daniels, Feb. 9, 1935, PPF 86, Roosevelt Papers.
[106]Quoted in Cronon, "Mexican Anticlericalism," 210.
[107]Daniels to Roosevelt, Dec. 6, 1934, PPF 86, Roosevelt Papers.
[108]Daniels to *Catholic Columbian,* Jan. 3, 1935, in clipping of Jan. 25, 1935, Reel 1, *Sel. Mat.*

Behind the scenes, Roosevelt did his best to ameliorate Catholic criticism. He was greatly assisted by the Reverend John Burke, and to a lesser extent by Judge Martin T. Manton and Bishop Francis Spellman. When a particular bishop requested the president's opinion on the Mexican situation, Roosevelt generally discussed the reply with Burke, who also kept Roosevelt up to date on developments in Mexico's attitude toward the Church and served as a liaison man to the Vatican.[109] Burke personally favored a settlement which would involve only the Mexican Church and government.[110] At the same time, in hopes of reaching a settlement, Judge Manton sought to arrange a meeting between Bishop Spellman, another supporter of the administration, and President Cardenas of Mexico. Roosevelt was advised of this move and agreed to arrange such a meeting, provided it was cleared with the Vatican. Spellman was personally willing to undertake the job, but the apostolic delegate to the United States, Archbishop Cicognani, preferred that all negotiations between the Church, Roosevelt, and Mexico be handled by Father Burke. All hopes of a meeting ended with this rebuttal. Judge Manton felt, according to Spellman, that the Church was "missing a good opportunity."[111]

Besides these maneuvers, Roosevelt himself made public statements favoring religious freedom on at least three different occasions in 1935. These included his reply to the congressional petition of July 18, his speech at San Diego on October 2, and his remarks at Notre Dame.

As the election year of 1936 approached, it was only natural that the administration should hope that Catholic criticism would abate. Certain elements in the Church,

[109]Confidential memorandum from Marvin McIntyre to Roosevelt, May 27, 1935, OF 146, Mexico 1933-1940, Box 1, Roosevelt Papers.

[110]Sumner Welles to Roosevelt, June 25, 1935, PSF, Diplomatic Correspondence, Mexico, Box 2, Roosevelt Papers.

[111]Gannon, Cardinal Spellman, cites diary, July 10, 1935, p. 118; Manton to Roosevelt, July 11, 1935, OF 28, Roosevelt Papers.

however, were interested in keeping the issue alive. The Knights of Columbus refused to accept Roosevelt's letter of November 13 as the last word on the subject of Mexico. Indeed, one Catholic priest called the letter "an affront to the sense of equity of the multitude of American Catholics."[112] Martin Carmody continued to take his case to the public over the radio and in public appearances. Over the Boston airwaves he insisted that the Knights had never called for intervention in Mexico and that the president had brought this up to confuse the issue.[113] In Philadelphia, Carmody spoke publicly against the administration. Here, however, he was confronted with a counterattack by Michael Francis Doyle, who had a rebuttal published in the local newspaper. Roosevelt was so impressed with Doyle's defense that he sent it to Father Burke "with the thought that it might be extensively used."[114]

The Catholic press also did a good job of keeping the Mexican issue alive in 1936. *Columbia* naturally reported faithfully the speeches of Carmody. The editor of the *Sign,* national Catholic monthly, felt that the Mexican government was now acting as if President Roosevelt had given his blessing to its anticlericalism. These critical ideas were shared by the Reverend Theophane Maguire, a contributor to the *Sign,* who warned that Roosevelt's "nice but innocuous" words did not confuse American Catholics about the extent of his sympathy.[115] As evidence of the United States' responsibility for the chaos in Mexico, *America* pointed to the fact that Daniels, who had demonstrated his incompetence, was still in office.[116]

[112]George J. Reid to the editor, *Commonweal,* Jan. 3, 1936, p. 274.

[113]Boston *Pilot,* Feb. 29, 1936, p. 1.

[114]Doyle to Marvin McIntyre, March 2, 1936; Roosevelt memorandum, March 14, 1936, Reel 2, *Sel. Mat.*

[115]*Columbia,* May 1936, p. 3; Clipping of the *Sign,* April 1936, p. 523, Box 777, Daniels Papers.

[116]Clipping of *America,* Feb. 29, 1936, p. 487, Box 777, Daniels Papers.

In another Catholic periodical, *Light*, Frederick V. Williams sought to answer pro-Cardenas views presented by Cram in *Commonweal*. Williams felt that Cram had been influenced by the propaganda put out by Washington, which was aimed at saving the Catholic vote. But Williams was sure that Roosevelt and the Democratic party had "no doubt lost this election year by the refusal of the President to check out Ambassador . . . in his flagrant support of the Communist persecution of the Church."[117]

There were certain signs developing, however, to indicate that this belligerent attitude by the Knights of Columbus and others had in reality antagonized more people than it had converted. The Knights were accused of having political motives behind their campaign against Roosevelt. Frank Picard of Saginaw, Michigan, wrote to Martin Carmody to express disappointment over the campaign against the first president to have given Catholics "a fair deal." He further accused the supreme knights of attempting to split the northern Catholic vote in order to throw the 1936 election to the Republicans. "I do resent," said Picard, "this damned Republican propaganda under the guise of religion."[118] This same charge was made by Joseph Leib of South Bend, Indiana. To both men Carmody gave assurance that "there has been nothing political, partisan, or personal in the position of the Knights of Columbus." Furthermore, he would not permit such an issue to be made a political football.[119]

---

[117]F. V. Williams, "An Answer to Cram," *Light*, July 1936, clipping in Box 777, Daniels Papers. This magazine was the official organ of the International Catholic Truth Society. Other evidence of continued disenchantment with the Roosevelt foreign policy appeared meanwhile in many diocesan papers. See also *Catholic World*, CXLIII (Aug. 1936), 620-21; *Commonweal*, Aug. 14, 1936, p. 388; Boston *Pilot*, Sept. 12, 1936, p. 1, and *Catholic Transcript*, March 12, 1936, p. 4.

[118]Picard to Carmody, April 12, 1935, OF 28, Roosevelt Papers.

[119]Leib to Roosevelt, Dec. 16, 1935, OF 28, Roosevelt Papers; New York *Times*, Dec. 13, 1935, p. 14.

Despite these comments by Carmody, many individuals still feared that the Mexican controversy was going to hurt Roosevelt with Catholic voters at the polls in 1936. Josephus Daniels, for one, was not worried about his own reputation among Catholics, but was chiefly concerned "lest some politicians might seek to arouse Church opposition to Roosevelt in the next presidential election."[120] Daniels, who expressed this opinion to President Roosevelt as early as August 1935, was not alone in this estimation. Frank Tannenbaum, a noted Columbia University economist who was an authority on Latin America, also feared Catholic political reprisal. With these fears in mind, he had even attempted to convince Mexican officials to grant more religious freedom to Catholics. The professor reported to Ambassador Daniels that he had verbal assurance from President Cardenas that Mexico would conduct its religious policy in such a way that it could not be used to hurt Roosevelt politically. Daniels himself suggested that Catholic opinion be soothed by "liberal dosages of patronage."[121]

At first, the Roosevelt administration was divided over how to combat the political problems raised by the Mexican affair. James Farley wanted Daniels to take an active part in the campaign because he thought the ambassador's influence would help the ticket in certain sections of the country. Secretary Hull and others, however, felt it would be best to keep Daniels out of the campaign and attempt to ignore the entire issue.[122]

While division of Catholic opinion no doubt had some effect on Roosevelt's method of handling this politically sensitive issue, it does not entirely explain his actions.

[120]Josephus Daniels, *Shirt-Sleeve Diplomat* (Chapel Hill, N.C., 1947), 179.
[121]Daniels to Roosevelt, Aug. 26, 1935, PSF I, Diplomatic Correspondence, Mexico, Box 2, Roosevelt Papers.
[122]Cronon, *Josephus Daniels,* 109.

Roosevelt was primarily interested in domestic issues in 1935 and 1936 and wanted to avoid any foreign squabbles.[123] But the president also was firmly convinced that any action similar to that requested by the Knights of Columbus could only hurt both the Catholic Church and United States-Mexican relations. Consummate politician that he was, Roosevelt correctly calculated that American Catholic opposition was divided and, therefore, unlikely to be of significance in the 1936 election. Indeed, his public statements and private actions, although undoubtedly sincere, were phrased in such a way as to retain the sympathy of many Catholics.[124] Of course, the overwhelming victory of 1936 clearly indicates that no large minority group, Catholic or otherwise, deserted Roosevelt at the polls.

Roosevelt's political acumen and actions, however, were only one reason why the Mexican issue was not significant in November 1936. The height of Mexican anticlericalism came in 1935. By 1936, some improvements in Mexican church-state relations had been made. One student of the period believes that "had the elections taken place some eighteen months earlier . . . Roosevelt would have lost some votes."[125] As it was, the divided opinion of American Catholics gave the administration tactical room to maneuver, and the solid cooperation of such men as Burke, Mundelein, Callahan, and Doyle was a valuable asset.

If the Mexican episode did not have political repercussions in 1936, it was still important for a number of reasons. The entire affair demonstrated the difficulties the

[123]Cronon, "Mexican Anticlericalism," 219, advances this view, but it could be argued that the difficulties Roosevelt was having with domestic issues would make him more prone to placate Catholic criticism at home. He would sacrifice a foreign policy, one not considered of prime importance at the time, to insure Catholic support for his New Deal legislation.

[124]Cronon, "Mexican Anticlericalism," 219.

[125]Ibid., 224.

Church experienced when it attempted to exert political leverage. It is true that Roosevelt was sympathetic to the Church and gave Catholics extensive recognition, but this did not mean that he could be pressured into actions that he considered contrary to the best interest of the country. Finally, the Mexican affair demonstrated a number of things about the American Catholic Church. Obviously this was no monolithic institution which could demand unity of thought and action by its members concerning a largely secular topic. Furthermore, when voting time arrived in 1936, Catholics reacted in much the same way as their fellow citizens; they agreed that foreign affairs should take a backseat to domestic problems.

9

The Campaign of 1936

I F Mexican anticlericalism was not to be a significant issue in the campaign of 1936, many other topics made both Roosevelt and the Catholic Church especially conscious of each other's existence and power. While Ambassador Daniels persisted in emphasizing that Mexico might still be an issue, James Farley was warning the president that the charge of communism in the administration was beginning to evoke sympathetic audiences, especially among Catholics. Father Charles Coughlin, an old supporter of the New Deal, had by this time become totally disenchanted and was sponsoring a third-party movement behind the political figurehead of William Lemke. Al Smith and the American Liberty League were pushing hard the theme of constitutional government, a phenomenon that they insisted had disappeared under FDR. On the bright side, however, the president could count on the support of such prominent prelates as Cardinal Mundelein of Chicago, Father John Ryan of Washington, and a number of influential Catholic laymen. The election results of 1936 showed clearly that fears of

American Catholics defecting from the Democratic party were unfounded.

The administration, however, had no way of foreseeing this in early 1936. Furthermore, on the horizon numerous signs pointed to a disenchantment of Catholics with the New Deal. Already a few leading figures had deserted the party over the Democrats' handling of Mexican anticlericalism. Now, from Mexico, Ambassador Daniels wrote to the president that he should make sure that there was a Catholic in his cabinet. Without one the administration would leave itself wide open for charges of religious discrimination. In addition, Daniels remarked that he was informed that Bishop Kelley of Oklahoma was actively campaigning for Landon, serving as an adviser for him. "If the Republican Catholics are going to be active for Landon," said Daniels, "I am sure you will do as you have been doing to show such recognition as their long devotion to the party deserves to able Democrats of that faith."[1] Specifically, Daniels felt that Michael Francis Doyle deserved recognition for the splendid work he was doing in combating the criticism of the Knights of Columbus regarding the Mexican question. The ambassador enthusiastically endorsed Doyle for the position of assistant secretary of the navy.[2]

Daniels and Farley were not the only ones to be concerned with the allegiance of American Catholics to the Democratic party during 1936. Their concern was now reinforced by Mary W. Dewson, Democratic national committeewoman. Miss Dewson had received letters from other politically active women which indicated that Ambassador Daniels' indifference toward Mexico's anticlericalism was hurting the party's image among Catholics.

[1]Daniels to Roosevelt, June 22, 1936, PPF 86, Roosevelt Papers. P. H. Callahan wrote Daniels frequently during 1936 expressing fear that Mexico would be used to win Catholics away from Roosevelt.
[2]Daniels to Roosevelt, March 30, 1936, OF 237, Roosevelt Papers.

She expressed the wish to Eleanor Roosevelt that the president might make Daniels "Secretary of War, or something."[3]

A number of other issues were raised during the course of the 1936 campaign which provoked strong interest among American Catholics. One of the most important was the defection from the Democratic party of Alfred E. Smith. The ex-governor had been moving away from the Roosevelt administration ever since the very beginnings of the New Deal. His discontent rested on the argument that it was necessary to fight for the preservation of states' rights against the ever-growing power of the central government. Smith's criticism reached its apogee on January 25, 1936, when he addressed a star-studded meeting of the American Liberty League at the Mayflower Hotel in Washington. In a speech that was praised by Pierre S. duPont and other leaders of American capitalism, Smith attacked the New Deal and Roosevelt as being Communist-oriented.[4]

Joseph T. Robinson, who ran on Smith's ticket for vice president in 1928, was designated as the administration's spokesman to reply to the "Happy Warrior." The main theme of Robinson's rebuttal was the fact that Smith had deserted the cause of progressivism, for which he had fought in New York State, to take the side of the barons of wealth. Roosevelt himself never once publicly attacked Smith and even tried to regain his friendship after the Liberty League speech.[5]

The actual political effect of Smith's defection and his subsequent support of Governor Landon is difficult to assess. Rexford Tugwell has stated that Smith probably

[3]Miss Mary W. Dewson to Mrs. Franklin D. Roosevelt, Oct. 19, 1936, OF 237, Roosevelt Papers.
[4]Arthur M. Schlesinger, Jr., *The Politics of Upheaval* (Boston, 1960), 519.
[5]*Ibid.*, 519, 520.

did not hurt Roosevelt among Catholic voters in 1936.[6] Smith's biographer, Oscar Handlin, is careful to point out that Smith chose to leave the New Deal at a time when the National Catholic Welfare Conference was praising Roosevelt's efforts, and that few people followed him.[7] There are other indications that most Catholics were embarrassed by the New Yorker's rebellion from the party. It is true that C. W. Thompson, political analyst for *Commonweal*, hailed the Liberty League speech by Smith as being significant because it started a movement away from Roosevelt among prominent southern and New England Democrats.[8] Yet Thompson's analysis was not shared by others. In Chicago, a meeting of the Catholic Conference on Social Problems was the occasion for strong criticism of Al Smith's speech.

Of more significance, because of its greater depth, was the criticism of Smith made by the Reverend Ignatius W. Cox, who gave a radio address called "The American Liberty League and Our Immoral Economic Order" on February 7, 1936, in New York City. Basing his remarks on the papal encyclicals, Cox asked the rhetorical question: "In reacting so strongly against the danger of collectivism, has the American Liberty League fallen into the lap of the opposite danger, branded by Pius XI as Individualism?" The league, said Cox, seemed to be interested primarily in the welfare of the individual, while Catholic social thought placed emphasis on the common welfare. The emphasis on rugged individualism, espoused by the league and by Smith, was an aspect of modern thought which "no Catholic who knows Catholic social doctrine can approve." As for Governor Smith, he had grossly oversimplified the issue by saying that the present strug-

---

[6]*The Democratic Roosevelt* (Garden City, N.Y., 1957), 172-73.

[7]*Al Smith and His America* (Boston, 1958), 181.

[8]C. W. Thompson, "As the Primaries Begin," *Commonweal*, March 6, 1936, p. 509.

gle was between communism and constitutional government. To Cox, plutocracy was just as dangerous as communism. He pointed out that "not all regimentation is
communistic," and that too long had economic forces
been unregulated in the United States. The priest chided
Smith for pointing to communism as the main danger facing America. In fact it was only a symptom of the economic liberalism favored by the Liberty League. This
latter force was the real danger to America, and he suggested that Smith direct his efforts against it rather than
sponsor it.[9] These remarks by Father Cox were widely
publicized as evidence that neither Smith nor the American Liberty League spoke for the Church on social
issues.[10]

The Reverend Maurice S. Sheehy of Catholic University
also took exception to the speech by ex-Governor Smith.
Writing to Marguerite LeHand, Sheehy said that he had
"given considerable thought to the possible effect of Governor Smith's speech on the Catholic following of President Roosevelt." The president might not consider it of
any significance, remarked the priest, but it "has been a
major heartache to those who expected nobler things of
Governor Smith." After all, Smith was not only condemning the president in his speech, he was indirectly criticizing "the leaders of his Church, including Cardinal Hayes."
This followed because Hayes and others had forthrightly
endorsed the aims of the New Deal on many occasions. It
was this same philosophy of the common good which
Smith now labeled "socialism." Clearly, said Sheehy,
"Governor Smith perhaps forgets that the greatest foe of
Communism was the Catholic Church, and the most ear-

---

[9]*Catholic Mind*, XXIV (March 8, 1936), 113-21; "Constitutional Liberty and our Immoral Economic Order," *Catholic Mind*, XXXIV
(March 8, 1936), 105-13.
[10]New York *Times*, Feb. 8, 1936, p. 2; *Commonweal*, March 20, 1936,
p. 577.

nest champions of President Roosevelt's social policies have been the Catholic bishops." As to the political implications of Smith's defection, Sheehy was sure, on the basis of his talks with three bishops, that Catholics were more than ever behind the president.[11] Others felt the same way. In the East, Edward J. Flynn, Senator Robert Wagner, and other New York politicos reported that Smith's decision would have little impact on the voters.[12]

Still, as the campaign progressed, it became clear that the major charges made by Smith—the disappearance of constitutional government and Communist influence in the administration—struck a sympathetic chord with some Catholic leaders. Certain elements in the Church were beginning to express dissatisfaction with the course of the New Deal. F. P. Kenkel, editor of the *Central-Blatt and Social Justice,* directed his attack more at Roosevelt's advisers than at the president himself. Kenkel felt the brain trust was attempting to foster a planned economy on the people, "despite the Constitution." Applauding the decisions of the Supreme Court on NRA and AAA, this editor felt that the New Deal was doomed to failure from the start "because its provisions were incompatible, not alone with the organic law of the land, . . . but with the traditions and the very spirit of the American people." Some relief was given to the people, but it was incorporated in a scheme of economic nationalism and state socialism. The main culprits in this scheme were not the elected officials but rather people like Hugh Johnson and James Warburg, who, Kenkel felt, aimed at the destruction of the middle class in America. As for the assertion that their ideas resembled the papal encyclicals, Kenkel insisted that this was a mere "enchanting fancy, which the men chiefly responsible for Mr. Roosevelt's planned

[11]Sheehy to Miss Marguerite LeHand, Jan. 30, 1936, Reel 2, *Sel. Mat.*
[12]Harold Ickes, *The Secret Diary of Harold Ickes* (New York, 1954), I, 687, 698-99.

economy . . . were at no pains to destroy." The pope's plan envisioned no such large exercise of state power, but rather, according to Kenkel, would have the state "discharge its obligations . . . through the professional organizations, accepting all the tasks they are able to fulfill."[13]

A number of other Catholic editors were also breaking away from the Roosevelt consensus. Patrick Scanlan of the Brooklyn *Tablet*, one of the president's strongest Mexican critics, wrote that Roosevelt's popularity was slipping. He attributed this decline to such things as continued high unemployment, prolific government spending, and poorly designed laws. The planned economy was an obvious fraud, so why not admit it, said Scanlan, instead of preaching class hatred and insinuating that it was a crime to make more money than one's neighbor. In New England, the Boston *Pilot* was crying out against what it considered another attempt by the government to over-regulate the private lives of its citizens, an idea that had recently proved futile in prohibition. The editor insisted that the same tendency was present in the "twenty thousand regulations . . . enacted since 1933." This constant growth of bureaucratic government should be checked, for it tended toward one-man rule. Indeed, remarked the editor, "it is possible that the country is somewhat nearer dictatorship than the average citizen realizes." The Reverend James Gillis, editor of the *Catholic World*, lamented the defection of Al Smith from the Roosevelt cause but could sympathize with him. Excessive government spending, continued unemployment, and the disrespect for the constitution which seemed to be characteristic of the New Deal were causing Gillis himself to have second thoughts about the president. Even *Commonweal*, a pro-Roosevelt publication, was concerned enough to question the president's political strength for reelection. The editor

[13]F. P. Kenkel, "New Deals," *Central-Blatt and Social Justice,* XXVIII (March 1936), 381-83; (July-Aug. 1936), 115-18.

remarked that "the essential dissatisfaction was . . . less with 'planned government' as such than with the evidence to show that the planning hadn't actually been planned."[14] The Reverend Edward Lodge Curran, president of the International Catholic Truth Society, was so disturbed about the course of New Deal legislation in 1936 that he suggested that Catholics ought to band together as a group to fight to preserve the constitution.[15]

The most dangerous indication of Catholic dissatisfaction, however, was seen in the political activities of Father Charles Coughlin, who was especially effective among people who feared Communist influence in government. Red infiltration of the New Deal was one of the priest's favorite themes. Before 1936, Coughlin was not significant in the story of Catholic relations with the New Deal. He represented primarily a personal movement which, while perhaps revealing certain aspects of Catholic thought, was not entirely within the mainstream of the Catholic Church.[16] Yet in 1935 and 1936 he entered the political scene in such direct fashion that he prompted many members of the Catholic Church to take a more active role in the presidential election.

A history of Father Coughlin's relations with the New Deal is not at issue here. It is clear that in the early stages of the Roosevelt administration, he was an enthusiastic backer of the president, and that his support was welcomed. The break in this relationship seems to have developed partially over the fight to have the United States join the World Court in January 1935. Roosevelt favored

[14]Brooklyn *Tablet*, April 6, 1935, p. 9; July 4, 1936, p. 9; Boston *Pilot*, Feb. 1, 1936, p. 4; *Catholic World*, CXLIII (April 1936), 1-9; *Commonweal*, April 17, 1936, p. 674.

[15]*Commonweal*, Oct. 30, 1936, p. 3.

[16]Charles J. Tull, "Father Coughlin, the New Deal, and the Election of 1936" (unpublished Ph.D. dissertation, University of Notre Dame, 1962), 217, writes that it is perfectly clear that the radio priest did not represent a concerted political effort on the part of the Catholic Church in America.

this move, but Coughlin is attributed with helping to defeat it in Congress. One should not, however, place too much emphasis on any one event, but rather consider the growing estrangement as inevitable in view of the strong personalities involved.[17]

As early as February 1935, Coughlin was charging that the administration had Communist tendencies. In the same speech, however, he paradoxically insisted that Roosevelt was a tool of capitalism.[18] On November 17, 1935, the priest seemed to take an irrevocable step when he publicly announced that the principles of his movement for social justice and the aims of the Roosevelt administration were "unalterably opposed." As long as the president entertained both communistic schemes and the support of the plutocrats (an unwitting compliment to Roosevelt's political dexterity), he would be unable effectively to bring relief to the American people. Later, on June 5, 1936, Coughlin retreated some by asserting that the president was probably not personally conscious of the communistic tendencies inherent in some of his new schemes, but was "being driven by sinister influences he does not fully comprehend."[19] This was only a momentary lapse, however, and as the campaign got under way, Coughlin, who was leading the support for William Lemke and his Union party, became even more vitriolic. In New Bedford, Massachusetts, the priest reached a high point of inanity when he publicly declared: "As I was instrumental in removing Herbert Hoover from the White House, so help me God, I will be instrumental in taking a

[17]Lowell Dyson, "The Quest for Power: Father Coughlin and the Election of 1936" (unpublished M.A. thesis, Columbia University, 1937), 29, points to two factors leading to the break: Coughlin favored inflation to cure the depression while FDR had already tried this and found it wanting; Coughlin wanted to be an intimate adviser and public spokesman for the New Deal, but FDR was not interested.
[18]Tull, "Father Coughlin," 107.
[19]Quoted in *ibid.*, 140, 167.

Communist out of the chair once occupied by Washington."[20] Later in the campaign, Coughlin was guilty of such indiscretions as calling the president a liar and a scab.

The main significance of this performance is not the neurosis that gripped this particular priest, but rather the reaction his performance prompted from both the Catholic Church and the administration. This reaction resulted not so much from concern with Coughlin the individual as with concern over his role as a Catholic priest and his impact upon the Catholic image in the United States. It is from this point of view that Coughlin should be viewed here, without reference to the merits or demerits of his philosophy and personality. He was an irritant, and as such both the Church and the administration had to deal with him.

The outbursts of Smith and Coughlin were not isolated phenomena. Both men had an effect on the Catholic populace of the nation. Perhaps not all priests were so influenced by Coughlin as was the Reverend James A. Smith, pastor of a Catholic church on Long Island, who urged his congregation not to vote for Roosevelt because of his "red" affiliations, but there is evidence of growing concern among Catholics with this charge.[21] In 1936 it appeared that the Church was in the midst of a crusade against communism. Lay organizations such as the Catholic Daughters of America, Notre Dame Alumni, and the Holy Name Society were all active in this denunciation of the "Red Menace."[22]

So widespread was the charge that Roosevelt himself

[20]*Ibid.*, 187.

[21]New York *Times*, Nov. 2, 1936, p. 2; Dyson, "The Quest for Power," 57, says that the priest's concentration on communism was especially attractive to Catholic voters.

[22]R. M. Darrow, "Catholic Political Power: A Study of the Activities of the American Catholic Church on Behalf of Franco During the Spanish Civil War, 1936-1939" (unpublished Ph.D. dissertation, Columbia University, 1937), 60.

became concerned with its effect on his public image. On September 29, 1936, in Syracuse, New York, he publicly disassociated himself from the Marxist movement. He said: "Here and now, once and for all, let us bury that red herring and destroy that false issue. . . . I have not sought, I do not seek, I repudiate the support of any advocate of Communism or of any other alien 'ism' which would by fair means or foul change our American democracy. That is my position. It has always been my position. It always will be my position."[23]

There was a prelude to this strong statement by the president which is worth mentioning here. Sumner Welles had reported to Roosevelt the substance of a conversation he had with Charles Taussig of New York. Taussig had called Welles to report that he and Adolph Berle had dined with Bishop Molloy of Brooklyn and "certain other prominent Catholics." The clerics had expressed sincere concern about the communism charges being leveled against the administration. Both Taussig and Berle were "deeply disturbed and worried" by the effect that Coughlin, with his wild accusations about Roosevelt's leftist proclivities, was producing among Roman Catholics. Welles suggested to Roosevelt that Berle write a speech dealing with this question for delivery by the president on Columbus Day. Apparently the administration was well aware of the situation because Secretary Hull replied to Welles that the president had decided to deal with this charge of communism in his address to the Democratic state convention of New York at Syracuse on September 29.[24]

The speech that Roosevelt gave on September 29 should have ended the matter. Unfortunately this was not the case. Despite Roosevelt's forthrightness, Father Gillis

[23]Quoted in Schlesinger, The Politics of Upheaval, 620.
[24]Welles to Roosevelt, Sept. 25, 1936, PPF 182, Roosevelt Papers.

of the *Catholic World* complained that the speech lacked precision in its condemnation of communism, a situation he attributed to a lack of complete intellectual honesty. The priest also pinpointed the issues of the campaign as "the decline of democracy, the increase in centralization of governmental powers, and the possible emergence of the absolute state."[25] James Farley was still so concerned over the effect of the Communist charges that he asked Roosevelt to consider asking Cardinal Mundelein to make a statement. While Farley did not expect the cardinal to come out publicly for Roosevelt, he did feel that Mundelein would announce that there were no Communists connected with the administration. Roosevelt, however, demurred on this suggestion, although he remained well aware of the importance of Cardinal Mundelein's support.[26]

Still, the administration had to evolve skillful tactics to deal with Coughlin and his charge of communism. Because of his unique status as a Roman Catholic priest in politics and because of his fanatical appeal, Coughlin presented special problems.[27] Roosevelt himself was certainly aware of the difficulties Coughlin could cause. During the debate on the Bonus Bill in January 1936, a measure which Coughlin vigorously supported and which Congress passed over Roosevelt's veto, the two men came into direct conflict. Roosevelt was reported to have been

[25]*Catholic World*, CXLIV (Nov. 1936), 129, 132.

[26]Farley to Roosevelt, Oct. 23, 1936, PPF 321, Roosevelt Papers. Roosevelt felt that Walter Cummings was a better man for the job suggested by Farley.

[27]Scholars have pointed out another reason why Roosevelt took notice of Father Coughlin's political activity: the possibility that he might be able to "bridge the gulf between the rural fundamentalist Protestants and the urban Irish Catholics." James Shenton, "The Coughlin Movement and the New Deal," *Political Science Quarterly*, LXXIII (1958), 354, and Peter Morris, "Father Coughlin and the New Deal" (unpublished M.A. thesis, Columbia University, 1938), 22 n., accept this, but Morris substitutes "old Populist agrarians" for "rural fundamentalist."

so upset over the priest's antics that he threatened to release incriminating material on Coughlin's financial dealings. The president also considered the idea of conferring with Cardinals Hayes, O'Connell, and Mundelein "to show them the attacks a priest had made on the President and ask them how this jibed with their theory that the Catholic Church should have an ambassador in each country."[28]

Roosevelt's political acumen, however, was too sharp to allow him to carry out this threat. He continued a policy of active silence which had earlier caused him to send Frank Murphy, just returned from his post as governor of the Philippines to run for governor of Michigan, to see Coughlin. Murphy, an old friend of the priest, was to try to dissuade Coughlin from engaging in political debate during 1936, a task comparable to stopping water from running downhill. Several long and fruitless talks between Murphy and the priest followed. The former even went on the radio to attempt to counteract some of Coughlin's charges against the president. All this had little effect, however, as Coughlin continued his barrage. The extent to which Murphy and Coughlin fell out over Roosevelt is revealed by the fact that the priest eventually supported the Republican candidate for governor of Michigan against his "old friend" Murphy.[29]

The official strategy of the administration throughout 1936 was to avoid public condemnation of the priest. When this rule was broken by Secretary Ickes, who gave a speech criticizing Coughlin, Roosevelt expressed displeasure over it at a cabinet meeting.[30] The president preferred to ignore the priest publicly but to exploit the

[28]John M. Blum, ed., *From the Morgenthau Diaries: Years of Crisis, 1928–1938* (New York, 1959), 255.

[29]Richard D. Lunt, "The High Ministry of Government: The Political Career of Frank Murphy" (unpublished Ph.D. dissertation, University of New Mexico, 1962), 137; Tull, "Father Coughlin," 124.

[30]Dyson, "The Quest for Power," 70.

sympathy among Catholics which his attacks produced. Ickes and Farley informally sounded out such political figures as Senator Robert Wagner and Edward J. Flynn on the effect among New York Catholics of Coughlin's and Smith's attacks.[31] The president was well advised not to attack Coughlin publicly, but to let him continue on his way until he had irritated his fellow Catholics with his tactics. This is precisely what happened in the Catholic circles that controlled most of the Church's public expression. Although there was never any official condemnation of Coughlin by the American bishops, most bishops, priests, and laymen grew more and more disillusioned as his tactics grew more and more vehement.

While it is difficult to abstract the motives that caused the Church to be critical of Coughlin, certain tendencies are evident. One central fact is that many of the clergy were avid supporters of Franklin Roosevelt. They recognized the president's contributions in attacking the depression and appreciated his liberal approach toward the Church. To hear Coughlin call the president a liar and a Communist was embarrassing to this element. Second, a number of Catholics expressed dismay that Coughlin's efforts were destroying the good relations that the Church had developed with the Roosevelt administration. This was the argument advanced by Sheehy of Catholic University.

In confronting the Coughlin movement, the Church faced somewhat of a dilemma. It was clear that the priest's attacks were alienating many non-Catholics and that many were looking upon him as the official spokesman of the Church. Walter Maier, professor at the Concordia Lutheran Theological Seminary of St. Louis, expressed a popular idea when he publicly stated that Coughlin had not been repudiated by his Church, but

[31]Tull, "Father Coughlin," 222; Ickes, *Diary,* I, 686.

rather that he "talks personally with Rome by radio phone." Furthermore, "If ever Coughlinism should triumph . . . his church would capitalize the triumph, for the voice behind that radio priest is the voice of his church." This was announced to a crowd of 4,500 at an annual Lutheran Day ceremony.[32]

Maier's outburst was supplemented by a more rational approach from the editor of the *New Republic,* who, in an article on the political significance of the Coughlin movement, judged it to signal the entrance of the Catholic Church into American politics. This evaluation he defended by claiming, first, that Coughlin was the best man to organize Christian socialism in the country. Second, the international influence of the Vatican was slipping, especially in European affairs, which made the conquest of the United States imperative. Third, Coughlin's attacks on Roosevelt had attracted Catholics, many of whom, on religious grounds, opposed the president because of his son's divorce, his wife's support of birth control, and his own handling of Mexican anticlericalism.[33]

It seemed that a growing number of Americans were beginning to equate Coughlin's remarks with the official position of the Catholic Church. Yet the Church could not officially silence the radio priest. A number of difficulties stood in the way of such an action. As long as Coughlin had the support of his bishop, Michael Gallagher of Detroit, he could not be touched short of papal intervention. Second, many priests were conscious that Coughlin had such a hold on his followers that many of them would desert the Church if he should be attacked. Finally, there was also the problem of publicity which would arise if the Church did silence Coughlin. Liberals would take this as proof of the Church's basic antipathy toward civil

[32]New York *Times,* Aug. 2, 1936, p. 12.
[33]Tull, "Father Coughlin," 178-79.

rights as expressed in the constitution.[34] Altogether, the Coughlin movement presented a rather delicate situation to the Church.

Despite the lack of an official position, there is abundant evidence of the Church's displeasure with Coughlin's political activities and with his attacks on the Roosevelt administration. This displeasure was expressed by a process of disassociation of portions of the Church from the Coughlin movement, by publicly deploring the priest's tactics, and by public and private support for the president.

Expressions by Catholic hierarchy seemed to indicate that a large number of bishops resented Coughlin's activities. Among the three cardinals in America there was unanimity regarding the radio priest. O'Connell of Boston, an old foe of Coughlin, spoke of "hysterical voices among the clergy" which were out of keeping with the priestly vocation.[35] Hayes also privately resented Coughlin's attacks on Roosevelt. Most significant, however, was the role played by Mundelein of Chicago. An old supporter of the president, Mundelein was eager to help erase the impression that the Catholic Church was speaking through the voice of Coughlin.[36] Publicly, Mundelein stated that Father Coughlin had a right to his own political view, by virtue of his American citizenship, "but he is not authorized to speak for the Catholic Church, nor does he repre-

[34]Dyson, "The Quest for Power," 71, 80, 81.

[35]Quoted by Tull, "Father Coughlin," 132.

[36]Later the president wrote Josephus Daniels that Mundelein had been "perfectly magnificent all through the campaign." See Roosevelt to Daniels, Nov. 9, 1936, PSF, Diplomatic Correspondence, Mexico, Box 2, Roosevelt Papers. In this same letter FDR suggested to Daniels that he look into the feasibility of opening a Catholic seminary in Mexico City to train natives for the priesthood. Mundelein had suggested such a seminary for Texas, but FDR felt it should be located in Mexico itself and suggested to Daniels that "the germ of the idea might be planted with good effect." These remarks are cited only to illustrate the close relationship that existed between Mundelein and FDR.

sent the doctrine or sentiments of the Church."[37] In September 1936 Mundelein publicly expressed his support for the Roosevelt administration and emphasized the prosperity which it had returned to the United States.[38]

These public remarks and private actions were not without their effect. Arthur Krock of the New York Times commented on the great reception given Roosevelt in Chicago during the campaign. Searching for reasons for this support, Krock pointed to "the sympathetic attitude toward him [FDR] of the eminent Catholic hierarchy in this city and State, chief of whom is Cardinal Mundelein." According to Krock, Mundelein felt that FDR's re-election was "necessary definitely to rout the forces of social radicalism."[39] Edward J. Kelly, mayor of Chicago, placed great emphasis upon the cardinal's support when analyzing FDR's political fortunes in Illinois. After the cardinal had publicly praised the New Deal, Kelly wrote to the president, stressing the high esteem in which Mundelein was held by millions of Catholics and non-Catholics in the area. "Even the slightest comment," said the mayor, "either direct or indirect, is accepted as a standard by his followers and admirers." Mundelein's words of praise would "therefore be highly productive in [FDR's] favor at the proper time."[40]

Other elements of the hierarchy were also sympathetic with the Roosevelt cause. Of significance in measuring this sympathy are the remarks of Father Sheehy. As early as July 18, 1936, Sheehy was writing to the administration on the political implications of the Coughlin movement. At this time Sheehy described a meeting at the Waldorf-Astoria of four bishops, three monsignori, and himself.

[37]Quoted in William V. Shannon, The American Irish (New York, 1964), 317.
[38]Clipping of Chicago Daily Times, Sept. 15, 1936, in Reel 1, Sel. Mat.
[39]October 20, 1936, p. 24.
[40]Kelly to Roosevelt, Sept. 16, 1936, Reel 1, Sel. Mat.

They discussed Coughlin's personal attacks on FDR. "We decided," said Sheehy, "how this action might be handled most effectively. We have taken action." Sheehy insisted that his group wanted nothing to do with the political, but simply wanted "to tell the President his friends are not ignoring the calumnies of Father Coughlin."[41]

What actions were contemplated at the Waldorf-Astoria meeting is difficult to discern. Two of the bishops present, Thomas O'Reilly of Scranton, Pennsylvania, and James H. Ryan of Omaha, Nebraska, began a campaign along with Sheehy to seek statements by American bishops defending Roosevelt against Coughlin's charges that the president was a Communist. In September 1936 Sheehy again wrote to Stephen Early that he could expect a number of letters from American bishops "affirming their faith in [FDR] despite the communist charges of Coughlin." Sheehy admitted that the charges did not deserve a reply but added that "in as much as the Catholic Church is the great foe of communism, these letters will be worthwhile."[42]

Roosevelt had already received such a telegram from Bishop Bernard J. Mahoney of Sioux Falls, South Dakota, in July 1936. Mahoney spoke "in the name of the priests and people of the diocese," and protested "against references to you [FDR] by clerical vulgarian."[43] In September, Mahoney telegraphed to Sheehy asking him to inform the president that he considered Coughlin's charges of communism in the administration "most unjust."[44] Bishop James H. Ryan of Omaha, Nebraska, also wrote to the

[41]Quoted in Tull, "Father Coughlin," 216. When asked about this meeting, Father Sheehy could not recall any specifics but indicated that "some of the bishops individually wrote the President saying that Father Coughlin did not represent the Catholic Church." Sheehy, Letter to author, June 21, 1965.

[42]Sheehy to Early, Sept. 29, 1936, Reel 3, *Sel. Mat.*

[43]Quoted by Tull, "Father Coughlin," 215.

[44]Mahoney to Sheehy, telegram, Sept. 26, 1936, Reel 3, *Sel. Mat.*

president in the same vein. Ryan spoke of his astonishment at the statements linking FDR with communism. He called these charges "unfair, unjust and untrue." "To affirm," said Ryan, "that the President of the U.S. is linked with communism is to speak irresponsibly and without knowledge of your true opinions."[45] Ryan's telegram was supplemented by an editorial he wrote for the *True Voice,* the official organ of his diocese. In this article of October 2, 1936, Ryan condemned certain parties who had forgotten ethical principles in their political attacks on the president. "There is not one shred of evidence," read the editorial, "direct or indirect, to connect the name of President Roosevelt with Communism, its principles, and its propaganda." Ryan concluded that FDR had always been an enemy of communism.[46]

Other members of the hierarchy also expressed disapproval of Coughlin's attack on FDR. In Cincinnati, Archbishop John T. McNicholas reacted quite violently to Coughlin's assertion that Roosevelt was anti-God. While he made clear that he was not making a political speech for or against the Democratic party and its candidate, the archbishop did insist that Coughlin transcended the bounds of decent morality by making such an accusation against the president. "There can be no objections to expressing condemnation of the acts of the administration in destroying crops and food," said the archbishop, but this did not justify Coughlin's conclusion that Roosevelt was anti-God, or that bullets should be used if the elec-

[45]Ryan to Roosevelt, Sept. 25, 1936, Reel 3, *Sel. Mat.* This letter was forwarded to Senator Joseph C. O'Mahoney by Early with a note that "none of the other letters from the Bishops has been received as yet, but copies will be sent to you as they come in."

[46]Clipping of the *True Voice,* Oct. 2, 1936, Reel 3, *Sel Mat.* Roosevelt, in reply to Ryan's telegram, expressed deep appreciation for having "so valiant a vindicator as yourself." FDR to Bishop Ryan, Oct. 6, 1936, Reel 3, *Sel. Mat.* It should be noted, however, that there is no evidence that any more letters from American bishops were forthcoming to the administration.

tion did not turn out the way Coughlin wanted. "The mere suggestion," said McNicholas, "of advocating a revolution even in the heat of oratory is most dangerous. Father Coughlin gives the impression that he appeals to force. In doing so he is morally in error."[47] Bishop Schrembs of Cleveland was equally upset about Coughlin's criticism of Roosevelt. While defending the priest's right to speak, he deplored Coughlin's tactics. Bishop Noll of Fort Wayne, Indiana, reacted with irritation when the press linked him with the Coughlin cause. Noll pointed out that no one had criticized the radio priest more than he had.[48]

Bishop Gallagher of Detroit took a rather ambiguous position toward Coughlin in 1936. Without Gallagher's tacit approval, Coughlin could never have continued his public campaign. Furthermore, Gallagher for some time had approved of Coughlin's interpretation of the papal encyclicals. Yet as the political campaign of 1936 developed, the bishop's position became somewhat confused. True, he repeatedly defended Coughlin's right to freedom of speech, even his statement on using bullets instead of ballots. Furthermore, on returning from Rome —a journey the American press insisted was taken because the Vatican wanted Coughlin silenced—Bishop Gallagher remarked that his famous priest was "just fighting communism." He always insisted that "there is nothing in Church doctrine to prevent a priest from taking part in public affairs."[49]

Yet other signs indicated that even Gallagher was getting a little upset about Coughlin's political activities. Upon returning from Rome, Gallagher was asked his

[47]Quoted in the New York Times, Sept. 27, 1936, p. 28; Commonweal, Oct. 9, 1936, p. 543.
[48]Tull, "Father Coughlin," 214-15.
[49]New York Times, Sept. 6, 1936, p. 19; Commonweal, July 31, 1936, p. 344.

opinion on the merits of the three presidential candidates. He replied: "As far as my present knowledge of the candidates goes, Roosevelt is the best of them."[50] In September, Gallagher went into more detail in a public broadcast. He attacked the money plank in the Lemke platform as being unsound.[51] He felt that Roosevelt was a better man to have in the White House because he "has a much better background to work out these monetary problems than this man from the Dakotas." This was a remarkable statement in view of the fact that the money plank in the Union party program was one of the main contributions of Father Coughlin. Gallagher ended his statement by insisting that the Union party was not the Catholic party and that there would never be such a Church party in America.[52]

Apparently Gallagher was trying to make clear that while he might defend Coughlin's right to freedom of speech, this did not mean that he agreed with his platform, or that the priest spoke for the Church. One news source suggested that Gallagher had even forced Coughlin to moderate his tone. When Coughlin publicly apologized for calling FDR a "scab President," some saw the bishop's hand at work. Gallagher, however, denied forcing any action, but subtly suggested that force was not the only way of achieving results.[53] Whatever his motives, many people were not surprised to see Gallagher join the Roosevelt campaign train when it stopped in Detroit during October. He joined the president for lunch and, according to one source, discussed the activities of the radio priest. Unfortunately, the details of the conversation are not available, but it is conjectured that Roosevelt warned

[50]Quoted in New York Times, Sept. 6, 1936, p. 19.

[51]Rep. William Lemke (Rep.–N.D.) ran as the Union party's candidate on a ticket that incorporated many of Coughlin's principles.

[52]Tull, "Father Coughlin," 202; Dyson, "The Quest for Power," 78.

[53]New York Times, Nov. 1, 1936, p. 48.

Gallagher that Coughlin was in a position to bring discredit upon the Church not only by his political activities but also by the financial dealings of some of his close associates.[54]

There was also a persistent rumor during 1936 that the Vatican was on the verge of censoring Father Coughlin for his political attacks on FDR. Gallagher's visit to Rome was looked upon as the beginning of this action. Roosevelt received word from Charlton Ogburn, a prominent New York attorney and close friend, that the Vatican was being informed "of the harm which Father Coughlin was doing to the Catholic Church in America by attacking you." A few days later *Osservatore Romano,* the Vatican newspaper, came out with a story criticizing Coughlin for his attacks on Roosevelt.[55]

On October 8, 1936, Cardinal Pacelli (the future Pope Pius XII), the Vatican secretary of state, arrived in the United States for a month's vacation and tour. This visit by such a high ranking Vatican official in the midst of a presidential election was the source of countless rumors. The New York *Times* insisted that he had come over to reassure Roosevelt of the Church's support despite the attacks by Coughlin. Others felt that his presence was to prevent Coughlin from making any more critical remarks about the president. Some students have even traced to Pacelli's arrival the starting point in the decline of Coughlin's fortunes. Unfortunately, Pacelli made no public statement regarding Father Coughlin or the election. Furthermore, Coughlin seemed to take little notice of the cardinal and continued his campaign unabated.[56]

[54]*Ibid.,* Oct. 16, 1936, p. 1; Grace Tully, Interview with author, June 2, 1965, Washington, D.C.

[55]Ogburn to Roosevelt, Sept. 10, 1936, PPF 3794, Roosevelt Papers; Ogburn spoke of having briefed Count Fumasoni Biodi, a powerful Italian nobleman, of the situation. Biodi promised to "transmit these views to the Vatican." Shenton, "The Coughlin Movement," 363 n.

[56]Dyson, "The Quest for Power," 79; Darrow, "Catholic Political

Speculation grew intense when Pacelli paid a social call on President Roosevelt in November 1936. The press had to guess at what was discussed because Bishop Spellman, who was acting as Pacelli's official guide while he was in the United States, refused to let reporters question him on the subject of the talk.[57] It seems unlikely that Coughlin was the main topic of conversation, since Roosevelt had already won a smashing victory at the polls. It is more likely that some cursory remarks were made about the feasibility of sending an ambassador from the United States to the Vatican.[58]

While the Vatican failed to take an official position toward Coughlin, such was not the case with significant elements of the American Catholic press. *Commonweal* was a longtime supporter of the administration. When the charge of communism first arose in the 1936 campaign, this magazine immediately denied such an influence in the Roosevelt government. The editor considered it a special burden of the Catholic press to refute such accusations because they emanated from two notable Catholics —Father Coughlin and Al Smith. Besides branding the

---

Power," 61, says the cardinal was primarily concerned with communism and the Spanish Civil War. Farley says the trip was made because of Coughlin. Farley, Interview with author, March 20, 1965, Washington, D.C.

[57]New York *Times*, Nov. 6, 1936, p. 1.

[58]Grace Tully, who was at Hyde Park at the time but not present for the interview, insists that it was merely a social call. Interview with author, June 2, 1965, Washington, D.C. An interesting aspect of Cardinal Pacelli's visit to the U.S. was the reaction it produced in the Nazi press. General Erich von Ludendorff, leading a neopagan movement in Germany, issued a statement, "Let us not forget that Brother Roosevelt is not only the representative of the Jews and Masons; he is also Cardinal Pacelli's man of confidence and will do everything possible to increase Rome's influence in the great democracy and to prepare for the conquest of the United States by Rome." The *National Socialist Angriff*, the German Labor Front's organ, published an article saying that FDR had made political commitments to Pacelli for which the cardinal promised to deliver the Catholic vote to the Democrats. New York *Times*, Nov. 4, 1936, p. 27; Dec. 6, 1936, p. 42.

charge false, the editor warned Smith and Coughlin of the danger of falling prey to their own rhetoric. According to Coughlin and Smith's definition of communism, much of the Church's social teaching would fail to pass the test of purity. "Yet it remains true," wrote the editor, "that the highest teaching authority in the Catholic Church, the Pope, has declared that the main evils of modern society in the sphere of economics are precisely those evils denounced by President Roosevelt." Smith and Coughlin had accused him of being a Communist because of his stand. Actually, the New Deal, according to *Commonweal,* was a rather conservative movement in that it sought to reform institutions of capital "which greed, and private and corporate dictatorship . . . have almost shattered." Only the emotionally disturbed could believe the charge that President Roosevelt was planning a red dictatorship.[59]

The Denver *Catholic Register,* one of the more influential diocesan papers, was also at odds with Coughlin's criticism of Roosevelt. Indeed, while Coughlin was calling FDR a Communist, the Denver paper's editor was praising him as a statesman of the highest order. To the charge that Catholics were antagonized by the way FDR handled the Mexican affair, the editor claimed that no Catholic leader of significance "doubted the sincerity of the Roosevelt administration in its handling of this vicious problem." While not officially supporting either candidate, the paper made clear that it could not stand silent but must call for a leader "who was in spirit with the Papal encyclicals." This did not mean that one should necessarily vote for Roosevelt, but it did mean that everyone should be aware that if the relief program instituted by the New Deal were cut off, "this country would be in the hands of revolutionists in less than a year." Catholics and others

[59]Feb. 7, 1936, p. 395; May 4, 1934, p. 2; July 10, 1936, p. 274; Oct. 9, 1936, pp. 541-42.

should recognize that laissez faire capitalism was dead and that it was proper for the government to interfere in business. *Quadragesimo Anno* called for precisely this program.[60]

The editor of *Extension* magazine, S. A. Baldus, also spoke out in defense of the president. Baldus labeled those elements which were preaching contempt against the president as "demagogs" and dangerous "crackpots." As for the claim by the American Liberty League and others that the constitution was in danger, this was "a lot of hokum" and political rabble-rousing at its lowest level. "Our Constitution," said the editor, "is in no danger—certainly not at the hands of President Roosevelt." Those politicians who felt they could capitalize on this fear as an issue in 1935 were in for a surprise because they would find that "the multitude will be more interested in getting jobs and something to eat, than in 'saving' the Constitution." A person might be too blind to give Roosevelt credit for the obvious improvement in America's economic situation over the last four years, but this should not blind anyone to the fact that there had been such an improvement.[61]

Besides these comments from the press, Roosevelt and the administration had other reasons for believing that Coughlin's efforts were not affecting the Democrats' hold on American Catholics. All during the campaign, letters and resolutions poured into the White House from various Catholic ethnic groups who expressed support for the New Deal. The Catholic Workman, a Bohemian Fraternal Mutual Benefit Association of St. Paul, Minnesota, wired its loyalty to the president. John Straka, president of the National Alliance of Bohemian Catholics, from the na-

[60]Denver *Catholic Register*, Jan. 19, 1936, p. 4; Jan. 26, 1936, p. 4; July 19, 1936, p. 1; Sept. 10, 1936, p. 4; Nov. 15, 1936, p. 4.
[61]*Extension*, July 1965, p. 17; Sept. 1936, p. 19; *Commonweal*, Feb. 7, 1936, p. 412; *Catholic Messenger* (Davenport), Oct. 29, 1936, p. 4, also expressed similar sentiments.

tional convention in Chicago, sent a similar message. The
chairman of the Lithuanian Roman Catholic Alliance of
America sent the greetings of that organization and
pledged "loyal support to [the] constructive program
which is successfully rebuilding economic structure of
this country." Elements of the Polish National Catholic
Church, meeting in Scranton, Pennsylvania, wired words
of "encouragement in your work for the good of the
working man through the New Deal." The Slovak Catholic Sokol of New Jersey adopted a resolution at its annual
convention endorsing the New Deal and especially the
CCC and NYA. The Croatian Catholic Union of America
sent similar greetings. The Reverend E. J. Higgins, the
national chaplain of the Catholic War Veterans, read an
open letter to Roosevelt over the New York radio. Higgins
praised Roosevelt for "opening the treasure vaults of
Uncle Sam," by which the president had "killed communism with one stroke" and restored faith in the under-
privileged. He concluded by saying that "no political
force will be able to destroy this image [as friend of the
poor] in the hearts of humanity." On the subject of communism, the board of directors of the National Alliance
of Bohemian Czech Catholics of America congratulated
FDR on his October speech in which he repudiated left-
wing political support. One of the remarkable things
about this rather diversified outpouring of support is that
Roosevelt saw fit to acknowledge almost all of them.
Busy as he was, he often wrote the acknowledgment from
his campaign train and in one case had the Department of
Commerce trace the Catholic Workman of St. Paul so he
could send a note of thanks to the proper people.[62]

[62]All these letters, and more, can be found in Reel 3, *Sel. Mat.* John
Straka to Roosevelt, June 10, 1936; The Catholic Workman to Roose-
velt, May 28, 1936; Alexander Aleksis to Roosevelt, July 1, 1936; Mrs.
Emily Sznyter to Roosevelt, Aug. 10, 1936; Roosevelt to Joseph G.
Prusa, Sept. 14, 1936; The Croatian Catholic Union to Roosevelt,
Oct. 11, 1936; Rev. E. J. Higgins to Roosevelt, Oct. 26, 1936.

Also important was the public and private support for Roosevelt which was expressed by many individual Catholics, both layman and priest. Some of this support was prompted by what Catholics considered an unjust campaign by Coughlin. Others were honestly convinced that Roosevelt had helped the country out of the depression. John B. Kelly, a millionaire and leader of the Democratic machine in Philadelphia, was dismayed over the political antics of Father Coughlin. Kelly felt that the priest was disgracing his vocation by his attacks on the president. Joseph P. Kennedy, Boston millionaire and loyal supporter of FDR, was a close friend of Coughlin, but he could not stand by and see the priest brand the president a Communist. In a speech to the Democratic Businessmen's League of Massachusetts in October, Kennedy called FDR "a God-fearing ruler who has given his people an increased measure of social justice." Kennedy criticized those who sought to mislead the public into believing that the social justice of the Roosevelt administration was communism. He pointed to two facts. First, FDR had insisted upon religious freedom when granting diplomatic recognition to Russia. Second, and more decisive, Kennedy reminded his audience that Cardinal Mundelein of Chicago had praised Roosevelt for his work. "Who in the face of the eloquent testimony of Cardinal Mundelein," asked Kennedy, "can doubt the President's stand on the great issues between man and his Maker?" Kennedy concluded by pointing out sardonically that if Roosevelt was the dictator some claimed, he would long ago have silenced the radio priest.[63]

A third layman who was active in the Roosevelt cause during 1936 was Frank P. Walsh of New York. Walsh was a longtime friend and supporter of the president and was active in the Catholic promotion of the child labor

[63]Quoted in New York *Times*, Oct. 25, 1936, p. 33; Tull, "Father Coughlin," 213; Shenton, "The Coughlin Movement," 367 n.

amendment. He was dismayed at the sympathy that the Coughlin charges of communism in the administration were receiving in Catholic circles. Walsh was interested in trying to stop what appeared as a move to set up the Catholic Church as the special institutional foe of international communism. As a member of the executive committee of the Progressive National Committee, he supported Roosevelt for reelection and publicly decried the smear tactics of his opponents.[64]

Among priests there was also a sizable segment ready to defend the president. The Reverend Bryan J. McEntegart, a director of the Catholic Charities of New York, expressed enthusiasm for the Social Security Act and for the NRA at the annual meeting of the National Conference of Catholic Charities held in Seattle, Washington. "Planning has replaced the laissez-faire idea," said McEntegart, and "this is good as long as it follows the mean suggested by Leo XIII (of) acting for the common good."[65] The Reverend Wilfrid Parsons, who had earlier attacked the idea that Father Coughlin was speaking for the Church in economic matters, went to great lengths in *America* in 1935 to emphasize this point and to show that Coughlin's ideas were loosely constructed.[66] As for Coughlin's assertion that the Roosevelt administration was filled with Communists, Monsignor Fulton J. Sheen of New York and the Reverend Francis J. Haas agreed with Frank Walsh that the Catholic Church should not be set up as a sort of anticommunist front. Sheen declared that rather than attacking Communists, Catholics should

[64]J. C. Walsh to F. P. Walsh, Oct. 5, 1936, Box 95, and Scrapbook No. 27, F. P. Walsh Papers; William E. Leuchtenburg, *Franklin D. Roosevelt and the New Deal* (New York, 1963), 182.

[65]McEntegart, "Catholicism and Social Welfare," *NCCC Proceedings*, Aug.2–5, 1936.

[66]Parsons to John A. Ryan, May 14, 1935, Ryan Papers; Tull, "Father Coughlin," 132.

"go out and find what is good in them."[67] Haas wrote to Father John J. Burke, secretary of the NCWC, expressing concern that the denunciations of communism being made by certain Catholics created the impression that the Church's own program was a negative one. "It is my judgment," wrote Haas, "that the cause of religion is hurt in our country by the fact that the secular press features only the condemnation of Communists and neglects reference to the paramount fact that the Church has an affirmative, constructive program for social justice."[68] Father Sheehy of Catholic University, at the suggestion of Senator O'Mahoney, toured the West, visiting a number of bishops and priests. Upon his return, he reported that "some extraordinary things" were underway to counteract Coughlin's efforts in the campaign.[69]

Equally robust were the efforts of the Reverend John A. Ryan. Indeed, this priest played the most active role of any during the campaign. His support took both private and public forms. In his private correspondence Ryan tried to allay the suspicions aroused by Coughlin and other opponents of the administration. On the charge that the administration favored communism and had demonstrated this in its dealings with Russia and Mexico, Ryan was quick to reply. The Mexican bishops, he pointed out, did not want any interference by the United States because it would hurt the Catholics in Mexico. Moreover, Roosevelt was president of the United States, not of Mexico, "and a Catholic's attitude toward him ought to be determined by the kind of administration he has given to our own country."[70] All this hysteria about Communists in government confirmed Ryan's suspicion that most

[67]Quoted in *Commonweal,* March 20, 1936, p. 576.
[68]Haas to Burke, June 3, 1936, Haas Correspondence.
[69]Quoted in Lunt, "Frank Murphy," 151.
[70]Ryan to Miss Kathryn Gazda, Oct. 28, 1936, Ryan Papers.

Catholics were "extremely gullible in their reactions to professional hunters of alleged Reds." He wondered how anyone who knew "anything about Catholic social teaching" could accept the charges being leveled against Roosevelt. The only "Reds" in the Roosevelt administration were those "who are sufficiently 'red' to believe in social justice."[71]

Ryan also supported the president in the Catholic press. When it appeared that James Gillis, editor of the *Catholic World,* was becoming disenchanted with the administration because of its fiscal policies, Ryan promptly wrote a letter to the editor. Using economic statistics, Ryan argued that the current national debt was not dangerous; that, in fact, it could go much higher. As for the constitutional integrity of the New Deal, Ryan argued that the Supreme Court had precedent on both sides of the issue and that the president had to take into consideration the needs of the people more than the subtle meanings of the constitution. Furthermore, the popes were more radical than the New Deal. If Roosevelt were defeated, wrote Ryan, the victors would not be men with either "the desire or competence to provide a more perfect program of social justice." If Roosevelt lost, it would be the Bourbons who triumphed.[72]

Ryan had less success when dealing with Patrick Scanlan, editor of the Brooklyn *Tablet,* who violently opposed the administration during the 1936 campaign. Scanlan's major charges were over the recognition of Russia and relations with Mexico. He filled his paper with anti-Roosevelt material during 1936, and he usually played up the comments of Father Coughlin. Ryan did not attempt to dissuade Scanlan from this course but rather sought to

[71]Ryan to R. F. McAuley, May 21, 1934, and to Mrs. Roy E. Grimmer, April 2, 1935, Ryan Papers.
[72]John Ryan, "Open Letter to the Editor," *Catholic World,* CXLIII (April 1936), 22-26.

make public the unreasonable bias of the editor. This led him into a personal feud with Scanlan which took the form of letter and counterletter published in the pages of the Brooklyn *Tablet*. Scanlan called Ryan a blind supporter of the president. Ryan replied that Scanlan was a professional "Roosevelt hater."[73]

While this dialogue was confined to the readers of the diocesan press (a rather select audience), Ryan did not restrict his activities to this narrow field. As early as February 1936 he publicly called for a program of social justice which would institutionalize many of the advances made under the New Deal. He dismissed as "silly" Al Smith's charge that the New Deal was communistic. In his peroration the priest remarked: "If the present administration is not continued in office, there will follow another orgy of excessive capital investment, excessive plant capacity and soon thereafter another depression. And that depression will be incomparably more devastating than the one from which we have now partially emerged."[74]

Ryan's most valuable service, however, was rendered later in the campaign as a semiofficial apologist for the administration against the attack by Father Coughlin. From an early position of sympathy for the radio priest, Ryan had come to view him as loose in his thinking and dangerous in his speech. In May 1936 he privately characterized Coughlin's economic program as being put together poorly. "It contains," wrote Ryan, "no definite proposals for practical and beneficial action in the field of social or economic reforms." The idea of a central banking scheme, which was the only definite part of Coughlin's program, Ryan termed "all wrong and futile."[75] Ryan

[73]Ryan to Scanlan [n.d.], Ryan Papers, 1936–1937; Brooklyn *Tablet*, May 29, 1937, p. 11.
[74]Quoted in the New York *Times*, Feb. 16, 1936, II, 1.
[75]Ryan to Richard A. Froehlinger, May 22, 1936, Ryan Papers.

had certainly become more politically active than he had been in 1932. Even more was ahead.

As the campaign of 1936 drew to a climax, more and more friends of the administration grew concerned over Father Coughlin's effectiveness with the voters. Even Farley, who later predicted that FDR would carry all but two states, was apprehensive over the attractiveness of the Communist charge made by Coughlin. In September 1936 Ryan received word from James J. Hoey, a New York politician and friend of Roosevelt, that he had attended a political conference at Hyde Park during which word was passed about that the president faced a greater danger from Coughlin than from Landon. This was obviously an exaggeration, but when Senator Joseph O'Mahoney of Wyoming also supported Hoey's contention, Father Ryan grew worried. Hoey and O'Mahoney's great fear was that Coughlin's charges of communism would stick in the Catholic mind. They pointed out that the radio priest had been received enthusiastically by Holy Name organizations when he made these accusations. They called on Ryan to speak out against Coughlin.[76]

It is difficult to explain why Ryan accepted this role of public defender of the administration. Although an admirer of the New Deal, he had never been an intimate of the president, nor had he contributed anything directly to the social reforms passed during the first administration. Some months after the 1936 election, Ryan explained his decision to take on the role suggested by Hoey. The priest insisted that someone had to prevent the imminent "diversion of millions of votes from Mr. Roosevelt to Mr. Lemke." While the election results hardly substantiate this contention, Ryan pointed out that "the managers of the national Democratic campaign were unanimous in the belief that this diversion of votes might defeat Roose-

[76]Hoey to Ryan, Sept. 23, 1936, Ryan Papers.

velt." Furthermore, if this defeat could be traced to the political activities of a Catholic priest, the consequences in terms of public resentment against the Church would be substantial. As Ryan saw the situation, many thousands of Catholics felt that Lemke's views, drawn from Coughlin, had the approval of the Catholic Church. Someone had to erase this impression, and Ryan did not regret for a minute that he had adopted this role. He concluded, "I am glad I made that radio speech. I regard it as one of the most effective and beneficial acts that I have ever performed in the interest of my religion and my country."[77]

After making his decision to speak for the administration, Ryan discovered that Hoey and others had certain definite ideas on what should be mentioned. Hoey suggested that Coughlin's name be mentioned in the speech, as the president was expecting this. Hoey, O'Mahoney, and Charles E. Michelson, Democratic publicity chairman, had a hand in revising Ryan's original draft. On October 8, 1936, Ryan went on a national radio hookup to speak on the subject "Roosevelt Safeguards America."[78]

Ryan offered two major themes: that there was no basis for the charge that Roosevelt was under Communist influence, and that Father Coughlin's economic thought was outdated and in no way connected with the papal encyclicals. In the first place, Ryan emphatically denied that Roosevelt or his advisers, such as Tugwell, Frankfurter, and Sidney Hillman, were under Communist influence. People who made such an accusation were breaking the eighth commandment. On the contrary, it was the work of the New Deal which had frustrated the growth of

[77]Letter to the editor, *Catholic Transcript*, June 17, 1937, p. 4; Francis L. Broderick, *The Right Reverend New Dealer: John A. Ryan* (New York, 1963), 229.

[78]Ryan to Hoey, Oct. 27, 1936, Ryan Papers; Broderick, *Right Reverend*, 225.

communism in the United States. As for Coughlin's economic theory, Ryan insisted that the radio priest's proposals were all wrong. If enacted, said Ryan, "they would prove disastrous to the great majority of the American people, particularly to the wage earners." Ryan insisted that these proposals found "no support in the encyclicals of either Pope Leo XIII or Pope Pius XI." He closed his address with an appeal that his listeners not vote "against the man who has shown a deeper and more sympathetic understanding of your needs and who has brought about more fundamental legislation for labor and for social justice than any other President in American history."[79]

The reaction to Ryan's speech was rapid in developing. Members of the administration were swift to forward their approval. James Farley wrote to Ryan that the speech had a "real effect in every section of the country." Farley, who did not "know of any address made during the campaign [that was] more effective," immediately had the Democratic party reproduce copies of the speech for distribution.[80] Josephus Daniels wrote from Mexico City that the speech had "heartened" him and that he was sure it "had a great effect with the voters." Homer S. Cummings, attorney general, called Ryan's remarks "admirable in every way." President Roosevelt sent a telegram of appreciation to Ryan.[81]

While the remarks of Farley and Daniels can be attributed to the generous nature of these men, there is some evidence that Ryan's speech was, in fact, used effectively during the campaign. In Washington, Joseph R. Burko, student director of the Roosevelt University Clubs, reported having distributed many copies. John W. Chase of

[79]"Roosevelt Safeguards America," Oct. 8, 1936, Pamphlet published by Democratic National Committee, Ryan Papers.

[80]Farley to Ryan, Oct. 31, 1936, Ryan Papers.

[81]Daniels to Ryan, Nov. 9, 1936, Ryan Papers; Broderick, *Right Reverend*, 228-29.

New York wrote to Ryan requesting copies of his speech to use in swinging Catholic voters behind Congressman Sisson, a Roosevelt supporter who was having difficulty.[82]

Meanwhile, the Catholic press displayed an ambivalent attitude toward the entire affair. The Pittsburgh *Catholic* mirrored the opinion of Bishop Hugh C. Boyle when it wrote that the speech would probably be beneficial.[83] The Omaha *True Voice* and *America* both agreed that Coughlin's economic thought was outdated and that Father Ryan was the most authoritative Catholic voice in this field.[84] The Baltimore *Catholic Review* and the Brooklyn *Tablet* agreed that neither Coughlin nor Ryan had any business in the political arena, although the Baltimore paper was not convinced by Ryan's claim that communism had not found a home in the Roosevelt administration.[85] The *Catholic Transcript* editorialized on the possibility of a bishop's supporting Landon so that all candidates would have a prominent prelate backing them. Yet the editor admitted that Coughlin had instigated Ryan's speech by his own continued intemperance of speech.[86] The editor of the Davenport *Catholic Messenger* gave no credence to Coughlin's charge that Ryan was a paid political spokesman for the New Deal. The *Catholic Telegraph*, while taking no editorial position, did display numerous political advertisements that used Ryan's address as a keynote to exhort the reader to vote Democratic.[87]

Commonweal, on the other hand, looked upon the entire affair as evidence that there was no "Catholic vote." If such prominent Catholics as Father Coughlin, Al Smith,

[82]Chase to Elizabeth Sweeney, telegram, Oct. 13, 1936, Ryan Papers.
[83]Broderick, *Right Reverend*, 228.
[84]*Ibid.*, 227-28.
[85]New York Times, Oct. 16, 1936, p. 21.
[86]Oct. 22, 1936, p. 4.
[87]*Catholic Messenger*, Oct. 15, 1936, p. 1; *Catholic Telegraph*, Oct. 29, 1936, p. 7.

and Father Ryan could all find themselves on different sides of the political fence, surely there was no "Catholic political solidarity," as the myth would have it. In any case, the editor was convinced that Ryan's remarks would have little effect upon Coughlin's followers, who had recourse to emotion rather than reason.[88]

Finally, in further estimation of Ryan's effort, some mention should be made of the volume of personal mail he received soon after October 8. The priest admitted to a correspondent that he had received at least 1200 letters from Coughlin's supporters and that most of these letters were filled with derogatory remarks. In contrast he could point to only 200 letters favoring his speech. Yet Ryan felt that even this small amount of approval justified his making the speech. Significantly, he mentioned that he had not received more than three or four letters of approval from priests. A closer examination of these pro-Ryan letters reveals a number of interesting characteristics. A few expressed sympathy for Roosevelt because he had appointed Catholics to his cabinet. Others insisted that Coughlin was distorting the social message of the Church and should be silenced. Such letters were generally from a rather well-educated audience. In contrast, the anti-Ryan mail revealed a poorly educated group. Some of the themes that dominated this correspondence were fear that communism was taking over the Roosevelt administration, distaste of recognition of Russia, criticism of the manner in which Roosevelt treated anticlericalism in Mexico, and the president's being a member of the Masonic order. The tone of these letters revealed extreme class bitterness and a note of anticlericalism.[89]

[88]Oct. 23, 1936, pp. 597-98.

[89]See Ryan's Papers where these items are all grouped together in the 1936 file. Shenton, "Coughlin Movement," 366, points out that most of the letters attacking Ryan were from Irish and German writers. At the same time, however, Roosevelt received mail critical of Coughlin from the same ethnic groups.

The smashing victory that Roosevelt achieved in 1936 made all the dire predictions appear chimerical. The president amassed over twenty-seven million popular votes compared to Landon's sixteen million and Lemke's 900,000. Even more impressive was the electoral vote where FDR captured all but two states for a grand total of 523. American Catholics voted overwhelmingly for Roosevelt in 1936. In this they simply followed the current of the times which affected their fellow citizens in like manner.

The evidence that Catholics supported the president is impressive. On one level is the testimony of numerous individuals. Father Ryan, working on the basis of his own circle, estimated that at least 70 percent of the Catholic clergy in the country voted for Roosevelt. He knew personally that a great number of his fellow professors at Catholic University supported the Democratic ticket.[90] Father Sheehy corroborated this estimate. Sheehy was proud of his own role in swinging an estimated 76 percent of the Catholic vote behind Roosevelt. In a letter to the president some years later, he outlined his role as threefold: contacting personally many bishops; supplying Democratic campaign material to the Catholic press; and sending the Ryan speech to 11,000 Catholic pastors.[91] Before the election results were in, Sheehy reported to Marguerite LeHand that his visits with numerous bishops and priests revealed a strong sentiment for the president. "There is a feeling prevalent among the priests," said Sheehy, "that the priesthood, through Father Coughlin, has betrayed the President, and some extraordinary things are being attempted to offset this betrayal."[92]

From Kentucky came the observations of P. H. Calla-

[90]Broderick, Right Reverend, 231-32; Ryan to Henry G. Leach, March 19, 1937, Ryan Papers.
[91]Sheehy to Roosevelt, May 13, 1940, Reel 3, Sel. Mat.
[92]Sheehy to LeHand, Oct. 5, 1936, Reel 3, Sel. Mat.

han, another friend of the administration. Callahan presented a detailed vote analysis. He examined areas in his own state where large religious congregations were located and found that in most cases these areas supported Roosevelt by large margins. On a nationwide basis, he delineated the voting of seven states that he characterized as having the largest Catholic populations: New Mexico, Arizona, Rhode Island, Massachusetts, Maryland, California, and Connecticut. By contrasting the voting record of these states in 1932 and 1936, Callahan demonstrated that all had given Roosevelt a larger majority in 1936 than in 1932.[93]

Monsignor Robert F. Keegan, Cardinal Hayes's assistant, wrote to the president after the election expressing congratulations. Keegan called Coughlin's activities "grossly intemperate" and concluded: "I am proud and happy that my vote and the vote of every friend whom I could influence, went to swell the magnificent total. . . . You are an answer to prayer—the prayer of all of us close to the man in the street, the factory, on the farm, and for whom any other result would have been the worst calamity that could have befallen America."[94]

There is more sophisticated evidence of Catholic support in 1936. Various public opinion polls indicated that the president received a large share of the ethnic and religious vote. One study concluded that 81 percent of all

[93]Callahan to Joseph Polin [n.d.], Ryan Papers, 1936; Callahan to Edward Keating [n.d.], Box 95, F. P. Walsh Papers. The Callahan figures are as follows:

	1932	1936
N.M.	40,772	47,380
Ariz.	36,860	51,930
R.I.	31,338	41,851
Mass.	63,189	172,417
Md.	130,130	148,000
Calif.	476,255	735,825
Conn.	6,788 (Hoover)	103,264

[94]Keegan to Roosevelt, Nov. 5, 1936, PPF 628, Roosevelt Papers.

Catholics who voted supported Roosevelt.[95] Both the Gallup and Roper polls indicated that Roosevelt had received substantial support from Catholics, Gallup estimating it at over 70 percent.[96] The vote of the large urban centers in the United States, where most Catholic votes were congregated, went to Roosevelt, who won with smashing majorities in Chicago, Detroit, New Orleans, St. Louis, New York, Philadelphia, and Milwaukee. Roosevelt won every one of the twelve cities in the United States with a population of over 500,000.[97]

Lemke and Coughlin were buried in this avalanche of votes. Yet some discussion of their support is relevant because of its special characteristics. Lemke received only 2 percent of all votes cast, but he was not on the ballot in every state. Samuel Lubell has analyzed Lemke's support and concluded that outside of his home state, he carried over 10 percent in only thirty-nine counties in the United States. Of these counties, twenty-one were more than 50 percent Catholic. Furthermore, twenty-eight of them were predominantly German. Lubell has concluded: "Drawn primarily from Irish and German Catholics,

[95]Darrow, "Catholic Political Power," 35 n.

[96]Harold F. Gosnell, *Champion Campaigner: Franklin D. Roosevelt* (New York, 1952), 166, who also says that FDR got only a bare majority of the Protestant vote in 1936. A Good Neighbor League was set up by the Democratic National Committee under the leadership of prominent Protestants such as Dr. Stanley High and Methodist Bishop Edgar Blake to offset the pro-Catholic image of the party. See Gosnell, 159.

[97]Edgar E. Robinson, *They Voted For Roosevelt* (Stanford, 1947), 82, 103, 110, 120, 130, 149, 180.

The following figures are indicative:

City	Dem.	Rep.
Chicago (Cook County)	1,253,164	701,206
New Orleans	108,012	10,254
Detroit	404,055	190,732
St. Louis	260,063	127,887
New York	1,454,590	480,302
Philadelphia	539,757	329,881
Milwaukee	221,512	54,811

Lemke's following represented the most belligerently isolationist voters in the country."[98]

Explaining why Catholics voted for Roosevelt is another matter. Some scholars attribute this support to gratitude for the welfare measures of the New Deal. It seems,
however, that more than welfare was at stake. As one
historian has remarked, "The newer ethnic groups in the
cities swung to Roosevelt, mostly out of gratitude for the
New Deal welfare measures, but partly out of delight
with being granted 'recognition.' "[99] This seems a balanced and judicious interpretation. If this analysis has
shown anything, it is that Roosevelt was solicitous of the
Catholic Church. He never failed to respond to a note of
gratitude or encouragement from Catholics. His appointment policy was enough to make anyone forget the bigotry of the past.

There were a myriad of reactions to the Roosevelt victory. Certainly the contention by *Commonweal* that
Roosevelt might be "in trouble among Catholic voters in
the industrial states" and that Lemke's vote "will be a
large one" seems ridiculous in retrospect.[100] When the
votes were counted, it was time for a reappraisal. Cardinal Hayes in New York wired his congratulations and
thanked the president for receiving Cardinal Pacelli.[101] In

[98]Samuel Lubell, *The Future of American Politics,* 2d ed., rev. (New
York, 1956), 152. Lubell's findings have been challenged, however, by
Leuchtenburg, *Franklin D. Roosevelt,* 195 n., 183 n., who feels it was
"unlikely that foreign affairs were that compelling in 1936." One
might ask how compelling an issue is required to be to sway 2 percent of the voters. Tull, "Father Coughlin," also challenges Lubell's
interpretation, attributing Lemke's vote as support for Coughlin's
ideas and disenchantment with the progress made under the New
Deal.
[99]Leuchtenburg, *Franklin D. Roosevelt,* 184-85, who also points out
that FDR made one judicial appointment in every four to a Catholic.
The ratio under Harding, Coolidge, and Hoover was one of every
twenty-five. On election day Roosevelt swept the urban areas of
over 10,000 by a count of 104 to 2.
[100]July 3, 1936, p. 254.
[101]Hayes to Roosevelt, Nov. 6, 1936, Reel 3, *Sel. Mat.*

Detroit, Father Coughlin announced on the radio that the election had convinced him to withdraw "from all radio activity in the best interest of all the people."[102] Naturally Father Ryan rejoiced at the results and accepted the president's invitation to render the benediction at the inauguration.

The Catholic press was varied in its reaction to the election. Commonweal dwelt at length upon the "truly representative" vote the president received. He had support from virtually every section of the United States and from every class and interest. Father Gillis, editor of the Catholic World, admitted that he voted for Roosevelt but was disturbed because he feared the president would use his victory to embark upon adventures such as taking the United States into the World Court. Remarkably, Gillis insisted that the president in the election of 1936 did not have a mandate for great change. The Brooklyn Tablet admitted that the people of the United States had expressed a "desire to allow the government to develop along new and modern ideas rather than according to the ideas of those who hold to the traditional constitutional form." The editor warned that now more than ever was it necessary to remain vigilant "to safeguard this nation against the dangers of an organized, militant Communism."[103]

Coughlin's personal attacks against the president had boomeranged. Roosevelt was a popular figure, and the intemperate language used against him by Coughlin only served to alienate many Catholics from the priest's cause. Others, perhaps neutral about the entire affair, became greatly embarrassed by the spectacle of a Catholic priest's attacking the president of the United States.

[102]Commonweal, Nov. 20, 1936, p. 100; in fact, Coughlin was shortly back on the air and remained active on the side of isolationism until the early 1940's.
[103]Commonweal, Nov. 13, 1936, p. 59; Catholic World, CXLIV (Dec. 1936), 258-60; Brooklyn Tablet, Nov. 7, 1936, p. 10.

There is little question that this embarrassment was instrumental in causing Ryan and other members of the hierarchy to take a more active pro-Roosevelt position in the campaign than had originally been anticipated.[104] Coughlin's political activities contributed to this shift. Of course, there were other major factors in Roosevelt's triumph which operated upon the Catholic voter in the same way they operated on all. These included the indisputable fact that economic improvement had been made, that Roosevelt was a better campaigner than his opponents, and that the Democrats had large shares of patronage with which to operate.[105]

In 1936 Franklin Roosevelt was once again in the White House, and American Catholics had played an active role in putting him there. In retrospect, it appears that the relationship between Roosevelt and the Church during the period from 1932 to 1936 had been mutually fruitful. Roosevelt won the political support of Catholics, while the Church became firmly integrated into American na-

[104]Josephus Daniels was so impressed "because the great loyalty to their party and their principles caused the large body of Catholic voters to turn a deaf ear to the pleas of Mr. Carmody, Fr. Coughlin and Al Smith" that he suggested to Roosevelt that either Cardinal Mundelein or Cardinal Hayes offer prayer before the inaugural address as a reward. He pointed to Mundelein's role as pivotal. Daniels to Roosevelt, Dec. 4, 1936, PSF I, Diplomatic Correspondence, Mexico, Box 2, Roosevelt Papers.

[105]Other reasons have been suggested as to why Coughlin failed to win large Catholic backing. Tull, "Father Coughlin," 224, emphasizes that many Catholics did not want to throw their vote on a hopeless cause. Shannon, American Irish, 313, has an interesting passage in which he points out that Coughlin lost his support when he threw off the special demeanor of a Catholic priest and engaged in bitter political diatribe. His followers were ambiguous in their feelings. "They wanted to be respectable and proper but they also wanted to rebel and protest. A priest who voiced radical, rebellious sentiments in dignified . . . tones and by use of religious imagery was uniquely positioned to heal this division. . . . When he abandoned his dignity and priestly manner, Father Coughlin lowered himself in the eyes of many to just another cheap, shouting politician."

tional life. In analyzing the rapport that developed between the president and American Catholics, a number of salient features are worth reemphasizing.

Roosevelt had begun his national political career with a favorable image in the minds of many Catholics. His role as supporter of Smith in 1928 and his many speeches against religious bigotry played a role in creating this image. As a politician in New York State Roosevelt had come into early contact with the political dimensions of the Church. He learned to understand and respect it as well as developing close personal contacts with many influential members of the hierarchy. In 1932 Roosevelt inherited most of the urban Catholic following that had supported Smith in 1928. After his election in 1932, FDR's patronage policies reflected the increased political power of American Catholics within the Democratic party.

Both Roosevelt and the Church shared a deep concern over the moral effect of the economic crisis facing the country in 1932. The public reaction of many prominent Catholics to the depression revealed a radicalism that surprised many observers. Catholic social spokesmen such as Father Ryan, Father Gillis, and members of the hierarchy stressed the need for federal action to combat the ravages of unemployment and economic suffering. They felt that national planning was a logical step to take during the crisis. Such an attitude made for a receptive state of mind toward the innovations that Roosevelt brought to Washington.

The advanced state of Catholic social thought was seen in the generally favorable reaction with which Catholics greeted the New Deal measures. Such legislation as NRA, AAA, and the labor policies of the New Deal were lauded by Catholics as being in complete accord with the papal encyclicals. Although the congruency between the pope's ideas and the New Deal was never as close as some imagined, the encyclicals were couched in such general terms that much was left to the imagination. Many Catholics undoubtedly assumed the pope's social ideas were unassailably true. Being Americans as well as Catholics they wanted to see the New Deal as part of the same tradition as the papal policy, and this helped to make a favorable reaction.

Yet the general terms of Catholic social principles produced some rather disturbing incidents when individuals attempted to express analogies between the pope's intention and the concrete measures of the New Deal. Catholics produced a startling variety of thought. Father John Ryan saw the New Deal as only a beginning and wanted more national planning. Father James Gillis felt the New Deal went too far in regimenting national life. There were often direct contradictions in the interpretation of the Church's social teaching. Some said that the pope wanted all laborers to join a union. Others insisted that forcing a man to join a union in order to get a job was against Catholic teaching. There was also an ambiguity in Catholic reaction to child labor and the role of the rural dweller in our society. While large segments of the Catholic hierarchy and many prominent prelates argued vigorously for the passage of the Wagner Labor Act, another element of the Church publicly lobbied against the child labor amendment. This latter group argued that the amendment would lead to federal control of children. Apparently the connection between the strengthening of American labor and the ending of exploitation of child labor was not readily apparent. Yet it should be emphasized that in this area, as in most, a large segment of Catholic thought was consistently progressive in outlook. Father Haas and Father Ryan both recognized the need to protest exploitation at all levels.

Another vivid example of the variety of attitudes in

Catholic social thought during this period was the contrast between Father Ryan and Father Luigi Ligutti Granger, Iowa, who had been a leading exponent of Catholic agrarianism. Ligutti was a Jeffersonian who felt that the only hope for society was to return to a nation of small family-owned farms. While admitting and accepting the need for federal assistance in his agricultural endeavors, Ligutti frowned upon any plan to combine farming operations into giant corporations. Ryan, on the other hand, worked more in the industrial field and felt that if small businesses could not compete with large ones in wages, the small ones should be allowed to die out.

Despite Roosevelt's awareness of the political strength of American Catholics and his sympathetic attitude toward their needs, he seldom let their advocacy of a particular line of action influence, to any significant degree, his own final decision. Whenever Roosevelt and the Church came into direct conflict, such as over the recognition of Russia and the anticlericalism in Mexico, the president always managed to have his way, while still maintaining Catholic support. By simply listening to their grievances, Roosevelt often took the sting out of much of the Catholic opposition. He opened the door of communication and made a point of considering Catholic sensibilities on an issue. In short, he was a master of tact when dealing with the Church. This was usually enough to satisfy most Catholic critics. In fact, Roosevelt's attentiveness to Catholic bishops occasionally paid off in terms of political reality. One such instance was his appearance at Catholic University. This event gained him valuable allies in the future debate over the recognition of Russia. His handling of Father Walsh in connection with the priest's protest over United States diplomatic relations with Russia is another example of the fruitfulness of FDR's tact and accessibility. The campaign of 1936 revealed a large num-

ber of influential Catholic supporters for the president who
had been won over primarily by his recognition of their
Church.

After four years of the New Deal, American Catholics
could look back upon a period that saw them make impressive gains politically, socially, and intellectually.
Catholics were now firmly established in the national
government and in the group surrounding the president.
Many Church leaders were in close personal contact with
the president. Catholic educators and reformers such as
Father Ryan and Father McGowan could reflect upon the
welfare measures of the New Deal as having brought the
general social teachings of the popes into the spectrum of
American reform. By 1936 it appeared that American
Catholics had reached a position of respect and integration in public life in the United States. Many problems
still remained, including the formation of a consistent
Catholic social philosophy that could be accepted by all
members of the Church. But they had come a long way
from the alienation that they had sensed after the 1928
election.

Bibliographical Essay

For a more detailed discussion of the sources used in this book the reader is referred to the various notes accompanying the text. This brief essay is designed to discuss those general sources which proved of some value, most of which are easily accessible for those readers who are not research-oriented. Before discussing these sources, however, a few preliminary remarks are required. One of the most profound disappointments associated with my research for this book was that the various archives of the Church are still closed. Despite this handicap I felt the story was worth telling because, from those few private Catholic sources I was able to work with, there did not seem to be a significant discrepancy between the private and public expressions of churchmen. There can be no question, however, that our knowledge will be broadened immeasurably when the Church archives in the United States are opened to legitimate scholarship. The papers of Cardinal Mundelein, Cardinal Spellman, Father Burke, and the back files of the NCWC will certainly help to fill out the story of American Catholics and the New Deal. It is regrettable that Vatican II's theme of opening new windows to the world has not extended to American chanceries in their attitude toward Church archives.

Fortunately, some manuscript collections are available which shed light on recent church history. The Franklin D. Roosevelt Papers at Hyde Park, New York, are of prime importance. Here a tremendous bulk of material has been carefully cross-indexed by a professional staff of archivists, who are willing and able to help the researcher. In June 1955 a team of photographers from the Catholic University of America visited Hyde Park to film material that related to "Roman Catholic Church Matters." The three reels of microfilm which resulted from this enterprise are available from the Catholic University of America. While much of the material is mere trivia, enough of value remains to help the researcher to evaluate the considerable cross section of the Catholic population to which FDR appealed.

The archives of the Catholic University of America, Washington, D.C., is another valuable depository of materials. The major collection here is the John Ryan Papers, which cover the entire career of this prolific and articulate clergyman. Other collections of some value are the papers of Father Francis Haas and William Montavon. These documents are valuable not simply because of the importance of the individuals concerned but because of the wide influence of Ryan and Haas throughout the Church. Their correspondence touched, directly and indirectly, most of the major church figures of their day.

Other collections consulted are scattered and of marginal value. The Josephus Daniels Papers at the Library of Congress are indispensable for a consideration of the dispute over anticlericalism in Mexico. The Thomas Walsh Papers, also at the Library of Congress, provide some information on the 1932 campaign. The David Walsh Papers at Holy Cross College, Worcester, Massachusetts, are sketchy for the 1932-1936 period. The Frank P. Walsh Papers at the New York Public Library are filled with material on the child labor dispute. At the time of my research the papers of Father Edmund Walsh were still in a rather disorganized state at the Georgetown University Library, Washington, D.C.

Published contemporary sources provide the bulk of information on Catholic attitudes during the Roosevelt administration. The Catholic University of America has a fine microfilm collection of newspapers and periodicals which proved invaluable as a source of Catholic opinion. These include the Boston *Pilot;* the Brooklyn *Tablet;* the *Catholic Herald* (Milwaukee); the *Catholic Messenger* (Davenport, Iowa); the *Catholic Telegraph* (Cincinnati); the *Catholic Transcript* (Hartford, Conn.); the Cleveland *Universe Bulletin;* the Denver *Catholic Register;* the *Michigan Catholic* (Detroit); the *Monitor* (San Francisco); the *New World* (Chicago); and *Our Sunday Visitor* (Fort Wayne, Ind.). The National Catholic Welfare Conference *News Service,* also available on microfilm from Catholic University, is a quite detailed source for virtually everything that happens in the Church. The fact that most diocesan papers subscribed to this news service makes it even more important for this period.

Contemporary Catholic periodicals are another key to church opinion. The two most important magazines in this category are *Commonweal*, edited by a group of New York laymen and generally representing liberal Catholicism, and *America*, a Jesuit weekly generally representing a more conservative Catholicism. The *Catholic World*, edited by the Paulist priest James Gillis during the 1930's, also had a wide circulation. The other periodicals are of varying importance. This category includes *Ave Maria*, the *Catholic Mind*, *Catholic Action*, official monthly of the NCWC; *Central-Blatt and Social Justice*, official journal of the Catholic Central Verein of St. Louis; *Columbia*, published by the Knights of Columbus; *Extension*, published by the Catholic Church Extension Society of Chicago; the *Interracial Review*, published by the Catholic Interracial Council; *Light*, official organ of the International Catholic Truth Society; *Pax*, a Benedictine organ; *Social Justice*, Father Coughlin's forum; and the *Proceedings* of the National Conference of Catholic Charities.

There are few secondary accounts that bear directly on the theme of Roosevelt and American Catholicism. Those that proved most valuable for the methodological framework include Will Herberg, *Protestant, Catholic, Jew* (1960); James Fenton, *The Catholic Vote* (1960); Samuel Lubell, *The Future of American Politics* (1956); Peter H. Odegard, ed., *Religion and Politics* (1960), which is filled with pertinent articles; Joseph Moody, ed., *Church and Society* (1953); James O'Gara, ed., *Catholicism in America: A Series of Articles from the Commonweal* (1954); James W. Smith and A. Leland Jamison, eds., *Religion in American Life* (4 vols., 1961). See also the writings of Robert D. Cross on "The Changing Image of Catholicism in America," *Yale Review* (June 1959); and Charles Glock, "The Political Role of the Church as Defined by Its Parishioners," *Public Opinion Quarterly* (1964-65).

On the political aspects of the Roosevelt period, a number of outstanding works are pertinent. First in any list dealing with the New Deal must be the brilliant survey by William Leuchtenburg, *Franklin D. Roosevelt and the New Deal* (1963). The following books are all more important for information on Roosevelt than on American Catholicism: James M. Burns, *Roosevelt: The Lion and the Fox* (1956), still the best one volume biography of the president; James Farley, *Behind the Ballots* (1938) and *Jim Farley's Story* (1948) are good on politics;

the still incomplete biography by Frank Freidel, *Franklin D. Roosevelt* (3 vols., 1952-1956); and three volumes by Arthur M. Schlesinger, Jr., *The Crisis of the Old Order* (1957), *The Coming of the New Deal* (1959), and *The Politics of Upheaval* (1960). Other books that treat particular aspects of the political story include Harold F. Gosnell, *Champion Campaigner: Franklin D. Roosevelt* (1952); Oscar Handlin, *Al Smith and His America* (1958); Richard Hofstadter, *The Age of Reform* (1955); J. Joseph Huthmacher, *Massachusetts People and Politics, 1919-1933* (1959); Harold Ickes, *The Secret Diary of Harold Ickes* (3 vols, 1954); Edmund A. Moore, *A Catholic Runs for President* (1956); Frances Perkins, *The Roosevelt I Knew* (1946); Edgar E. Robinson, *They Voted for Roosevelt* (1947); William V. Shannon, *The American Irish* (1964); Rexford Tugwell, *The Democratic Roosevelt* (1957). A recent monograph by Edward M. Levine, *The Irish and Irish Politicians* (1967), discusses the changing image of one type of Catholic politician, but has little to say about the New Deal period. Readers interested in a more detailed bibliography on the New Deal should consult Leuchtenburg's book.

Information on American Catholic social thought comes primarily from the papers of Father Ryan, Father Haas, and from the various church periodicals listed above. Of capital importance in this area is a manuscript by David O'Brien, "American Catholic Social Thought in the 1930's" (unpublished Ph.D. dissertation, University of Rochester, 1965), which will soon be available in published form. Other secondary accounts of interest include Charles Tull, *Father Coughlin and the New Deal* (1966); Aaron I. Abell, *American Catholicism and Social Action* (1960); Frederick L. Broderick, *The Right Reverend New Dealer: John A. Ryan* (1963); Daniel Callahan, *The Mind of the Catholic Layman* (1963); Dorothy Day, *The Long Loneliness* (1952); John T. Ellis, *American Catholicism* (1956); Donald P. Gavin, *The National Conference of Catholic Charities, 1910-1960* (1962); William Cardinal O'Connell, *Recollections of Seventy Years* (1934); John Ryan, *Social Doctrine in Action: A Personal History* (1941); Raymond P. Witte, *Twenty-five Years of Crusading: A History of the National Catholic Rural Life Conference* (1948). The reactions of American Catholics to the various actions of the New Deal are most fully outlined in the various papers and periodicals already mentioned. In these various organs, such as *America* and *Commonweal*, men like

Ryan, McGowan, Haas, and others discussed and criticized the different New Deal measures. See also the published editions of the papal encyclicals: Pope Leo XIII, *Rerum Novarum* (1942 ed.) and Pope Pius XI, *Quadragesimo Anno* (1942 ed.).

For the chapters dealing with the recognition of Russia and anticlericalism in Mexico, the most relevant material will be found in the contemporary journals and newspapers. Especially fruitful is the magazine *Columbia*, sponsored by the Knights of Columbus. Other secondary works of some pertinence are the excellent study by E. David Cronon, *Josephus Daniels in Mexico* (1960); Robert Browder, *The Origins of Soviet-American Diplomacy* (1953); Josephus Daniels, *Shirt-Sleeve Diplomat* (1947); Robert A. Devine, *The Illusions of Neutrality* (1962); a rather uncritical sketch by Louis Gallagher, *Edmund A. Walsh, S.J.* (1962); and what appears to be an official biography by Robert I. Gannon, *The Cardinal Spellman Story* (1962), which has some new material on the Roosevelt period.

A number of edited works were consulted with profit. These include John M. Blum, *From the Morgenthau Diaries: Years of Crisis, 1928-1938* (1959); Waldemar Gurian and M. S. Fitzsimmons, *The Catholic Church in World Affairs* (1954); Raphael M. Huber, *Our Bishops Speak: National Pastorals and Annual Statements of the Hierarchy of the United States, 1919-1951* (1952); Elliott Roosevelt, *F.D.R.: His Personal Letters* (3 vols, 1947-1950); and the invaluable collection by Samuel Rosenman, *The Public Papers and Addresses of Franklin D. Roosevelt* (13 vols., 1938-1950).

The following works were of some miscellaneous value: *American Catholics Who's Who* (1934-35); John T. Ellis, *A Selected Bibliography of the History of the Catholic Church in the United States* (1947).

Index

Columbia: on regulation of Wall Street, 64; on Russian recognition, 128; on Mexican policy, 188, 190. *See also* Knights of Columbus

Commerce, American, 127, 131

Committee for Mobilization for Human Needs, 99

Common good: interpretation of, xiv; as goal of pope and president, 24, 40, 90, 92, 94; as restriction on private property, 34, 56-58, 96; definition of, 55

Commonweal: on 1932 election campaign, 8, 12, 16; on New Deal legislation, 33, 41, 42, 63, 70, 75, 82, 100, 120, 121, 217, 218; on Russian recognition, 128, 133, 140, 144, 148; on Mexican policy, 154, 158, 161, 182n; on 1936 election campaign, 201, 217, 234, 235; on Catholic vote, 229, 234; mentioned, 183, 186, 191

Communism: relationship to NRA, 96, 97, 102; and child labor amendment, 110; and Catholicism, 126, 134, 138, 149, 199, 212, 218, 222; as threat to U.S., 127, 131; as factor in Russian recognition, 129-30, 132, 134, 137, 144; influence in Roosevelt administration, 148, 174, 186, 195, 199, 200, 202-203, 204-205, 212-13, 223, 225, 227-28; mentioned, 25, 28, 32, 98, 124, 206, 224. *See also* Russia; Campaign of 1936

Competition: role in modern economy, 18, 32, 34; Catholic economic thought on, 25, 30-31, 55, 89-90; NRA's approach to, 88

Congress, U.S.: and New Deal legislation, 64, 69, 95; on child labor amendment, 109; pressure on administration over Mexico, 156-57, 161-62, 165, 173, 189; on World Court, 203;

mentioned, 5. *See also* Mexico; Knights of Columbus; Borah resolution

Connecticut: on child labor amendment, 111; and Catholic voting pattern, 232

Connery, W. P., 105

Connolly, W. F., 19

Constitution: religious test under, 5, 7, 8; Supreme Court's view of 100-101; and New Deal legislation, 101-102, 121, 200; as issue in 1936 campaign, 195, 199, 200; mentioned, 109, 136

Convention of 1932, Democratic: Catholic reaction to, 7, 10, 14; issues at, 9, 11; mentioned, 8

Coolidge, Marcus A., 130

Co-ops: in agriculture, 68, 72; in industry, 100

Corcoran, Thomas G: on FDR and Catholics, 6n, 48n, 51n; and Mundelein, 38n

Corrigan, Jones I.: on Roosevelt, 40; on AAA, 70-71; supports NRA, 86, 88; on child labor amendment, 110; on Russian recognition, 129

Coughlin, Charles E.: relations with Roosevelt administration, 20, 202, 203, 204, 207, 210, 212, 213, 214, 216, 223, 235; on New Deal measures, 28, 57, 62, 63, 71, 96, 156, 183, 202, 203n; economic teaching of, 33, 45, 48, 203, 213-14, 222, 225, 227, 228, 230; on communism and Roosevelt's foreign policy, 129, 155-56, 202, 203, 204, 206, 208, 212, 214, 222, 226; impact on American Catholics, 185-86, 202, 204, 205, 206, 208-209, 212, 214-15, 216-17, 221-22, 226, 229, 232, 235, 236; political activities of, 195, 203-204, 207, 209-10, 211, 214-15, 227, 229, 233, 235; tactics of, 204, 206, 208, 212, 213, 215, 229, 230; relations with Frank Murphy, 207. *See also* Campaign of

rights under NRA, 93-94; freedom to join, 106; rights under Wagner Act, 107-108. *See also* Section 7a, NRA; Wagner Labor Relations Act

United States: fear of revolution in, 32; relations with Soviet Union, 124, 130, 137; relations with Mexico, 155, 163, 190, 193; place of American Catholics in, 204, 240; and communism, 228; and World Court, 235

Vatican: on FDR and New Deal reform, 38; role in Russian recognition, 130, 134, 140-41; role in Mexican anticlericalism dispute, 158, 189; international influence of, 209; and Coughlin movement, 214, 216-17; ambassador to, 217; mentioned, 178

Vocational groups: Pius XI promotes as economic panacea, 25, 32; similar ideas of papacy and NRA on, 90, 91, 94, 95. *See also* Guild system

Von Ludendorff, General Erich, 217n

Vote, Catholic: existence of, xiii, xiv, 21; and 1928 election, 8; and 1932 Democratic nomination, 11; and Socialist ticket in 1932, 11-13; and 1932 election, 13, 16, 21; motivation behind, 14, 236; and FDR's appointment policy, 54; and Russian recognition, 124; FDR's awareness of, 124, 198; and FDR's Mexican policy, 172, 191-92; and FDR at Notre Dame, 186; and Knights of Columbus, 191; and 1936 election, 192, 194, 198-200, 228-29, 234; and John Ryan's speech, 228; and Lemke, 234

Voting: influenced by clergy, xiv; analysis by historians, xiii; electoral strength of East, 10; results in 1932 election, 20; and 1936 election, 232

Wages: Hayes on, 57; NRA effect on, 93; and Coughlin economics, 228

Wagner, Robert: sponsors labor legislation, 107; and Catholic protest over Mexico, 157, 162; and 1936 election campaign, 200, 208

Wagner Labor Relations Act: FDR's attitude toward, 107; Catholic support of, 107-108, 116, 238; effect of, 108. *See also* Labor; Wagner, Robert

Wagner-Lewis Act. *See* Social Security

Walker, Frank: advises FDR over Knights of Columbus protest, 167; arranges honorary degree for FDR, 183

Wallace, Henry: and papal social encyclicals, 48-49, 70; and Agricultural Adjustment Act, 69-70; Catholic support of, 69, 72; and Russian recognition, 125

Wall Street: Catholic attitude toward, 61; investigation of, 63-64

Walsh, David I.: role in 1932 election campaign, 15-16; and Mundelein, 37; and Wagner Act, 108; and Russian recognition, 130; and Knights of Columbus criticism of FDR, 157-58, 162; and Borah resolution, 158; mentioned, 107

Walsh, Edmund A.: and economic reform in U.S., 28, 86; identified, 124; 1932 election campaign, 124; role in U.S.-Russian negotiations, 129, 131-43 *passim*, 146, 149, 239; relations with FDR, 135-36, 138, 239. *See also* Russia, recognition of